the
accidental
footballer

PAT NEVIN

the
accidental
footballer

a memoir

monoray

First published in Great Britain in 2021 by Monoray,
an imprint of Octopus Publishing Group Ltd
Carmelite House
50 Victoria Embankment
London EC4Y 0DZ
www.octopusbooks.co.uk

An Hachette UK Company
www.hachette.co.uk

First published in paperback in 2021

Photographic credits: pages 2a & b, 3, 5, 10a courtesy Herald and Times Group;
4b, 7b Hugh Hastings/Chelsea FC; 6 Duncan Raban/Popperfoto/Getty Images;
7a Ben Radford/Visionhaus; 8bl Nick White Photography;
8br Sunday Express/Reach Licensing; 9 Mirrorpix/Alamy Stock Photo;
10b Peter Robinson/EMPICS Sport/PA Images; 11a S&G/EMPICS Sport/PA Images;
11b Howard Wiker/Mirrorpix; 12 Clive Arrowsmith; 14a & b Bob Thomas/Getty Images;
15 Allstar Picture Library Ltd/Alamy Stock Photo; 16 Courtesy Scared to Dance.
All other images are courtesy of the author.

Every effort has been made to trace copyright.
If any omissions have been made please contact the publishers.

ISBN 978-1-80096-013-8

A CIP catalogue record for this book is available from the British Library.

Printed and bound in the United Kingdom

10 9 8 7 6 5 4 3

This FSC® label means that materials used for the product
have been responsibly sourced.

For Annabel, for being the love of my life,
our son Simon, who never ceases to amaze us with his
willingness to do his best in adversity,
and our beautiful, smart, caring daughter Lucy, who
has been an inspiration every day since coming into
our lives.

Contents

Prologue   1

PART ONE
GLASGOW

1	Do You Remember the First Time?	8
2	Kids	18
3	The Story of the Blues	29
4	Everything's Gone Green	32
5	Don't Mess Up a Good Thing	45
6	I Don't Want to Go to Chelsea	54
7	Changes	66

PART TWO
LONDON

8	London Calling	80
9	A New Career in a New Town	90
10	Eighties Fan	103
11	Bigmouth Strikes Again	110
12	This is the Day	118
13	Black Star	126
14	All Together Now	135
15	Knives Out	146
16	Back to Black	161
17	Fame	174
18	Crash	185
19	Kicker Conspiracy	201
20	New Dawn Fades	208

PART THREE
EVERTON

21	Hit the North	222
22	Doubts Even Here	231
23	Shine On You Crazy Diamond	245
24	This Charming Man	258
25	Here Comes the Summer	266
26	I'll Be Honest	276
27	Let's Stick Together	288
28	Leaving Blues	298
29	With a Little Help from My Friends	304
30	Take a Chance on Me	310
31	Never Understand	321
32	Ferry 'Cross the Mersey	327

Epilogue	332
Chapter Titles Playlist	336
Index	337
Acknowledgements	343

Prologue

Last year I was in an office in London discussing the next run of articles I was about to write for an online publication. There was a very new, very young marketing chap in control of the output and he wanted to know what this old man was thinking about producing this year. I gave what would be the stock, if worthy sounding, answer for me.

'Well, as ever I will try to write things that are hopefully interesting, I will use any insight I have from my own experiences in the game and with a bit of luck add a little humour alongside any informative points I can muster. I will try to look at each subject from a different angle than those you might read elsewhere, and hopefully I will be considering topics that aren't being done to death by everyone else. At the very least I like to give an alternative viewpoint on issues, with the aim of making the reader think in a different way. How does that sound?'

I had fallen into his trap. After waiting a moment, he looked at me and kindly, almost sympathetically, explained where I was going wrong.

'What I would like you to do is precisely the opposite of that.'

I was surprised and not a little confused. 'What? I'm not sure I understand.'

With a patient sigh he carried on as if talking to an infant. 'I want you to go online, be it Twitter or any social media platform, see what the most topical thing trending at the moment is, and then write about that.'

1

Being a reasonable chap, and also being no more than a lowly employee these days, I said, 'That sounds a bit restrictive, but I suppose I could look at those topics and give my perspective.'

'Oh no, I don't want your perspective, what I want you to do is gauge what the prevailing mood is from the majority of the people online and then mirror that argument in your article.'

This concept had never even occurred to me.

'You want me to write, but you are not interested in what I think or believe to be true?'

Having personally written thousands of columns over three decades, many for national newspapers and magazines as well as a bunch of websites, this was indeed the opposite of my previous thinking, and I still didn't fully understand why. He saw my confusion and enlightened me.

'People just like to have their own ideas reflected back at them, particularly online. They don't want to think too much and certainly do not want to be challenged. Tell them what they want to hear, say it in as short and as simple a way as possible and if you do that, we will get more clicks. The more views we get on the site, the more advertising we can sell. That's how it works, do you understand?'

I now understood the idea perfectly as a concept. I had studied marketing as well as economics to degree level, I had also been a chief executive of a football club and chairman of the PFA, though I suspect he wouldn't have known any of that.

The premise is perfectly reasonable in a purely business sense, but only if looked at through the prism of me being a mercenary hack, my readers being a bit stupid and the short-term advertising figures that he can present to his boss being more important than everything else put together. Unfortunately, I've never really bought into this cynical world view. It is a pretty neat summation of everything I dislike about how the business world looks down at the rest of us. To use Abraham Lincoln's age-old adage, 'You can fool all of the people some of the time and some of the people all of the time, but you can't fool all of the people all of the time.'

So, I was surprised but also angry at this conversation, not just for me but for any writer and indeed every reader who I think is being short-changed by the presumption that we are nothing but click-bait clowns. I said I would think about the new direction of travel, although I knew perfectly well that I would do no such thing. Minutes later I was out of the office and into the cool air, heading back up home to Scotland, wondering if every modern, young, thrusting, marketing department of every big data-driven organisation was now thinking like this to a greater or lesser extent. I suspect they are. I was even more annoyed by the time I got on the train to Gatwick airport. 'I don't think most people are thick and I am certainly not going to treat them as though they are. I'm not that arrogant!' I grumbled away to myself.

I got to Gatwick but had a five-hour wait for my plane. I opened my laptop and let the contents of my addled mind gush out. It was a barrier that had clearly been waiting to burst for a while: the afternoon's conversation had breached it as spectacularly as the RAF 617 'Dambusters' Squadron of World War Two would have done. By the time I got on board my flight I had written over 10,000 words of this memoir and less than three weeks later the first draft of the book you are holding was finished.

As I wrote, all the frustration quickly dissipated. I enjoyed the writing and loved looking back on what was a strange and totally unplanned first twenty-eight years of my life. It took me back to my days growing up in Glasgow, and playing for Celtic Boys Club and Clyde FC, and the more I wrote, the more I realised I wanted to explore those days at Chelsea and Everton, when I played at the most high-profile clubs of my career – a career that, initially, had never crossed my mind.

So, now, here it is. I just hope that you will also find some interest, fun, enjoyment and maybe even a little insight into the world into which I found myself catapulted. It was certainly enlightening for me as I dredged up memories I hadn't considered since they had happened, some of them fifty years old.

I have made no attempt to reflect your own views back at you. While you may not agree with the things I say or attitudes I have, hopefully you will understand that I treat you with respect as I share my perspective.

Am I still annoyed with the marketing man? Absolutely not; I would have prevaricated over this book and indeed may never have written it had that discussion not happened. I had considered writing my story for a long time, after many people had suggested I should at least have a go, but I was always too busy working on my, admittedly, very enjoyable jobs. So the months quickly passed, and the years, then the decades and, like that messy bit at the bottom corner of the garden just out of sight from the front door, I never quite got round to working on it.

So, this is an honest thank you to the marketing man. Maybe we can even talk about it now, a little.

Did I ever change my style in the articles I wrote for his publication? Not even slightly, and within months they were among the best trending features on the site.

Is there a message? Try and stick to what you believe to be right, if you possibly can. There is nothing wrong with failure on your own terms if you have given it your best shot. But there's a great deal to regret if you fail doing something you don't believe in. In my life, that is something I discovered during the first half, as you will discover in the following pages.

PART ONE
GLASGOW

1/
DO YOU REMEMBER THE FIRST TIME?

Two serious-looking coaches at Celtic Football Club sit me down, one of maybe a dozen kids who have waited in the dressing rooms at Barrowfield, the club's shabby training ground. I am sixteen and had been signed by Celtic on a schoolboy (S) form four years earlier. I have already watched a couple of the other lads trudge out trying to hold back the tears, failing pathetically, having been told they were not getting a professional contract. They knew in that moment that their dreams were smashed, their futures forever changed.

Barrowfield had been my Celtic Boys Club home ground for the previous four years. There had been many great victories and personal triumphs celebrated in those same sparse rooms, but all those memories suddenly seemed hazy and distant. The only light seeping in on that early summer evening was from the small barred windows about twelve feet above the floor as one by one, like prisoners, we were called from the home dressing room to the away one to be given our verdicts. Those brash, confident young players I had known, who always had something to say and plenty to laugh about, were suddenly silent, vulnerable and more youthful-looking. Not one was able to make eye contact with another.

When it was my turn to face the judges, I was ushered into the small room that still reeked of the sharp scent of wintergreen oil mixed with the dull smell of stale sweat. I walked those few yards and closed the door slowly behind me. With only me and the two Celtic officials in the room, I suddenly heard its echo for the first time, in a way it never did when it was filled by pumped-up players preparing for games.

It was an odd arrangement: there was no table, I was on an old wooden bench at the corner of one wall and they sat at a 90-degree angle on an identical bench along the adjacent wall. Maybe they had arranged it that way, so they didn't have to look directly into the eyes of the hopefuls they were crushing. Before they even started talking, I found myself feeling quite sorry for them. What a horrible job to have to do.

The first to talk was the trainer Frank Connor, who I never believed was 'on my side' anyway. For the first time in years the habitual look of a gruff sergeant major he wore with pride was removed to reveal his more human, caring side. I hadn't witnessed him wearing this part of his personality before and it looked an uncomfortable fit. I didn't expect him to be fighting to give me a contract – I wasn't his type of player – but he was honest with his appraisal and I appreciated that from him.

The other man was Jimmy Lumsden, Celtic's then chief scout and the one I reckoned was the real decision-maker. This was a tougher call. He clearly liked me and favoured my playing style more than Frank did, so as I sat there, I thought that maybe it was all still in the balance. Jimmy wasn't playing a role, it clearly affected him deeply having to break the bad news to unlucky young men who had worked so hard to get this far.

Between them they kindly explained that although I had been top scorer and Player of the Year at Celtic Boys Club that season and nearly every season before, having scored 160 goals in one of those campaigns, sadly I wasn't going to be signed up either. 'We don't feel you will make it as a professional footballer. Maybe you are talented enough to deserve a contract with some other team, but you aren't tall enough to make the grade at the top level anyway.' Helpfully they added, 'You are a bright lad, concentrate on your education and forget about the football.'

I was caught in a very difficult situation, but somehow I managed to keep the emotions and thoughts safely under control. I nodded, said thank you for the wise advice and walked out. I managed to get out of the door, round the corner of the dressing rooms and all the way out into the London Road before I gave way to my true feelings. I smiled. There was no devastation, not even a little disappointment and there certainly weren't any tears. I had already turned my back on that possible life, long before they had made their decision.

I didn't want to seem ungrateful, but I had already decided that had they offered me a contract as a youth apprentice at Celtic Football Club, I would definitely be turning them down flat. Their considerate words didn't deserve my lack of interest, but it had never even crossed my mind to become a professional footballer and there was no reason why they should know that.

My vision was much simpler. I wanted to follow my older brothers and sister into higher education and then on to a sensible job. I knew football was a precarious career, one in which only the smallest percentage ever made a living. I didn't fancy the odds and certainly didn't want to give up on all the other possibilities life had to offer.

The truth was I had only ever played football for the sheer joy and love of the game. I loved the skills, the creativity, the fitness and, yes, winning was fun too. You can be as competitive as anyone and still value the artistry.

But this is why I loved the game. The idea of chasing fame and self-aggrandising glory seemed ridiculous to me. OK, earning decent money would have been a good bonus if I had become a professional player. But in my earnest sixteen-year-old mind all that paled in comparison to the good you could do if you became a teacher, like my three older siblings, and helped other people improve themselves. It may seem particularly strange that I couldn't care less about being let go by Celtic because I was a committed supporter. I loved the club and its ethos. It encompassed an exciting, skilful, vibrant and hard-working philosophy allied with an overwhelming belief in the importance of the group, an ideology that had been promoted by the legendary Jock Stein. I had watched Jimmy Johnstone, Bobby Lennox, Billy McNeill and Bertie Auld alongside the other Lisbon Lions as a youngster and then had the good fortune to see Kenny Dalglish, Danny McGrain, Lou Macari, George Connelly and David Hay (my own personal favourite) breaking through and becoming brilliant players. So, how could I be so unaffected by being released and not even getting a chance to try to follow in their footsteps?

Well, first, I never felt I could be as good as any of them, which was probably proved right in time. Few players in Scottish history were ever as good as that bunch of world-class talents. More importantly, back then I would be just as happy to don my green-and-white scarf and get back on the terracing to support my team. I could still get my fix of playing by turning out for some Sunday league outfit.

Having said that, there was one dark cloud hovering over me as I made my way home on the bus after Celtic's rejection. I had to tell my father that I had been dumped.

I knew he would be devastated, and he had good reason to be – he had put thousands and thousands of hours into training me up and helping me improve my skills.

When I informed him that night, he was outwardly very stoical, and it was a fairly short conversation. In hindsight, both of us were far more concerned about the other's feelings to go into any real depth.

To understand how important that moment was to him, we have to skip back ten years to 1969.

At that time we lived in Easterhouse, in the east end of Glasgow. Some would go on to call the area a 'slum' but to my young eyes that is not how it felt. Glasgow had decided to level the worst parts of the central area such as the Gorbals and build new estates on the edge of the city: Pollok, Drumchapel, Castlemilk and Easterhouse. The housing was to be of a better standard and located near open countryside, which would also help the health of those young families. As usual many things went wrong, with the town planners forgetting to consider important concepts like adding any amenities or integrating the transport system. Initially there were very few things for poor kids to do so far away from the city, so a gang culture erupted. There was no decent shopping in the area, so business was slow to flourish. There was also the fact that when Easterhouse was built, they had one pub for over 50,000 people, which is a bizarre idea anywhere, but particularly daft for working-class Glasgow!

It was a deprived area and like the others Easterhouse became known as a sink estate, but there were good people there and one thing not lacking was space to play football. Because there were so many schools built for these young families moving out of the city centre, schools and their playing fields were abundant. This was all I and many others really needed for our happiness and those estates at the time produced many talented footballers.

At the age of six, I would run home every day after attending the local Catholic primary school Blessed John Ogilvie. My mum would make me some food, which I would wolf down before dashing outside to play football.

An hour later my dad, Patrick senior, would arrive home from his work. He'd have been labouring since 6.30am with British Rail. By 5.30 in the evening I had to be on the football field conveniently situated in the 'other' school (the non-denominational or 'Protestant School' as it was called by everyone) right behind our tenement.

At least an hour of coaching from Dad would follow. Dribbling, keepy-ups,* shooting into him as goalkeeper and learning tricks we had gleaned from studying the Celtic stars we had watched at Parkhead the week before.

He read coaching manuals from around the world and during the summer would sometimes go down to Barrowfield to glean information from Jock Stein's training techniques with the Celtic team. I got the

---

* I could do 10,000 by the age of eight.

benefit of all that knowledge. Dad also coached, trained and managed a raft of local youth and school teams himself and was engaged in that, unpaid, every other night and during the weekends. For a man who was out the front door to go to his very arduous job at British Rail by 6.30am and wasn't back home again until well after 5pm – except when he was on the night shift, which was worse – I have no idea where he got the energy. Somehow in the midst of all that he still had time for all of us.

My mum would be forever washing the strips of entire football teams that my dad was dealing with. That washing line was always teeming with shirts she had hung out in the shared backyard at the bottom of the tenement. I am still amazed that none was ever stolen, though she did keep an eagle eye on them all day from our top-floor flat along with Auntie Josie, Mum's twin sister who lived through the wall in the next-door tenement with her fabulous family of gorgeous girls.

My mum Mary was one of those selfless people who, if heaven exists, are born to be angels. A typical day would be: providing breakfast for all six children before school, taking care of her own mother even in her long difficult dementia years, going to the Catholic church for Mass, helping clean the priests' house, cleaning the church, doing the flowers at the church, getting back home and keeping our house clean, shopping for the entire family, carrying that heavy shopping up the three flights of stairs as well as doing all the washing for the family, then getting a load of football strips washed as well!

After all that, us kids would be back from school and we all had to be cooked for again and then sorted out for the next day. Looking back I have no idea how my parents managed, especially when I consider the limited budget they had. They both cared selflessly for their own children, but they also helped hundreds, maybe thousands of others over the years as well. Crucially they never did any of it looking for recognition, they did it because they believed it was the right thing to do.

Maybe I got a little special attention from my dad because I was so committed to his beloved football. I used to religiously practise every football skill you could think of with him, including penalties, and it soon led to a couple of unexpected outings. The first time I ever appeared on a football pitch in front of many thousands of fans was particularly special. I managed to get to the final of the Glasgow schools penalty kick competition, to take penalties before a league game at Celtic Park one Wednesday night. I was only ten, but oddly not at all fazed by the surroundings. How perfect that it was at Celtic where I was used to standing on the terraces. I scored all ten against a professional goalkeeper to get me into the final and then managed to score all five at half-time to win the competition in front of 30,000 fans. Denis Connaghan of Celtic was the goalkeeper. That got me into the national final, which was to be held at half-time during the Scottish Cup final at Hampden Park in front of over 75,000 there for the Celtic v Airdrie game. The keeper for our penalty competition was the Scottish international Stewart Kennedy. I managed to win after scoring every single one again after a shoot-out against another youngster. I knew this lad, Scott McGarvey, well through the Boys Club football in Easterhouse.*

It was tough for Scott. As we faced up, shooting into the 'Celtic End' of supporters, they announced our names and which schools we attended. For some reason the strongly Catholic Celtic fans booed every penalty taken by Scott from Provanhall Primary School and cheered every single one taken by Patrick from Saint Jude's.

I loved winning and getting presented with the trophy, but the most extraordinary thing in hindsight was that even though I was a quiet kid, those 75,000 people watching didn't affect me or my confidence in the slightest. There was no nervousness, I just believed I could do it. In retrospect that's a bit unusual for an introspective ten-year-old. But I had practised thousands of penalties with my dad, even at that young age. The whole thing simply felt like second nature.

---

* If that name sounds vaguely familiar, he went on to play for Manchester United for a short time and more recently was cast as the guy who brought down Sam Allardyce when he was England manager in a *Daily Telegraph* sting.

Maybe penalties weren't that important in my later career (spoiler alert – I became a professional footballer!) but dribbling around the cones, sticks or bricks for all those thousands of hours with my dad really was vital for my future success. That specific training regime was the one we practised most often and it became the base of my control of the football. If you do it often enough you then no longer have to look at the ball when it is at your feet. It's just like becoming a good driver. After enough time you don't even consider your feet on the pedals or hands moving through the gears. Your concentration and your eyes are, as they should be, focused on the road and the surrounding dangers. Football is similar; it is best if you can keep your head up all the time, looking at opponents trying to tackle you, seeing what opportunities are developing or just as importantly spotting where your teammates are. It gives you a massive advantage. Have a look at Kevin De Bruyne or David Silva playing and see how rarely they look down at the ball in comparison with other players.*

Every day, month after month, year after year, Dad and I trained throughout my childhood. I loved it and even when I started playing organised football for boys' clubs or the school team – sometimes with my dad as manager (and boy, was he ten times harder on me than anyone else) – we still trained every day when I wasn't involved in a real game.

Then every Saturday morning I played for the school team followed by another 90 minutes with Celtic Boys Club in the afternoon. On Sunday there would be a game for a different boys' club. There were Glasgow Schools representative games and then in the summertime there

---

* There are a few other similar ways of getting that skill imprinted. The Will Coerver method is an easy-to-learn version but there are others too. The one thing they each have in common all the way from ball games on the Brazilian beaches to tiki-taka and the Cruyff-Ajax-Barcelona coaching style, is the huge number of hours you need with a football at your feet if you are going to be truly at one with the ball. There isn't really a short cut to developing that sort of skill set.

would be a couple of extra midweek games into the bargain.*

All those thousands of hours, all that sacrifice that my father and I had given to the joy of playing football. All those times when he travelled to watch me, he hardly missed a match, wherever it was played. How could I have been so callous, not to be overly upset for him when that dream had died?

I kept it to myself, but I never shared his dream and back then, while I knew he wanted me to get better at the game I loved, I didn't know that he believed I could be a professional footballer. You might find it hard to believe, but in our family it was simply never spoken about. I thought the fitness and health benefits we gained, and the joy of playing, were enough in his eyes. I knew he wanted all his children to be happy, fit and healthy: surely that was the real reason for doing it?

But unbeknown to me and not spoken of for another decade, he had told my older brothers when I was very young that he thought I would play internationally one day. I know what my reaction would have been then had he said it to me: 'Poor old Dad, you haven't got a clue, you really do see my abilities through the rosiest of rose-tinted glasses.' The arrogance of youth and the wisdom of age are clearly unchanged by the passing of the decades. He was going to have the last laugh on that one.

---

* There were countless games in those years and they all blur into one another, but because most were in the east end of Glasgow, the gang warfare that was going on sometimes interrupted the matches. In one game for St Clare's Boys Club up at Lochend in Easterhouse, play had to be stopped on several occasions when gangs of maybe fifty lads chased each other back and forth across the pitch. They were carrying baseball bats, golf clubs and the odd sword, which was a fashionable accessory with the gang leaders. There was, however, no consideration of abandoning the match and rightly no thought that the players were in danger; we were just in the way momentarily as they charged past. When they had passed through the referee just blew his whistle and we started again, with me reminding him to add the extra time on at the end. I imagine it would be considered differently now; it would probably make the national news. Back then it was not unusual in Easterhouse.

When I was ten, Dad and I walked about half a mile or so to the only grass pitch in the area, between Springboig and Barlanark; it's covered by a housing estate now. We were there doing our drills and suddenly three lads in their late teens or early twenties came over and spoke to my dad:

'Hey auld man, get aff the pitch, we're usin' it noo.'

'Don't worry, lads,' said my dad, 'we will be gone in about twenty minutes and you can have it then.'

The wannabe bully boys looked at this old man and said, 'Get aff noo, ya auld c***.'

My dad, in his mid-fifties (which I'm sure you'll agree isn't old!) was seething. 'You will have to make me,' was his calm, firm and, to be honest, slightly menacing reply.

At this point you should know that at certain moments my dad looked not unlike a young Clint Eastwood. He might as well have said, 'Go on punk, make my day.' You should also know that in his time Dad had been a handy boxer in the Navy, a Mediterranean Champion with an infamous knockout punch. He was only about five foot six, but perfectly built, good-looking in that 1940s film star kind of way and even in the winter he looked tanned and toned.

Moments later, having launched their attack, the lads dragged their battered bodies away dazed and confused. I looked on, mouth open, in awe of what I'd just seen.

But Dad turned to me and fixed me with his firm, no-nonsense eyes and said, 'Pat! What are you doing? *Why have you stopped dribbling round the sticks?*'

2/
KIDS

In those early days of my youth I was surrounded by a loving and sometimes, I accept, an over-protective family, who were not only passionate about sport but just as passionate about education. Our generation was the first not to leave school at fourteen years of age, but even from the 'deprived' working-class area of Easterhouse, our parents ensured all six of us went into higher education. In some ways I am the family failure because in the end I didn't finish my degree.

For their part our parents taught us about the importance of fairness, honesty, hard work, giving your best at all times and kindness to others no matter the circumstances. This they did not with long worthy speeches but by the way they led their lives, with every action of every day. They were loving and giving people who showed me and my five siblings exactly what parents should be. Growing up in the third floor of a tenement in a housing scheme in Glasgow's east end may not seem ideal for future opportunities, but I loved it and somehow we all prospered.

There was an honour and respect about the way my parents always behaved and expected us to behave. The gang culture was a major problem at the time and there were fights all around, but we were never part of it or of Glasgow's infamous drinking culture either. We were educated to be apart from all that madness – not above it, just apart. Swearing at home was unthinkable, and we were expected to use the best English we could, which led to us all having much softer accents than most of our neighbours. No member of the family was ever in trouble with the authorities – that would have been unthinkable for us.*

My dad worked those long hard hours for British Rail, taking all the overtime he could get to provide for us.

My needs were limited, however; a ball and a pair of football boots were enough for me. Any other clothes apart from the school uniform were functional aside from the odd football top we could get our hands on.

One thing that did grate sometimes was at the weekend when Mum and Dad would say, 'Right, we are all going out for a walk.' This 'wee donner', as it was called, could last anything up to six or seven hours! The upside of Easterhouse was that it was right on the edge of the city, so the countryside and long walks along country lanes and canals paths were only minutes away. At the time I probably didn't realise all the reasons why these hikes were so prominent in our lives. Yes, there was health, fitness and an appreciation of nature to be gained as well as quality time together with all the family.†

But the real reason was almost certainly that there was absolutely no financial cost to these marathon marches, and it was the cheapest way to keep us entertained. With eight of us squashed into that three-bedroom apartment, maybe it was a sensible idea to get us out of there for long periods, hail, rain or shine, otherwise we might have been at each other's throats.

On the top floor at number 7 Eddlewood Road in Easterhouse there

---

* My worst misdemeanour was to sneak into Archie Macpherson's garden – the legendary Scottish football commentator lived in the posher estate nearby – and steal apples from his trees. He commentated on me many years later when I played for Scotland, but I thought it best not to mention the apples until I retired.

† I am ashamed to admit I collected birds' eggs out on those walks. I was very young and knew no better.

were the four boys sleeping in bunk beds in one room (Thomas, Michael, Joseph and me), the two girls (Mary and Kathleen) in another, then Mum and Dad in the third. It might sound awfully cramped but it felt normal and cosy to a youngster who knew nothing else.

Thomas was the oldest and back then he was super-protective of us all. That was ingrained in his personality along with his constant generosity and little has changed to this day. He was mild-mannered like all of us but unlike the rest of us you could not meddle with him. From deep beneath and on rare occasions there was a dark menacing danger that lurked and might arise, when he had to defend something or someone dear to him. He became a teacher then a headmaster soon after. To my mind he was good enough with a fair wind to have become a pro footballer too, in a left-midfield box-to-box style.*

Big sister Mary was caring, diligent and quiet but with an unspoken iron will to finish off anything she started. She never flinched at anything the boys did, didn't ask for or expect any special treatment. She was calmly our equal and often our better. She went into special needs schooling and became a teacher and lecturer in Glasgow. She also taught me how to read and by the age of three, long before I went to school, she had me perusing the newspapers, giving me a great start in education, which was more of a help than she could ever imagine. She also used to go to see Celtic with us all, so was as well versed as anyone else in the family with the football chat. She stayed with the rest of the family on the long sea swims that we

---

* He ended up in Hong Kong and every person in football I have ever introduced him to, within minutes, says the same thing: 'The wrong one became a footballer.' He would have been much better suited to the lads' banter style; he is utterly comfortable in any company. Because of the expat community circles he moves in, it is no exaggeration to say that every single country I go to anywhere on this planet, someone eventually comes up and says, 'Are you Tommy Nevin's brother?' The question is never asked the other way around. The inference being he is far more important and well known than I am in the real world!

would go on, even though at the time an outsider might have considered it inappropriate as she was 'only' a girl.*

My other older brother Michael and I played football together for almost as many thousands of hours as I did with my dad. I loved his personality mostly because of his humour, which just grew more pronounced the older he got. Back then it was dark enough and strange enough to always make me laugh. If one of our short-lived cats walked into the room wearing a gold lamé jacket, borrowed from one of little sister Kathleen's dolls, I knew it would have been Michael's doing, even as he sat there totally straight-faced on the settee. Football was an altogether more serious business. I would never have made it as a pro without those long evenings when we played against each other, especially up in the grass area behind the tennis courts in Barlanark. Being four years older, bigger, stronger and a very good player himself, he made me better because we would compete as equals. Deep down he probably knows how thankful I am.† I definitely wouldn't have improved as quickly without him. Like my other older brother Thomas, he was probably good enough to make it as a pro, in the Kenny Dalglish forward sort of position, but in football you need the stars to align just at the right time as well as having the talent. The stars didn't align for either of them.

Joe was the artistic, talented one and fifteen months my junior. If he was interested in something then he would be totally immersed in it for that time and would become supremely knowledgeable very quickly. He had an ability to bore deep into any subject to a microscopic level, which eventually helped his art. I would have chosen his degree at Glasgow School of Art over any other degree, but I had nowhere near his talent – few have.

Then there was my little sister Kathleen who I completely doted on.

---

* A swim straight out to sea lasting hours was not unusual for my dad and the older kids to do. This was on Scotland's west coast, long before wet suits were commonplace, so it would be freezing to start with, but we were a hardy bunch.

† Well, he does know now as I have just called him to say it.

It couldn't have been easy being last of the six of us, each with their own big separate personalities, but she fought her corner well. She still amazes me with her stoicism but will forever be the kid sister who I wanted to spoil, even if she did get bored with me sometimes.

The family also spent a good deal of time in another part of the east end of Glasgow: Celtic Park. When younger I can never remember paying to get in; it was accepted that all young kids would be lifted over the turnstiles. There was a little problem with us in that you could only lift one kid at a time, but Dad sometimes would have two, three or four of us with him. So other men in the queue would be asked to lift us over with the accepted phrase, 'Gi' uz a lift in, mister?' My siblings and I had to ham up the accent if I am being totally honest.

There were so many great times following Celtic with my family as we grew up. They were in the middle of winning nine titles in a row, so there was a lot of celebrating. Dad and I saw them win the league at Brockville and at Easter Road as well as lifting quite a few cups at Hampden Park. He even took me along to Hampden for the second leg of the European Cup semi-final against Leeds United in 1970.*

There was allegedly a crowd of 136,000 squashed in there that night. Actually, there was more than that: I got lifted over the turnstile as usual, so that is one more for certain and I wasn't the only kid there. But it was very frightening; the crush was incredibly dangerous and I could see that my dad was very worried. It was only a year later that the Ibrox disaster

---

* Within a few months I had acquired the first football top of my very own – weirdly it was a blue Chelsea strip. They had also beaten Leeds United, this time in the FA Cup final that season, and I thought they were the coolest, most stylish team in England. Considering my family's love of Celtic's green and dislike of the blue team on the other side of the city, it was a bold but in time portentous choice by me to go for a Rangers lookalike top. I got more enquiring glances when I next acquired a Hibernian top and got my mum to sew a home-made white number 4 on the back, so I could be like Pat Stanton. My Celtic supporting friends must have thought my football fancies were a bit strange, so finally I relented and the next one was the green-and-white hooped classic.

happened, killing sixty-six, and there but for the grace of God went many football fans of that era. A few years later I was again at Celtic Park before the most amazing title win when from being 2-1 down against Rangers with only ten men, Celtic managed to win 4-2 and take the flag. It was so moving, more like a religious experience than a game of football. Walking back to Bellgrove train station after the match with thousands of other Celtic fans, I sang more that night than I have ever sung in my life, so much so that I couldn't speak at school for the whole of the next day.

When I was about nine years old we moved out of the three-bedroom tenement we had previously been squashed into in Easterhouse. The council agreed it would be a healthier option for the eight of us to have a semi-detached house in nearby Barlanark – just twenty minutes' walk away, but much better conditions for us all. We had the end house in the street, it was semi-detached, had four bedrooms over the two floors, with a garden that stretched from the front round one side and out to the back. From the front windows there was a view to a play park with swings, roundabout and a slide. Beyond that there was a decent-sized communal park that had tennis courts and a bowling green but, more importantly, lots of space and grass to play football on. Compared to the view onto other tenements back in Easterhouse it felt seriously upmarket, even if it was still a council house.

Another incredibly useful addition to the family arrived then, one that not many other budding football players would have been lucky enough to own: Shandy the family dog. He was a medium-sized mongrel, had a perfect temperament, was as intelligent as any dog could be and was as big a character as any kid in the area. His stories are local legends. He went to Mass every day with my mum and being very intelligent he quickly learned when to stand, sit and kneel (well, he laid down at that point) with the congregation. When the priest was asked by a parishioner one Sunday why Shandy, a dog, was allowed into the church, he said, 'That dog is never away from the chapel, in fact he is a better Catholic than most of you lot, his devotion should be an inspiration!'

Shandy would sit in the middle of our road and the cars would simply treat him as a roundabout. He just didn't fancy moving when he was enjoying a lie-down on a sunny day. I once watched the coal lorry play chicken with him. When he wouldn't move the lorry just drove over the top of him, wheels either side, with Shandy doing no more than looking disdainfully as the high-axle truck went over, inconveniently blocking the sun for a few moments.

As the years went by he would sometimes follow me onto the local train service when I was a student going into Glasgow, calmly getting off at the next stop and casually finding his own way home. I could go on but more importantly he loved to accompany me on my long runs, and it made those hours so much more fun.

Shandy also played football with me in our garden whenever I wanted to. Being a dog and sharp with his reflexes, if I let him get a sight of the ball he would get it off me. So I had to move it quickly. Unlike most tacklers he never fell for dummies and always kept his eye on the ball, and he never got bored or tired so was the perfect training companion. The speed I could move the ball with my feet improved massively but that wasn't the reason I did it, I just enjoyed it and so did he. I could do this for hour after hour after hour.

On paper, you might think that at primary school you would have hated me. I was never anything other than top of my class at every subject! But being seen as clever and also good at football was a winning combination in the popularity stakes and somehow I seemed to have plenty of friends and got on with just about everyone.

Even from the age of six or seven I had the desperate need to get everyone involved, particularly any outsiders who were left on their own, lonely and apart from the group. If I witnessed anyone bullying another boy or girl in the class I immediately took the side of the victim. With me around bullying became a rarity; we were all friends, or at least we all had to be kind to each other – whether they liked it or not. I always knew that if the bullies were in control they would make everyone's life a misery, so, responsible little lad that I was, I saw it as my job to make sure that that didn't happen.

As you can see, my earnestness started early! It was almost certainly picked up by osmosis from my family who were Christian and socialist in their outlook. The focus of our lives was on the basic caring side of those two ideologies – much more important than taking sides in battles between other religions or political ideals. Those who take well-meaning concepts and ruin them with hatred and bigotry have always been anathema to my entire family.

At St Jude's, in Barlanark, there was no let-up in the constant playing of football. I had the good fortune that one of my teachers took the school football team and also the Glasgow Catholic schools' representative team. Mr (Roddy) Shaw made sure I was given every opportunity in class and in the teams, but only if I worked hard.*

---

*· One player who stuck out in those primary school days was Maurice Johnston. He went on to play for, among others, Watford, Celtic, Rangers and Everton, and thirty-eight times for Scotland. Mo was an extraordinary character whose biggest impacts were cultural and social. In 1989 he became the first Catholic to sign for Rangers in over a hundred years of the club's existence.

His school played mine in a cup game. The first game was 6-6 after extra time. He scored all their goals and I scored all ours. In the replay they won 10-5. Guess who scored all the goals again? We then played together for the representative side known as the GCSFA, which stood for the Glasgow Catholic Schools Football Association. This is one of Mo's former teams that might not have been well received by some Rangers fans when he signed for them. We won a centenary tournament against the other (non-Catholic) schools associations in Glasgow and I have an abiding memory of the night we went to the City Chambers to receive our trophy and medals. Off to the side of the stage behind a curtain Mo and I ended up trading blows about who should be in front of whom. What we didn't realise was that the curtain was opening while we were grappling in view of the audience, including the Lord Provost, who just stood there with his mouth gaping, astonished by these apparent 'wee Neds'' inability to behave in that august room. Mo and I eventually played for Scotland together and there was even a short spell shared at Everton. The curtain incident was never mentioned.

In fact, the more I think about it, I can hardly believe how much football was going on. There was a period at primary school when I was playing for my school team, St Jude's in Barlanark, Tommy was manager of St Colette's team in Easterhouse (where he was teaching), and my dad was the manager of the Blessed John Ogilvie school team, also from Easterhouse. We were all in the same league, so those Saturday morning breakfasts were interesting affairs. There was no tension, just good-natured wind-ups. Obviously Dad's team 'The Ogilvie' always won everything. He was a very good coach!

Back then a lot of teachers like Tommy managed the school football teams, giving up their time at the weekends. That eventually ended following a strike – or, more specifically, a period of 'work to rule', where the teachers refused to do unpaid work after school or at the weekends – and many people in Scotland feel it had a dramatic if delayed effect on the throughput of talent to the top level. The national team didn't qualify for anything for generations so there may well be something in that argument, but there was much more to it than just the teachers' action. What a system, having to rely on teachers giving their spare time for free!*

Primary school was a cake walk and great fun but by the time I got to the secondary school I wasn't always top of the class even if I was still passing each exam fairly easily. It was a bit of a surprise to come across plenty of kids who were at least as good at exams as I was. They were also willing to study a whole lot more than me, which gave them an advantage. I got into the habit of doing enough to get good grades and no more. There were fun things to be done other than studying all the time and at that age it usually

---

* My slightly rotund but very cool French master Mr Smith took the football team at Under-16 level at my secondary school, but he couldn't always rustle up enough players on a Saturday morning. He was a lugubrious chap. We were walking one frosty morning towards another school, knowing that with only nine players we didn't stand much of a chance. 'Sir,' I asked him, 'do you think you could pass for under 15?' His lightning reply: 'What, stone?'

involved a football. It did frustrate some of the teachers but the English department, Miss O'Rourke in particular, were dedicated and caring and they fuelled my love of literature. The Modern Studies department with John McLauchlan and Chris Nairn knew how to entertain while teaching, which makes education fun, inspiring and, just as importantly, engaging. Learning and passing exams is much easier when you are engaged by an enthusiastic tutor.

In my mid-teens there was something of a political awakening. The family was obviously socialist but not in a bolshie, overtly party-political kind of way, just committed to a fairer, more equal society. Some of my cousins, though, were very radical in comparison. One of my uncles helped write speeches for Jimmy Reid, the famous Red Clydesider union man.

At school there was a political edge to some of the classes. The Modern Studies and Economics department tested us and got us to challenge our own ideas. Head of department John McLauchlan had a great schtick of winding people up with what sounded like perfectly good logical arguments that we all knew to be totally 'wrong' for us young socialist liberal types. Many years later I found the arguments and indeed the delivery precisely replicated when I got to know Tony Wilson, the owner of Factory Records. Throughout my life I found it easier to question the social attitudes and politics of my 'right-on' self because of Mr McLauchlan's rigorous testing by alternative arguments at school. When push came to shove though, I think we knew where the department's politics lay. Our school didn't go to a nice little French town on the school trip, they decided to go to Moscow instead. That was pretty radical during the Cold War of the 1970s.

As time went by there were the usual anti-apartheid badges along with button badges of my favourite bands pinned on my lapels. There were always earnest political debates alongside the odd political march, to 'fight' for the underdogs, the outsiders and the workers. Glasgow was and is a very political city with a well-developed social responsibility and my entire family were passionate about equal rights and equality of opportunity. Even then the anti-apartheid sympathies were strong. I was as likely to have a poster of Steve Biko as I was of Celtic's genius winger Jimmy Johnstone on my wall.

And yet there was bigotry on our own doorstep, not just in South Africa.

My dad was never promoted at work even though he toiled forty years for British Rail and was intelligent, diligent, trustworthy and incredibly hard-working. The problem was that in his workplace the Catholics were routinely overlooked for wage rises and particularly for promotions. He was disappointed because he couldn't provide more financially for his family, but he was never openly bitter about the discrimination. He felt that his integrity and his work ethic were the ways to show people how you should really behave. Most of his workmates respected him in the end, I believe, even if the youngest, rawest non-Catholics on the scene continued to be promoted ahead of him as the decades rolled by.

The real education was for his children; we learnt so many of our attitudes and developed so much of our personalities from watching him. This was the indelible grounding for my lifelong campaigning for equality, be it race, colour, creed, gender, sexuality, religious beliefs or whatever. If you or those close to you have experienced unfair discrimination, the bitter taste never fully leaves you.

For all that religion in the background – Dad was a committed Catholic and Mum was by any description devout – they would never accept any prejudice towards other religions. They were all about love not hatred. That there was to be no discrimination from them or from any of their children was unspoken but always understood. None of us ever went down that dark road. The thought of us joining in any sectarian songs at Celtic Park was utterly unthinkable.

3/
THE STORY OF THE BLUES

At eleven I joined a boys' club in my neighbourhood called Blue Star, probably so named because the founders were Rangers men at heart. This irked my dad a bit. 'Couldn't you find a team called Green Star?' he grumbled. Those Celtic roots ran very deep in my family.

Just about all of us came from in or around that little Barlanark scheme.

Paul McKenzie was my best mate at the little club and then Paul Kelly became my best mate for a while after he joined. There was Foxy, Mad Nugget (and he was delightfully mad) and a bunch of other lads with equally daft nicknames. I, like all of my brothers, was only ever known as 'Nifty'. We were a very good little team.

The manager was a man called Alex Neil. There were good reasons why he was the coach. First, he was another one of those selfless men like my dad and brother Tommy who gave up his time for no other reason than to help local kids. There was no pay or even local acknowledgement, just pure altruism from his side. He didn't even have a son in the team!

The other crucial factor was that he owned a tiny ancient blue minibus that thirteen of us could squeeze into, perched on the two slatted wooden benches facing each other along the sides in the back. It was a modern health and safety officer's worst nightmare. But we were such a good little team that amazingly we won almost every tournament we entered, including the 1975 Scottish Cup for Under-12s, playing against many well-established, bigger and better-funded clubs from around the country.

We travelled all the way up to Dundee for the quarter-final match. It seemed like a huge journey going all the way up to what then felt like the Highlands to us, squeezed of course into that little minibus for nearly three hours. It is hard to explain how excited we were to discover that in Dundee they played on grass pitches, not ash! That a hundred or so locals had turned up to see the game and that they also actually had nets on the goals – wow! That just added more excitement to the day and made me more desperate to score so that I could hear that delicious sound of a ball lashing into a rippling net. We must have been in shock during the first half, as we were 3-1 down at the break, but we eventually won 6-3 with me hearing my favourite sound three times as I got my hat-trick.

Another 'crack' Dundonian side had previously come all the way to Barlanark and were seen off 9-3, but to be fair they looked very apprehensive about everything, from the red ash pitch to the surrounding intimidating tenements and their raucous occupants. In the final we became Scottish champions by beating Whitehill Welfare 7-4 at a junior ground in Blantyre, where I got my usual hat-trick, but it was the semi-final of that Scottish Cup that sticks in my mind all these years later. We played the biggest team in the city, the ones to beat – Celtic Boys Club – at Helenvale, on a beautiful Wembley-like grass pitch. Grass wasn't something we often got to play on, red or black ash pitches were used 99 per cent of the time for youth football in Glasgow back then. This, however, was lush and beautiful, and it had a real stadium built around it.

It was a beautiful sunny mid-summer's day and Celtic were wearing their famous green-and-white hooped shirts, no doubt expecting to intimidate these little upstarts from the east end. They may have had the pick of any youngsters in Scotland's entire central belt but we still hammered them 5-2 and I managed to bag my customary hat-trick.*

This tells you a lot about how big Celtic Boys Club was in Glasgow in those days. After the game their coach walked straight into our dressing room and magnanimously proclaimed, 'You done well, lads, you were the better team, best of luck and I hope you win the final.'

Then, rather less magnanimously, he turned around to me and added, 'And you, son, you're playing for us next season.' And off he breezed as if this was the most natural thing in the world to do. But Celtic were that powerful, that confident, that arrogant and, to be fair, that right.

Next season I was his new centre-forward.

---

* I was always centre-forward or second striker (i.e. number 10) until I turned pro, but I'm not bitter about being stuck out wide for an entire career – honestly!

4/
EVERYTHING'S GONE GREEN

Celtic Boys Club at that time was an incredible winning machine at every age group.

I honestly think that in some ways it was better organised than some professional clubs I went on to play for. From Under-13s all the way through to Under-16s they were expected to win every game and every trophy. They didn't always manage to win every game but came damn close most of the time in that period.

The club called themselves 'The' Boys Club. Not just any old boys club but '*The*' Boys Club. You know the arrogant way that you can get the Brazilian Football Confederation or the Scottish FA but in England they are always known only as 'The' FA. Well, the Boys Club had that same swagger and confidence about itself as an organisation. Once you were there, you were without doubt at the best possible place in Scotland to learn how to play football.

I loved wearing those classic cotton hooped green-and-white shirts and numbered white shorts. They were sometimes handed down from the Celtic FC first team to the older Boys Club age groups to wear. That is sacrilegious for some to consider now and even physically painful for some memorabilia collectors to contemplate. I could have been running around wearing and ruining Jimmy Johnstone's old shorts or Kenny Dalglish's old top from the previous season! These were pieces of history ruined by a bunch of 'weans' sliding around on red cinder pitches!

That first season was the one where I scored 160 goals as a centre-forward. My dad's earlier promise of paying me a shilling (5p) for every goal I scored was waived for that campaign for fear of bankrupting the family. The coaches for me in that age group were professional and caring. They were good football coaches as well; they always gave positive advice and considerate support. Every week the Celtic FC newspaper, called *The Celtic View,* would have a section on 'The Boys Club' and though I would not have admitted it then, I can say now that it was a delight to see my name printed with the number of goals I had scored as part of the brief report.

Even though I was doing well for the Boys Club this didn't mean I was signed yet for Celtic itself under their 'S' Form scheme. The clubs were linked but they were not exactly the same organisation as far as we were concerned. We all knew that only the very best players would be taken on by the main football club. The Boys Club was an unofficial feeder club, but if you wanted to sign for someone else, you could. And indeed I almost did.

After watching me for a couple of games, the scout for Dundee United sidled up to me afterwards and said, 'Have you signed for the Celtic yet?'

'No I haven't,' I answered honestly.

'Would you like to come up to Dundee United and train with us during the Easter holidays?'

How exciting was that for a thirteen-year-old? Naturally, I really wanted to. At that time United's first team were a very good side. Players such as Andy Gray, Paul Sturrock, Dave Narey and Paul Hegarty were all Scottish internationals and little Graeme Payne was a personal favourite of mine to watch, due to his small stature and large skill set. They were often in the top three or four in the league chasing down Celtic and Rangers alongside Aberdeen as the 'New Firm'.

What a week it was. They quickly moved me through the ranks and even as a very small thirteen-year-old they had me training with their Under-16 squad by the Thursday. I knew I was doing well as I was the only one moved up like that. I was still finding it easy enough to beat players and score goals against these lads who were three years older than me.

At one point a player-coach from the first team, who were training on the adjacent field, walked over and asked me to come off the pitch and follow him.

He said, 'I have been watching you from over there.'

I was waiting with bated breath for the compliment that was surely about to come.

'You are pretty rubbish at kicking a ball aren't you, son?'

He then took my shooting action apart and reconstructed it in the same way Butch Harmon might have done with Tiger Woods's golf swing. He was absolutely right, and it was a huge help in getting me to strike the ball harder when I needed to. Most of all it was impressive that he spotted it while coaching others in the first team and he wasn't dazzled by the fancy skilful stuff I was doing either.*

On the Friday, the first-team manager Jim McClean asked me into his office and personally offered to sign me on a coveted 'S' Form. It was a bit of a surprise to be given the honour of an audience with the actual manager of the club in the first place. After all I was still only thirteen, not exactly a first-team certainty in the making. Jim had an infamous reputation for dressing-room rages that allegedly made Sir Alex Ferguson's rants sound like the whispers of a shy ingenue. With me in that room,

---

* In retrospect it is no wonder that this player-coach, Walter Smith, would go on to be a highly respected manager of Rangers, Everton and Scotland. Like all the best coaches he cared first and foremost about improving and getting the best from anyone he worked with.

however, he couldn't have been more polite or softly spoken. I replied to his offer with what you will come to see as a typical Pat Nevin response. I didn't bite his hand off as a lot of lads would, but instead said:

'I would like that but would have to go home and check with my dad first.' I may have thought myself streetwise, my dad was that too, but he also had wisdom in a wider sense.

For the record, Dad was delighted that I had obviously performed so well at a real professional club, but he wasn't desperately keen for me to sign on the dotted line right away. He said he would think about it for a while before he gave his consent. It was a canny move; we both probably knew deep down that this might raise interest at a certain other professional club.

At training with Celtic Boys Club a few days later I semi-innocently mentioned to a couple of the lads that I was going to sign for Dundee United, mostly to get trips to Dundee, to be fair. Going anywhere – and being paid 'expenses' to go – was as good as a free holiday, and who doesn't like a little adventure in life? The jungle drums obviously went into overdrive and by the next night the Celtic FC assistant coach, the lovely Sean Fallon, was in our house with orders not to leave without my signature. His old Irish charm was never going to fail with my mum and dad and, of course, I was just as keen too. This was Celtic after all, the club me and my whole family would be expected to follow religiously from cradle to grave.

I didn't tell anyone at school that I had just signed for Celtic. With hindsight maybe it does sound a bit odd that it wouldn't have crossed my mind to let the two worlds of football and the rest of my life collide. But I genuinely would have hated the interest from all the other school kids. So, for a while the training sessions that I subsequently had with Celtic FC and 'The Boys Club' were totally separate and secret from my school life. It got out eventually when it was reported in *The Celtic View*, but it wasn't something I ever talked about with my friends if I could help it. Even at that young age I wanted to be liked for who I was, not what I did.

The football club and the Boys Club were two entirely separate propositions, with different coaches, playing at different grounds. I would now play for both. The 'S' Forms trained at Celtic Park on Wednesday or Thursday nights and the Boys Club trained at Barrowfield on the other nights. I also played for the Boys Club at the weekends as the 'S' Forms only had a handful of organised games each season.

The training at the football club itself was awful, always on the cinder track or patch of muddy grass at the back of the goals at Celtic Park. We were training inside the stadium, which was a buzz, so that was something at least, but for the purposes of technical improvement it was close to useless. We did change in the first-team dressing rooms, getting a glimpse of how the real game looked for real players, but sometimes there was no training organised when we arrived. If it was the night after a big European game, we just swept up the rubbish left on the terraces from the night before, which was a horrible job.

Not every man in those days fancied fighting his way through 60,000 other fans jam-packed together to get to the grotty loos, so peeing into empty cans or bottles and leaving them behind was not uncommon. It was a smelly, sloppy sweeping job made worse because not all of the terracing was concreted: the 'away' end was built of wooden slats with fine, now moist, dirt to stand on. Maybe we were given these jobs to toughen up us young emerging players, but in reality it was probably nothing more than cheap labour for the club instead of employing real sweepers. It was gross. But there was one upside. Now and again you would find money dropped by celebrating fans and not found by them in the darkness of the evening game.

The Boys Club players always wore green blazers, grey trousers, white shirts and green Boys Club ties when going to games. When every single opposition team turned up in their old jeans or any other assorted scruffy clothes, it certainly gave us a psychological advantage over them. Personally, I thought we looked silly, but even when I played against them before I joined, I could see the effect it had on some of my teammates –

they were cowed before a ball was kicked. So, it was good psychology. However, the club uniform wasn't quite as good for travelling to and from the games on public transport in the rough east end of Glasgow.

There were a few dodgy moments, but on one occasion in particular I had to take a short cut and was caught by a gang of kids around my own age who weren't over-impressed by the emerald-green Celtic tie, green blazer with Celtic BC badge and then there was the shamrock badge on my kit bag, which seemed to particularly rile them. One good beating-up later I fortunately managed to get away with no bones broken. I went to a friend's house nearby and she let me get cleaned up. When I eventually got home later, I told one of my older brothers, I will not name which one, so as to keep his current respected character intact. We popped out in a battered old car with a couple of his friends, found the lads and 'interviewed' them robustly one by one. Oddly enough they never bothered me again after that.

I should say here that my family were never violent, never sought trouble, but in the east end of Glasgow back then you simply had to protect your own in those circumstances. If you didn't you were considered weak and became a target.

We didn't think of ourselves as targets at Celtic; we were winners. In fact, the most constructive thing that you had drilled into you again and again at Celtic was that you were a winner. There were two positions in football with Celtic: first and worst. Like the All Blacks or the US Women's football team, it was almost Jesuitical; you were the best of the best and being the elite was nothing to be ashamed of on the field.

The bit I really bought into, however, was that it should not just be about winning but winning with style, with panache and most importantly within the rules. A catchphrase used early on and used consistently through the years by all those in the sphere was 'Score an early goal and press on regardless.' I had no vestige of arrogance or superiority in any part of my being, but put me on a pitch with a ball at my feet and I didn't think anyone could get the better of me. That's why I was perfectly suited to playing there. A minute after the final whistle that ultra-confidence evaporated, but on the field during games it was a different world where the rules of who I could be were different – in fact they were diametrically opposite.

That ethos built around winning and winning the right way infected everyone. I remember playing for Celtic Boys Club Under-14 side one rainy Saturday afternoon, and I walked off at half-time having scored a couple of goals. I hadn't even reached our coach or the half-time oranges before I was stopped by a tall red-headed obstruction. For the first 45 minutes I had been kicked around constantly by a couple of thuggish centre-backs who were much taller and much more developed than me. I had 'shirked' (jumped out of) one tackle because I thought I was going to get injured by one of the 'hammer throwers'. The centre-half from our Under-16 team had come along to watch from the sidelines and he grabbed me roughly by the hooped shirt. The piercing blue eyes blazing at me belonged to David Moyes, who would in time become coach of Everton and Manchester United among others.

'Don't you ever do that again, I saw that,' he said. 'You might have scored a few goals and we might be winning but now they think you're scared of them. You have just given them a massive psychological lift. It might not help them today but they will always see that as a weakness in you in the future, especially if you shirk another tackle in the second half, so never do that again!'

The words and sentiment were seared into my consciousness, but what kid of sixteen spends his free time watching the younger teams, mentors them, coaches them and looks after their psychological wellbeing? Shouldn't he have been concentrating on his own burgeoning career instead of worrying about a skinny wee centre-forward in the younger side? That was the Celtic way, though: we all play the right way, we all help each other, we all win together. You could have stamped MGR on his forehead when he was sixteen and it wouldn't have made it more obvious than it already was; he was born for the job of being a top football manager. And I never 'shirked' a tackle again.

At the Boys Club there were an extraordinary number of players that made it through to Celtic FC: internationals such as Tommy Burns, Roy Aitken, Charlie Nicholas, Paul McStay, as well as the likes of Davie Moyes. There were many others who went on to have great careers but didn't play for Celtic, such as Jim McInally from my team who went on to play for Nottingham Forest and Scotland. Billy McKinlay was another player who made the same journey all the way to the national team and I could go on for pages with more names. There was a problem though, that most of us didn't discover until many years later. There were paedophiles operating within the confines of the club.

It should sadly be no surprise that no one who was being abused talked about it to the others around them at the time; that's how grooming predatory paedophiles operate. Certainly, I can recall thinking that one of the men, Jim Torbett, was a pretty creepy guy even if he always tried to come across as kind and interested. I didn't often speak to him and as a youngster I wouldn't have been able to verbalise it, but I just didn't feel comfortable in his company. He was in some role at the Boys Club but not chairman at the time I was there. I had no idea or no interest in his level of involvement, he was a distant figure to me and the phrase 'too smarmy by half' would have been the limit of my thoughts. There would have been nothing more than that level of concern from most of us young lads back in the mid-1970s.

He has since been convicted and everyone there will have asked themselves: what did they know, what did they suspect, what they could have done or said and to whom? I don't mean that the boys should have asked those questions. But what about the more worldly adults who were around at the time? I do understand that predatory paedophiles are by nature secretive and sly in their depraved actions. But was it really completely concealed and invisible to those who should have been protecting us all?

Maybe I just got lucky. Certainly one slice of luck was that my dad was ever-present at games and even regularly came down to watch the training sessions. Did he ever have knowledge or suspicions of what was going on? Is that why he was so present? I'll never know, but I doubt it strongly. His presence there then, as it was through my entire life in football, was for support and it didn't matter who I played for. He was there for all my games half a decade before I arrived at Celtic Boys Club – it is just what he did. I think if he had ever learned all about what happened in those days it would have broken his heart. That certainly has been the case of so many of his generation who revered the Boys Club.

If you think of all the settings where predatory paedophiles have infiltrated groups of young people – the churches, the Scouts, the BBC, public schools, every sort of organised youth sports club you could name – it is hard to blame each entire organisation. They had good people there too among the monsters. For the most part there was a deep naivety in the public, and an unquestioning belief in these organisations. I also think there was an ignorance about these evil people. I am sure it still exists but at least we are more vigilant in safeguarding young people in today's society, and also more educated compared to those dark times. The tragedy is the lives that have been ruined, that cannot be recovered – but an acceptance and admission by those who knew would be a good start as the historic cases come to light.

The only other man to have been convicted that I knew was Frank Cairney, the coach of our Under-16s side. Because of anonymity in court proceedings, to this day I cannot tell you if he has been found guilty of sexual abuse of anyone who was in my team. It has not even been made clear to me what he specifically did to be jailed for three years – the reporting was infuriatingly unspecific. I know in hindsight he behaved in a way that would now be deemed totally inappropriate, but any more than that honestly shocked me when the allegations arose. Some players didn't like sitting in the passenger seat of his car, fearing he might put his hand on their knee in a 'friendly' way. If they had to sit there, they would put their big green Celtic Boys Club sports bags on their laps.

There were also the showers after the games and not all young boys were keen on showers. But Frank insisted everyone had to get in and shower post-match and after training. Now that sounds very inappropriate today, though back then it seemed less so to most young naive kids; in truth, all coaches at all clubs encouraged you to shower after games. Parents would have wanted their kids to shower after training to get clean and that would be the reason given to demand everyone showered. In hindsight, from a different angle, with what we know now, it feels deeply uncomfortable at best.

I wish I had been more worldly; I wish like everyone else that I had known and could have done something or said something to save those victims, but it really wasn't any child's position to stop it at the time or indeed to fully understand. It was the adults in charge who knew, if indeed they did, who should have got involved. Surely some of them must have had an idea?

What Frank Cairney actually did to me, was bawl at me.

Playing those four years at the Boys Club, the only maltreatment I got was a huge amount of verbal abuse from him. Only ever known as Big Frank, he shouted and roared during every single game at Under-16 level and it felt as though it was constantly aimed at me, though one or two others got a bit. That was the culture in football back then in Scotland with some coaches. We have all heard of the 'hairdryer' treatment from Sir Alex Ferguson. It was considered a perfectly normal way of ensuring the players were motivated to give their best.

Things are very different now but up and down the country, even in professional dressing rooms, the bawling-out of players will still be common enough, even if it seems old-fashioned and is often counterproductive to creative play. It has doubtless delivered the required results on occasions, but in my view it should only ever be used sparingly if at all. Too much shouting too easily becomes bullying and quickly kills off any short-term productiveness the technique might arguably have had.

The constant barrage of shouting from the sidelines during these games, at half-time and post-match too, eventually began to wear me down. It started limiting my enjoyment of the game, especially in my last season at Celtic Boys Club. I had learned to block it out most of the time, but it wasn't pleasant, and I couldn't see the point because it wasn't helping me.

In fact, I was so hacked off with the constant barracking that by the time my Boys Club career was coming to an end, as I approached my sixteenth birthday, I made my mind up not to even go to the end-of-season Player of the Year function. This was ordinarily something that everyone looked forward to at the Boys Club. We'd collect all the medals and trophies we had won over the year and there would be awards for each age group's Player of the Year. But it says something about how worn down I was by all the shouting that I'd decided I'd had enough and in perhaps some small act of rebellion decided that I didn't want to go.

In any case I had been let go by Celtic FC by this point and when the Boys Club ended, I had basically decided to give up on playing football altogether. For a while anyway.

But in the end, perhaps out of a feeling of duty, or perhaps from some ghoulish interest, I caved in and turned up on the night, even dragging some of my school friends along, something I had never done before. It was a final farewell to the footballing life, I guessed, so I might as well do it properly.

Anyway, there was one specific individual trophy to be presented that night that caught everyone's imagination – the Chairman's Trophy for overall best individual player at the club – and we all wanted to see who was going to win it. Nearly all the players in the history of the club who went on to have stellar careers, for Celtic usually, had won this award. Roy Aitken, Tommy Burns, Charlie Nicholas, they'd all won it – so we could very well be in the presence of a star of the future.

Well, I knew I wasn't getting it, for two obvious reasons. One was that Celtic had decided not to take me on, and the other was that all I ever got was negativity from Frank Cairney, the very manager whose job it was to choose the winner! But, like everyone, I was intrigued to know who would win it.

The dinner was at the Plaza Ballroom on Eglinton Toll just on the south side of the Clyde in Glasgow, on the road out to Hampden Park.

It had been an ornate dance hall in its glory days and was still clinging on grimly to some of its previous grandeur. There could have been as many as six or seven hundred in the hall and everyone was dressed up for the occasion with shirts and ties or best dresses. The first-team manager would have been there as well as some of the players.

You'll have got there before me, I'm sure, but as the chairman stood up to name the winner and read out my name, I felt utterly confused and bewildered. As I walked through the hundreds of people there up towards the stage I had no idea what was going on.

Surely there must be some mistake, I thought. *Is this an elaborate wind-up? No one else seems surprised though, except maybe my school friends. Do they think I set this up so they could witness my glory?* If they did, they were wrong. Even my dad didn't seem too shocked by this accolade, but for one of the first times in my life I felt totally wrong-footed and had no idea what to do, think or say.

Approaching the stage in front of hundreds of people applauding, I noticed the Celtic FC contingent, the same people who had just got rid of me. I thought to myself, *Whoa, that's a bit embarrassing for them. But I'll think about that later, I have to get up the stage steps first without tripping over.*

As I walked by Big Frank, he stopped me and said quietly:

'You do know I only scream and shout at good players. There's no point in shouting at the others – they can't help not being good enough, but you could and did. More importantly I think you have a big future in this game, and you are going to have to deal with some very harsh words by managers, players and fans. After what I put you through, no one will ever be able to affect you by screaming and shouting at you.'

It was very old-school thinking, but if I am brutally honest, whether I like it or not, it was totally effective. There's no doubt in my mind now that Frank did in fact inure me to that brutalist simplistic method of 'coaching'.

He then did an extraordinary thing. He leaned into the microphone and said in front of the shuffling shoe-gazing Celtic FC representatives:

'You are making a big mistake letting this lad go and I have no idea why you are doing it. He is an exceptional player with a perfect attitude, and this is very wrong.'

I have very mixed feelings about Celtic Boys Club.

In our current society if someone or some organisation has been convicted of wrongdoing the established thing to do is distance yourself from them and decry everything that has been done by them, whether good, bad or indeed awful. But it would be a lie to suggest that the good things that happened within that organisation were in the end all tainted beyond redemption by the actions of a few.

For those who suffered I am distraught; I share their anger. For those of us who prospered while it happened, I can only say there was good among the bad.

We just got lucky.

5/
DON'T MESS UP
A GOOD THING

School work and passing exams was seen as vitally important in our house and Mum would never let us forget it. She had left school very young but passionately believed in education and the help it would give to all of her children. With a modicum of effort I was able to get accepted onto a few courses at a few universities, but I chose Glasgow College of Technology* because it had the course that gave most opportunities for most jobs, as far as I could see.

My English teachers, particularly Kathleen O'Rourke, might have been a bit disappointed in me for choosing a Business Studies degree instead of taking an arts course. But that encouragement to have an interest in reading and writing meant that I have been passionate about English and European classic literature throughout my life. I guess it was one of the reasons why I didn't exactly fit in with the footballer types as I reached my mid-to-late teens. We had very different interests and hobbies

---

* Now Caledonian University.

by then. These lads wanted to be footballers, buying expensive clothes, trying hard to look wealthier than they really were to impress as many pretty girls as possible. In the US they would have been called jocks and I would not have been hanging out with them.

Me, I had been a music lover all my life, and had been going to gigs by the likes of Genesis and Thin Lizzy while loving David Bowie. Then, in 1977, punk changed the entire musical landscape. Soon I was listening to the John Peel show on Radio 1, loving the post-punk scene that was fabulous in Glasgow at the time while immersing myself in literature and study.

My musical tastes were always a bit left field, even as a young kid. When I was six or seven my older brother Tommy got a Rolling Stones greatest hits album called *Through The Past, Darkly* with its octagonal sleeve. I listened to all the classic rock and R'n'B songs but was only transfixed by one track, the psychedelia of '2,000 Light Years from Home'. I loved the dark side and the odd different sounds more than the cheery pop on daytime radio. So it would be no surprise a few years later to find me at an early Siouxsie and the Banshees gig or even early New Order or The Cure, alongside any act Peely had played that seemed interesting. I was a regular at Tiffany's between 1979 and 1981, where young post-punk bands regularly played. At that time Simple Minds were releasing some great music, even though they were scarcely known outside Glasgow, and I loved what they were doing. Even now listening to 'Celebrate', 'Love Song' or 'This Fear of Gods' transports me back to those nights when Jim Kerr dominated the stage with his strange movements while the band played this dark, powerful, foreboding European post-punk electronica that seemed timeless. Those nights and that scene felt innovative and cool with an interesting group of followers, many of whom became friends. We went along to see another raw young band who turned up at Tiffany's in '81 and they seemed to show some promise in front of a small sparse crowd of us. In all honesty that incredibly youthful U2 put on an exceptional performance. Alongside that there was also the burgeoning Postcard Records scene with Orange Juice, Aztec Camera, The Bluebells, Altered Images, Josef K – the list goes on. It was a golden era for Scottish music, maybe *the* golden era of Scottish music and creativity.

I was also with my long-term girlfriend Alice and as such had absolutely no interest in going to nightclubs to chase other girls. That was how the football folk were behaving but I was having none of it. Neither outlook was right or wrong, better or worse. They were just different life choices and that is how I always felt about footballers. I didn't feel above them, just a little different to them.

On the course at 'The Tech' I studied economics, accounts, business studies, computer programming, marketing, contract law. I learned to type at speed and there was even a decent psychology module thrown in. Apart from the computer programming, I put every single one of those subjects to good use during my career and after it. So, it turned out that it wasn't a bad course to go for in the end.

At Glasgow Tech life was good. And it was exactly where I wanted to be. The plan, such as it was, was running smoothly. Each weekday morning I walked twenty minutes to the train station, or ran if I was late, usually accompanied by Shandy.*

Getting off at Glasgow Queen Street station in the centre of town it

---

* On one occasion I got on the train at Shettleston station to go into college only to catch a glimpse of Shandy casually jumping onto a train going the other way. He knew how to get back from the next station going into town, but he was going east not west, the fool! I got into Glasgow Queen Street station twenty minutes later and sprinted to the nearest payphone to call home in a panic with the bad news.

'Mum, Shandy's lost. He has just got on a train and might end up going all the way to Airdrie. He'll never find his way home.'

Mum sounded too calm. 'Oh, don't worry—'

I cut across her. 'You don't understand, he will never find his way home, he has gone the wrong way, he will be disorientated and confused.'

Mum sighed, 'You don't understand. Shandy isn't in Airdrie, he is sitting beside me right now in the hallway and we are just about to head up to the chapel.'

Clearly Shandy just thought he would try a different route home, getting off the train at Garrowhill station and trotting nonchalantly straight back to the house. He was too clever.

was a short walk up to Glasgow Tech, which I looked forward to every single day. The anticipation had more to do with the fun I had with the friends I had there than the education I was getting. I guess that is not uncommon for students of any age anywhere.

The first weeks were not great as I struggled to find the right group to hang out with but soon enough a few like-minded souls gravitated together. It wasn't that we liked the same music or football teams or even had similar political outlooks, we just had the same humour and relaxed outlook on life.

The closest friends were John Roche, Peter Welsh, Jim Morrison, Suzanne Smy and John Campbell. Rochey had a huge personality with an unfiltered, unselfconscious humour that cracked us up constantly, particularly but not exclusively when he'd had a few drinks. Peter was sensible, quiet, morbidly obsessed with Celtic FC, a decent footballer and eventually my flatmate. He also didn't have a bad bone in his body. Jim was an extremely talented basketball player who towered above us all and regularly came in with a broken nose from his sport. This was strapped with tape from one cheek across to the other to keep it in place. This looked silly enough, but when you consider the make-up the world-famous Adam Ant was wearing at the time, and the fact that at six foot seven Jim already stood out from the crowd, I am amazed he bore it so well. When we weren't humming 'Prince Charming' within his earshot, we were calling him Herman Munster.

Like me Suzanne was an indie muso kid, but she was also another one of those people so rare in the world who never appears to have a negative word to say about anyone. She had a bright, sunny outlook that I haven't seen drop in the almost four decades of knowing her, alongside a constant consideration for other people that reminded me of my mum, who was also an angel. John Campbell was the fifth member of the group and did tend to be the butt of the majority of the jokes, but he took it well and gave it back as good as he got. He was another who had a sunny, positive disposition, which is the thing, alongside the humour, that has kept us all friends to this day.

Out of the blue, I got asked to play for an Under-18 team called Gartcosh United, which was a nice way to keep playing football on the side. It turned out that the man running it was David Skinner, who had helped build an impressive little club virtually from scratch in just a few years. So much so that they had been Celtic Boys Club's biggest challengers the year I left at Under-16 level.

David was seen as the enemy the year before and from a distance seemed the incarnation of evil and arrogance – he was certainly portrayed that way. He turned out to be a funny, warm guy with that light heart absolutely in the right place, on top of which he was clearly an astute judge of players. By halfway through the first season there were more scouts from the professional clubs watching our little team than parents and supporters.

After one game, a cup final where I had scored all four in a 4-0 win, I could see the Glasgow Rangers scout making a beeline towards me. There were maybe a hundred people around and most of them could see the daftness that was about to ensue. He came up to me directly, everyone stopped and the buzz died down to silence, not unlike that in a wild west saloon when the gunslinger walks in.

He said proudly, 'I am from Glasgow Rangers and my name is…'

I answered, 'I'm from Gartcosh United and my name is Patrick Kevin Francis Michael Nevin…goodbye!'

I turned and walked away, shoulders bobbing up and down, while everyone else, including my teammates, chuckled at the guy's predicament. Back in those days Rangers had infamously never signed anyone born a Catholic, so in approaching me he had made a cardinal error, even if he wouldn't have approved of the word cardinal. In the west of Scotland my name was evidence enough of my family history and unsuitability for the mighty Gers. His first question should have been, 'What school did you go to?' and that would have given the game away, but he didn't even get that far with me.

By then I had already ditched religion, but that wasn't the point. Even being baptised or born into a Catholic family was enough to disallow you from being signed by Rangers. We Celtic fans all laughed at it because we all knew that Rangers were idiotically depriving themselves of access to about 50 per cent of the country's talent. It was a form of religious apartheid and it no longer happens at Rangers, but even back then I knew it was clearly disgraceful. The scout made the best of a bad job, turned on his heels and signed up our centre-half David McPherson instead. To be fair, 'Big Slim' went on to play over 300 times for Rangers as well as getting 27 Scotland caps, so he didn't have a completely wasted journey.

While at Gartcosh I trained briefly with Airdrieonians and realised quickly, to my amazement, that I was fitter than all of these part-time pros, especially the older ones who told me not to go too fast in the longer runs as it would show them up. I ignored them; the Celtic background would not allow me to do anything less than my best, whatever anyone else said. I played one game for their reserves as a trialist against St Mirren, but they didn't bring me on until the last ten minutes when they were already 3-0 down. I was fuming that I had given up a game with my mates at Gartcosh for ten measly minutes at Broomfield Park, even if it was on a real professional team's pitch. I came on, scored and spent every second on the ball embarrassing not just the opposition defenders but also the Airdrie manager who was watching. He said afterwards he was worried I was too young and too small – that old one again – which is why he hadn't brought me on earlier. I never went back.

Partick Thistle also got in touch around this time and asked me to go along for an Under-21s match. Always keen to play with new people, I accepted the invitation. When I turned up they said, 'Look we know you play centrally but can you play out on the wing tonight as we already have a couple of strikers.'

'Who are they then?' It was Kenny McDowall (who went on to be a Thistle legend) and Maurice Johnston! Again, I did OK, but this time I wasn't asked back. If I had serious desires to be a pro, I might have been crushed by these failures, but fortunately they had no effect on me at all. Had there been a good gig on that night, I would almost certainly have skipped the trial and gone to that instead. In fact, I wouldn't be surprised if I went straight from Firhill the couple of miles into town after the game to see a band, I was that casual about it.

Even so, if I wasn't interested in being a pro, why bother going to these trials?

Well, each had been arranged by David Skinner without me knowing, and his continuing efforts to get me opportunities were constant and selfless. In fact, as I clearly wasn't showing any great interest in becoming a pro, they were bordering on saintly on his part!

I suspect now that he and my dad might have been in cahoots. That would make a lot of sense. As it was, if I was asked to go and play football with some team one afternoon, I would! I just packed my kit into my bag and got on with it. Others would have considered these trials a big deal, but for me it was nothing more than another game of football and a chance to have some fun.

The next thing I knew was that I was being sent down to Ipswich Town. At that time they were a top-level side with England internationals Terry Butcher, Paul Mariner and Eric Gates, who was a fine number 10, as well as Scottish international John Wark. The manager was the great Bobby Robson. They had come second in the league around then and went on to win the UEFA Cup in 1981, not that I would have cared. They weren't Celtic so it meant virtually nothing to me.

I went down for a week and I guess they must have been giving me a trial ostensibly as a youth trainee, or YTS as it was called at the time. The first day I trained with the Under-18s. The next they moved me up to the Under-21s. By Wednesday I was with the reserves and on Thursday I was playing directly against Terry Butcher from the first team.

Now to be fair there were a number of things in my favour in that session. I was relaxed and the England captain-in-waiting didn't know my style. I was exactly the wrong type of small tricky player for him. He was also my cousin (through marriage), though he didn't know that yet either! I had heard there was a family tie there somewhere, but it certainly wasn't close and I didn't even consider mentioning it to Terry that morning.

I had some fun with big Terry, using every trick and dummy I had. I enjoyed it even more when the English legend started trying to kick lumps out of this young whippersnapper who appeared not to be taking his respected position at the club very seriously at all. 'Annoying little git', or words to that effect, were his only interactions with me. His increasing anger had the effect of making me realise I had him concerned and the other pros taunting Terry just spurred me on. Seventeen-year-old scrawny student versus top English league club captain – I liked that challenge and of course I knew I had nothing to lose. Terry doesn't remember it now, but why should he? It was only a training session for him, one of thousands, but I loved it and it must have bolstered my self-belief no end. Somewhere hidden deep in my psyche, I must have been thinking, *Maybe I am good enough*, but it still didn't come close to seriously piercing the surface or affecting my plans.

I really enjoyed my week at Ipswich, and on the final day I could see that the manager Bobby Robson was keeping a close eye on me during the sessions. Afterwards he called me into his office, and I could see that same serious frowning face I had witnessed before at Celtic but this time I listened with some interest. I was a student with no club, still very small and waif-like, I didn't look close to my seventeen summers and I also dressed very differently to the others in my punky biker jacket and ripped jeans. But maybe I was also maturing just a little and had a bit more respect for the situation than I had at Celtic. I had clearly done well enough again to get asked into the manager's office for a one-to-one. For a busy top-level manager it was an honour I appreciated but more importantly it showed Bobby Robson's decency.

'You know son, I think you might be good enough to make it and I am very torn about what to do,' he said. 'The problem is if I signed you, you would have to be better than Eric Gates and that is a tall order, lad.'

I took that as a huge compliment because I did like Gates as a player. I decided to make it easier for him and explained that although it had been a very nice week and I had thoroughly enjoyed myself, I didn't really see myself as a pro footballer, so I wouldn't have said yes even if he had offered me something. I told him I'd really just come down to see what it was like to play with English pros. But I was doing a degree and wasn't really looking to become a pro player myself, or move away from Scotland at all, for that matter. Looking back, he did seem quite surprised by all this! But he handled the conversation like a true gentleman and seemed genuinely interested in what I was saying. He even said he respected my thinking – though in a way, I suppose, I'd been completely wasting his time.*

I went back to Glasgow after that week and resumed my carefree life as a love-struck student. I was spending most of my spare time with Alice and I was laughing constantly every day with my student mates. There were also a few close school pals still around, in John Maguire, John and Christine Flynn and Brendan O'Hara. I was busy, happy, still living at home with my family and the world seemed just fine and dandy.

But everything was about to change.

---

* Four years later when he was England manager, Bobby Robson chose me as the First Division (now Premier League) Player of the Month on one occasion. Later still he picked me for the English League select XI in a game at Wembley against a Rest of the World team that included Diego Maradona, Gary Lineker (then of Barcelona), Paulo Futre and the Brazilian Josimar. I never did mention to him that I was that wee guy who didn't want to be a footballer and I am sure he had no idea. By the way, there is also no truth whatsoever in the rumour that when I was forced to pull on that white 'England' shirt at Wembley, it was the most embarrassing moment of my career. It was an honour to play the match.

6/
I DON'T WANT TO GO TO CHELSEA

I was seventeen and still playing for Gartcosh United when we found ourselves with a weekend off. The manager Davie Skinner decided to accept a bounce game against Clyde FC reserves at Shawfield, the home of the 'Bully Wee'. David told us he was just doing the Clyde manager a favour as a few of their reserve games had been cancelled and their players were getting a bit rusty. It was no big deal even if they were a professional club, it was just a bounce game to make the best of a spare weekend. We didn't know it then but that was absolute nonsense from David. He knew we were a pretty decent team. We had won every competition we had entered that season, including an international tournament that summer in Toronto, and he doubtless suspected that his little boys' club could impress this (part-time) professional outfit. We got a fantastic lift from that two-week run to glory in Canada. We won every game and I scored for fun against teams from the USA, Canada, Mexico and all over Europe, on top of which the local media loved us. So Clyde at Shawfield was just another game for us.

I was playing in my favourite number 10 role and before we trotted out onto the pitch, my closest friend in the team, Brian Sweeney, and I were laughing away distractedly in this real professional dressing room, not taking it at all seriously. We decided to have a bet, something I never do, but this was for fun. Whoever scored the best goal against this lot by beating the most players had to buy the other an album. I probably had my eye on *Wilder* by The Teardrop Explodes or *Heaven Up Here* by Echo and The Bunnymen having already just bought *Movement* by New Order and *Faith* by The Cure. I admit they were not the cheeriest of albums; I was going through my existentialist, Albert Camus-worshipping phase.

On the pitch, Brian scored a good goal. But I managed to beat four players before scoring mine and I thought I had won the bet. We walked off at the end of the game still laughing at the silliness of it all and arguing the piece.

'There was no way your goal was better than mine.'

'What do you mean? I beat four of them before dummying the keeper.'

'Yeah but I hit mine from twenty yards, yours was just a tap-in after beating them four, and they were rubbish anyway.'

We were not disrespectful, making sure we were out of earshot of their players but not of their manager, Craig Brown, who stopped me before I even got to the dressing room and asked for a word.

'Do you want to sign for Clyde and play for us professionally?' It was a bit blunt and totally unexpected. Of course, I got the Patrick Sensible head on quickly and explained that I was in the first year of my degree course and full-time football didn't appeal to me, I just liked playing for fun. You know the spiel by now! I expected him to meander off, but he thought for a moment then said:

'So, you're a student and you get a grant – you are pretty skint then, I guess?'

'Well, er, yes, I suppose.'

'Well, Clyde are part-time,' he explained. 'We only train two nights a week and then we play on Saturdays. That will not affect your studies, we could give you £30 per week, which you could treble in a good week with bonuses if you get in the first team and we win.'

'What if I can't get in the first team?'

'Well, you've just dribbled round most of them and scored a goal, so you've got a chance.'

So it wasn't a reserve team game! Well, in theory it was, but it turns out there were plenty of first team players in there too. 'So you are offering £30 per week as well as my grant?'

'Yes.'

'All right, you're on! Where do I sign?'

So much for the high-minded football lover with the pure thoughts! Thirty quid a week and I'm yours. What a tart! I would have argued that it all made sense and I wasn't doing it for the money – well, not solely – but if I'm honest, the dosh did play a rather large part. I mean, how many gigs could I go to and albums could I buy with £30 back then!* I could also take my girlfriend out to those gigs, to a restaurant or to the movies and not have concerns in the back of my mind whether I could afford to offer to pay. I had never really considered this dream scenario of being paid to play football and study at the same time, but it just fell into my lap.†

A few months later another three of my Gartcosh teammates had signed

---

* Brian never did buy me that album I won in the bet.

† I mention financial matters in this book only because I have been told it would interest some people to know about them. I had to remind myself of most of the numbers other than my first contract at Chelsea, which I could actually remember. For historical record and relevance, they are included, or some of them anyway. For someone who studied economics I had a very laid-back attitude about my own financial situation. As long as I had enough money to just about get by, I was happy.

As an example of why you shouldn't dwell on it too much if you are a former player, I played for five years at Chelsea and I earned so much money that if you add it all together it is roughly equivalent to two weeks' wages of one of their current players!

for Clyde and were all in and around the first team – quite a profitable little friendly for Craig Brown then. He seemed to have a decent handle on student thinking and didn't seem to find me as weird as other football folk did. I soon found out that Craig was a lecturer at a college in Glasgow as well as being the Clyde coach. He had played for Rangers, would go on to manage Scotland's national team and he even gave me a good number of games for my country. That little friendly totally changed my life in so many different and long-lasting ways.

I still had absolutely no intention of being a professional footballer, even though now I technically was one. This was part-time in the third tier of Scottish football, and though we now had 500 fans turning up to see us, it still wasn't totally serious big-league stuff and I could still have fun while I played.

Now don't get me wrong, I'm fully aware that there was a strange dichotomy going on here. I was a fanatical trainer – my 'other' sport was middle- and long-distance running and Sebastian Coe was a bit of a hero when I was younger. So even though I spent a lot of time laughing, trying tricksy skills and not being interested in being a full-time pro I was utterly dedicated to my fitness and my craft. I could only enjoy football when I was playing well, so I trained far more than anyone else around me to make sure I was in shape and in the team. That was the reason for being the best, not some desperate desire to 'make the big time'.

It took a little while for me to get a start in Clyde's first XI. I was on the bench and only used as a sub for the first few months and, in truth, the frustration was killing me. I thought I could have made a difference in some of those games and in training I was showing that I could cope with the tough tackles from the seasoned pros. I loved playing football and here I was sitting on a bench when I could have been playing a game somewhere else. Also, when it was a midweek game there was probably a gig on somewhere that night that I wanted to see. I was prepared to miss the gig to play football but less happy about missing it to sit on a bench frustrated.

It seemed like an eternity, but it was only a couple of months. When I eventually got to start against Cowdenbeath it went well immediately, and I stayed in the side. I scored six in the next six games as Craig Brown finally let me loose. Not that I was counting the goals and assists at the time, I just wanted to play football again. More importantly we also managed to win the league that season. This football lark was surprisingly easy! It was glorious, fun, unpressured and exactly how I wanted it to be. I even liked the players around me; they were normal working guys with full-time jobs, who just happened to be pretty good at football. None of them seemed to have any real expectations of becoming high-profile star players either, so I wasn't odd in that sense. Few had any pretentions about anything and they also took it upon themselves to look after me on the pitch. When I got kicked, they would be down on the perpetrator like a ton of bricks. The fans took to me quickly as well, which also helped.

At the time I hadn't quite discovered my obsessive compulsion to be early for everything in life. So getting to the game on Saturday usually meant jogging from my home to the train station, getting off two stops later at Bellgrove station and then running to Shawfield (sometimes at a sprint if the train was delayed) where Clyde then played. That sometimes meant running past Celtic fans on their way to their game. So before even starting the 90 minutes I had already run three miles. It was badly organised of me but quite a good warm-up and the fact that it didn't affect me during the games underlined how fit I was.

There is a photo taken on the final day after we had won the Second Division title where each of the first-team players had to hold up a letter spelling out 'THANKS FANS' to our 500 or so acolytes. I sneakily grabbed the second 'S' and when we were asked to hold them up, I managed to forget accidentally on purpose to lift mine. The manager wasn't amused.

I also got into the habit of sneaking up to the DJ booth at the back of the stand, locking myself in for ten minutes before the game like the scene from *The Shawshank Redemption*. The fans would be subjected to the latest single from New Order or the like. I am sure a very young Simple Minds got the track 'Celebrate' aired a few times as well.

Things were, however, beginning to run slightly out of control regarding my non-career. At college I had to take and, more importantly, pass, my first-year exams if I was to stay on the course. And in addition to playing for Clyde, I had been chosen for the Scotland Under-18s youth side and had played a few games that seemed to put me safely in the squad for each gathering.

An early youth game was against West Germany, who had Berti Vogts, the former World Cup-winning defender, as their coach. It was to be played at Hibernian's Easter Road ground and I was delighted to be there, Hibs at that time being the 'other' team that I favoured after Celtic.

In those days any big event meant being sent telegrams from well-wishers. Beside the neatly laid-out kit some of the lads had telegrams with homely messages saying 'Good luck' or 'We are all so proud of you on your first cap' or 'Play Your Heart Out'. Three arrived for me in the dressing room: the first one simply said, 'Give Jerry what for old boy' and the second said, 'Bosh the Bosch'. Knowing the senders, I knew it was satirical and not xenophobic. But it did sum up the different kinds of background and humour my lot had from the others. Even my old schoolteachers were at it: theirs read, 'Congratulations and score or you'll get belted. From the lower staff room.'

We won the match 2-1, I scored with a mazy dribble that I was very proud of, my mate Brian McClair scored our other goal and Michael Rummenigge scored for them.

I was one of the few part-timers in the team, as most of the others were from the likes of Celtic, Rangers, Dundee United and Aberdeen. We qualified for the European Championships to be held in Finland, getting past England on the way, but there was still some concern about the little lightweight oddball. The manager of the U18s was Andy Roxburgh, who went on to become the Scotland coach and latterly head honcho with UEFA and FIFA's coaching divisions; his assistant was Walter Smith. The day before we left for Helsinki, we were tested for our fat levels with a body mass index check, which was a bit pointless on my fat-free (and muscle-free) body. There was also a middle-distance run organised around a local track; it was to last twenty minutes with the entire squad running together.

I was quietly confident because of the distance running that I was still doing each week. I had run for the school in cross-country competitions a few times and ten- or fifteen-mile runs were not unusual or particularly difficult for me. However, these guys were full-time professionals so I didn't know for sure if I could keep up. With seven minutes to go Roxy shouted, 'Right lads, give it everything you've got for this last bit.' I lapped just about every player except Paul McStay, but I did take a couple of hundred yards off him very quickly. It sounds small beer but from that moment on my belief in my fitness never wavered. Just as importantly, Andy Roxburgh never again doubted my strength or endurance capabilities. Thankfully he was always a backer of my style and skills.

There were problems on the horizon, however, and I was trying to work out what I should do. *If we get to the final of these Euros in Helsinki, it is the night before one of my major exams in Glasgow. Can I really mess about with my real career for this football lark? Then again, we probably won't get to the final anyway, Scottish teams never do.* I decided to put it to the back of my mind. Then another 'problem' arose.

After only half a season in the Clyde first team, a club from down south made it known they were interested in buying me. Granted we had won the league and I'd also somehow managed to get divisional Player of the Year, but this was madness. The southern club was the famous Chelsea, and it was nice to have their interest, but it was still an easy decision for me. I wasn't even vaguely interested because that would mean going full-time as a footballer, leaving Glasgow to live in London and giving up on my studies and friends. There was no chance that was going to happen. I didn't consider it seriously.

Off I went over to Finland and decided to keep the trip quiet – there was no point mentioning it to the course tutors. I was supposedly studying in the library as the exams approached and they would be none the wiser if I was playing in a little U18 foreign tournament and studying in a hotel over there instead.

Even my girlfriend Alice was informed I'd be busy studying for a couple of weeks and might have to fit in a football game or two, so we should just meet up after the exams. She would be none the wiser about my travels either. I had everything under control.

Except I didn't, of course. We got into the final and even won the thing, the only Scottish national team to ever win a major tournament! Typical! More surprising still is that I was named Player of the Tournament after scoring against Albania, Turkey and then Czechoslovakia in the final. (I didn't notch against Marco van Basten's Netherlands side, sadly.) It was a magical time because every game seemed to go incredibly well for me and the Turks in particular seemed keen on me not going back to Scotland but coming with them to sign for one of the big clubs in Istanbul.*

While everyone on the team might have been getting very excited about the tournament as we progressed, maybe also having the odd night out in Helsinki, I was back in my room at every opportunity cramming for the exams that were closing in too quickly for comfort. It was one of the few times I travelled to a country and got to see very little, other than one hell of a lot of trees on the long drives between the Finnish cities. It might also be the case that not thinking about the relative importance of the tournament relaxed me even further; playing was the joyful release from the real stress of the upcoming exams.

The final against Czechoslovakia was special for me personally because of the goal I scored. We set up one of those complex training ground free-kick routines just outside their penalty area. We made a total mess of it and I immediately had four Czech heavies bearing down on me at top speed. There was only one option left: run straight at them with the ball and try to trick my way through. Much to my amazement it worked and I then only had to round the keeper to score; easy. From the side it

---

* All the games were televised and if there were any matches from my career I would like to have discovered on tape to watch again now, it would be the ones at this tournament. I had so much going on back then that with a couple of exceptions my memories are vague, which is a shame. Sadly, I have never seen even a second's worth of clips, as they were doubtless all wiped by Finnish TV.

looked brilliant, but it came from my own awful mistake initially. Even my screw-ups seemed to work in my favour at the time.

So my plan to keep my football life quiet hadn't really worked, especially as my picture was splashed across the back pages of all the national newspapers for days on end. I also had quite a bit of explaining to do to my girlfriend on my return about this little pastime of mine, but it was the lecturers at college who were having a field day. Most had scarcely noticed the wee guy up the back taking notes, but 150 students in a lecture theatre were alerted on my return that they had 'a star in their midst'. Maybe I shouldn't have used those marketing books in the photo for the Scottish *Daily Record*, but the marketing lecturer loved it…I hated the notoriety and the attention. I desperately wanted my two lives to be totally separate.

My disinterest, dislike and, let's face it, fear of fame looked to be in a bit of jeopardy right at that moment. Juggling sport and student life was looking like a decidedly hectic option.

The good news was that I did manage to pass those crucial first-year exams, even the one I flew in to sit the afternoon after winning the trophy in Finland.

And so it was that I decided to do the sensible thing – well, in my eyes anyway.

It was the summertime, the close season, and two college friends and I bought a couple of tents, three Interrail cards and set off to rough it round Europe for a month. I had met these two guys outside the refectory one afternoon: George had known my older brother Michael, and (yet another) Brian, his mate, seemed a good guy too. By the end of that first chat in late spring we had agreed on this trip around the continent in the summer. You can do spontaneous things like that when you are a student. I wanted to get back to student normality after all this superficial football madness and this still felt like the best plan.

The Clyde manager Craig Brown didn't agree. 'Are you mad?' he cried. 'Why don't you go on a football coaching course here in Scotland instead? You get it free with the divisional Player of the Year award. If you go interrailing, you will get ill staying in those rough rundown places. You can't afford to lose weight; you look like a rake as it is. It is also dangerous, and you could get injured.'

I tried to calm him and reassure him. 'I never want to be a football manager and that is certain so forget the coaching courses. And I will not get ill, and I will not lose weight, and will not have any accidents. I just want to live a normal life.'

Yup. I got ill, I lost a lot of weight with food poisoning in a hellhole in Brindisi en route to Corfu and then injured my leg falling off a motorbike on the island. However, I did keep my word never to become a manager!

Before we crossed the Channel on that trip around Europe, George, Brian and I agreed to go to some gigs. My gig was some post-punk indie band that cancelled at the last minute. Brian took us to see Jools Holland and George got us tickets to see Talking Heads at Wembley and sorted out Simon and Garfunkel tickets when we hit London on the way back. To pay back those favours, a little while later I took them to see a favourite band of mine, the then unknown punky indie band, The Jesus and Mary Chain. On the night it sounded like they could barely play their instruments and certainly didn't play anything recognisable as a tune above the raucous white noise, while they stood with their backs to the audience throughout for the entire twenty-five minutes that the gig lasted. (They were brilliant and I loved it.) They were thought to be very cool by the *NME* and by me at the time, but my travelling companions were unimpressed. In retrospect I think I owe George an apology! Simon and Garfunkel played much longer, the tickets were more expensive and to be fair they had a few good tunes!

The European trip was a blast. In the old days before the internet, bank machines and even credit or debit cards for us, the money was always a problem. It was a case of French francs for today, Swiss francs tomorrow, Italian lire for a while before getting some drachmas for the trip over to the Greek Islands. The night we arrived in Rome we discovered we had no lire at all and no banks were open to change currency. Accommodation wasn't a problem: I was carrying my tent on top of my rucksack. The metal pointed tent poles sticking out from either side were trailing a line of other travellers' blood across the continent behind me. The problem was that we needed food and we needed it badly having not eaten since Paris.

Sitting in the warm evening air I suddenly hatched a plan. Each of us had one luxury we could bring, à la *Desert Island Discs*, and obviously mine was a football. I went into the middle of the square and started doing keepy-up skills with plenty of tricks thrown in, something I had done all my young life, just for the joy of it. These days freestyle footballers are 'a thing', but it wasn't the case back then. I put the cap out and hoped the locals in the square would appreciate it. Being football-mad Italians they did and thirty minutes later I had enough lire to buy us each a lasagne from a cheap *ristorante*. It tasted fantastic, as anything does when you are that hungry and you have worked for it!

Despite my manager's protestations, travelling around Europe was definitely the right thing to do. I needed space to think, to make sure I remembered who I was. George (who went on to become a headmaster in a West of Scotland High School) summed it up on the way back when he said he finally understood why I was turning down a pro career at Chelsea, pointing out with a smile, 'Football just isn't your forte, is it?' The thing is playing football was, but *being a footballer*, living the typical footballer's life, wasn't. And I really didn't want anything spoiling my love of playing.

It was as simple as that.

At the end of that season I was given the Scottish Youth Player of the Year award. There was a lunch in my honour down at Largs where the Scottish FA coaching centre was based. The rest of the Scottish youth team was there, but I was to sit beside the then Scotland coach and former legendary Celtic manager Jock Stein. To explain the true significance of this you have to understand that in my family there was a holy trinity of God, the Pope and Jock Stein (but not necessarily in that order). Big Jock bombarded me with questions for an hour during lunch as if the thoughts and opinions of this teenager were the most important things in the world to him. When I attempted to ask him a question he just laughed, ignored it and kept on with his own interrogation. He had an insatiable appetite for understanding how people ticked, how they could be motivated and even manipulated as players. I found out more about this genius later.

After the lunch I got the train back to Glasgow, went into the college library to do a few hours' studying, met up with my student friends and settled back into reality. I put the trophy, which I was very proud of, in a locker, but I never saw it again. Someone must have been watching me putting it there, broke the lock while I had my head in a book and swiped it. Oh well, easy come easy go.

In that first season playing for Clyde, and Scotland Youths, I had scored 14 goals in 30 league starts and created quite a few more on top of that. I'd created more goals than I scored, for the likes of Danny Masterton, our brilliant old-school striker, and I'd really enjoyed that, sometimes more than scoring goals myself. I had felt that pleasure before I joined Clyde and nothing had changed now that I was playing for a real football club.

Clyde had won the league, which was amazing. And I'd played for Scotland, albeit at youth level, and we'd won the Under-18s European Championships and I'd been awarded Player of the Tournament! I'd also won the Players' Player of the Year for the Second Division, and the Scottish Youth Player of the Year, presented by Jock Stein himself. I had also turned Chelsea down.

Maybe an important reason for that was that I'd also really enjoyed my college course, believe it or not; and I had loved hanging out with Alice and all my other mates at least as much as I loved the football. I was close to my family; I was going to gigs and living the student life in Glasgow with some money in my pocket. My attitude was simple: 'I am happy with my life, why change it?'

But when you look at the evidence, however much I was trying to ignore it, something was going on and changes were afoot.

7 /
CHANGES

After that glorious summer I went back for my second year at college, desperate to spend time with my best friends on the course.

We spent most of our time laughing or stifling laughter in seminars. Typical students, my happy memories are of various idiots doing daft things, usually under the influence of alcohol. Like the time we were in Glasgow late at night after a fancy-dress party and we each decided to leapfrog over a three-foot-high post in the middle of the pavement. Then watching, as if in slow motion, the final member of the gang, kitted out in full-length Monsignor's cassock, try to do the same, with the inevitable consequence of almost hospitalising himself but being saved by his inebriated bounce-ability. You can't leapfrog in a cassock.

One afternoon John Roche and I were on a train home after he had seriously misjudged the effects of an afternoon's student cheese and wine party. Much to his surprise two bottles of wine had a more marked effect than two bottles of beer. With his good-sense filter surgically removed, he thought it would be a good idea to approach four very big, very tough looking, hairy Hells Angels-type bikers and ask, 'Hey, where are your bikes, children? Did your mammies not let you out on them today? Oh, you poor wee souls. Will yer mammies let you out to play with your bikes tomorrow? What happened, did you get home late from the Brownies last night?' Fortunately, I wrestled him away before he got both of us chain-whipped.

Another night Roche and I went back to my folks' place a little the worse for wear, trying to tiptoe in noiselessly at 4am to get a few hours' kip. That was the night of the crushed Bisodol incident. One of our party had been scammed into thinking they'd bought some white powder. When he was told that his high must be fake because it was Bisodol, he said, 'Don't you think you would be spaced out if you had half a pound of Bisodol up your nose?' Fair point. We crept into the sitting room only to see Shandy the dog sitting up on the couch, watching us with a quizzical eye while wearing an Arran jumper with the sleeves rolled up, as was the hip style at the time. I think we woke up the entire house with our attempts to stifle the laughter through the tears.

Being a student was a joy, especially with such good friends around me.

Jim Morrison's girlfriend Julie was great but the first time I met her, only two sentences into our conversation, she said, 'I have a flatmate who is at Glasgow University with me, you haven't met her yet but you two are perfect for each other. In fact, you and Annabel will get married one day.' What a stupid thing to say when I hadn't even met this girl and I had a girlfriend at the time who I was head over heels in love with to boot.

Nevertheless, Julie had set wheels in motion.

After I put some weight back on, I figured the new football season would take care of itself. But even though we were stepping up to a higher division with Clyde, I still wasn't overly concerned. I thought I could manage, and so what if I didn't? I was only doing it for the joy, the love and the fun of it anyway. I had literally nothing to lose. This attitude was working and if only I could retain it, I thought I would do OK.

That second season with Clyde was never going to be another promotion season, though. It soon became apparent that it would be more about survival. We did survive but only just, we were three points clear of relegation in the end. But it was a memorable time and most importantly a happy one. Our striker Danny Masterton was a brilliant natural finisher, not unlike Chelsea's Kerry Dixon years later. He was that talented in front of goal, good in the air and lightning quick too. There were two midfielders, Jimmy Sinclair and Tommy O'Neil, who I realised had that very rare thing, real game awareness.

There are lots of fine footballers out there but the ones I am always most impressed with are the ones who have that quality. It is hard to quantify, but you know it when you see it and especially when you play beside it. These players can develop situations; they always see the right pass and they can generally deliver it at precisely the right moment. They read games in a way most people don't even understand when they are watching it. Think Kevin De Bruyne or David Silva again. OK, so Tommy and Sinky weren't at that standard, but they could play. More importantly, they and all the rest of the players at Clyde seemed to want to help the youngsters. This was not always the case in every club I went on to play for!

After one game against Hearts, I was walking off at the end, extremely disappointed with my performance, having struggled to get past the 38-year-old defender Sandy Jardine. To be fair to the young me, he had been a Rangers and Scotland great, but even so I was fed up that I had not beaten this 'old' man more often. As I traipsed towards the dressing rooms, he came over and explained what I should have done to beat him. It was fairly technical stuff but it made perfect sense. The thing I didn't understand was why on earth an experienced opponent was helping this boy in his teens.

I was so intrigued I asked him outright, 'Surely telling me this will help me beat you next time?'

He smiled. 'There will not be a next time, you will be gone from here very soon, you're too good for this level already. But remember you should always help those coming up behind you too, for the wider benefit of our game.'

OK, I accept that he was probably going to retire at the end of the season anyway, but he was a true gentleman and though sadly no longer with us, he is fondly remembered by everyone in the Scottish game. He wasn't the only one to give that sort of advice on the pitch. Eric Tait at Berwick Rangers did precisely the same thing.

In the media it was being reported that there was a lot of interest in me from other clubs, but I was doing my level best to ignore it, or at least keep it in its rightful position. Family, girlfriend, friends, studying and probably even my love of music were taking up all my time.

However, bit by bit, even I couldn't ignore the fact that I was getting more and more involved in the pro football world. And then one day I was told that the Celtic manager, the late great Billy McNeill, was coming along to watch me at Alloa Athletic. Now a transfer back to Celtic would fit nicely! No need to move anywhere and I could maybe keep on studying. Hey, I wouldn't even need to pay to get into Celtic games if I was playing for them! So, I can't deny I was excited about playing in front of Billy McNeill.

When the night came it was freezing cold and we were playing on a rock-hard, ice-covered pitch. Yes, in those days you would just play and get on with it. It wasn't perfectly suited to my sort of game, however, and I couldn't get a kick as both sides launched the ball like a barrage of howitzers. When I did get the ball, I was beyond hopeless on that surface. Frustrated and with only five minutes to go, someone must have made a pass on the ground by mistake because I finally got the ball at my feet, but I was still well inside my own half. I went on a mazy dribble and finished by taking it round their goalkeeper, stopping on the line and then tapping it into the goal, the way you would in a school playground game. Years later our manager Craig Brown described it as the best goal he had ever seen. It was certainly the most impressive goal I ever scored.

The frustration and even anger I had felt dissipated as I ran back to the halfway line and stole a glance up to see what Billy McNeill had thought of the goal. There, where he had been sitting was an empty seat. He had gone home early having decided he had seen enough. Not for the first or indeed the last time, Celtic and I managed to miss each other.

The truth is that I loved that club and this was really disappointing. Celtic was always the main draw for me. One night, when I should have been playing for Clyde I wasn't feeling very well, and Clyde had an away game at Stranraer. I had a heavy cold and maybe at a push I could have played, but I would probably have let the side down. That is what I told myself and the manager anyway. So, as the Bully Wee struggled their way down to the south-west of Scotland, I stood in the jungle at Celtic Park cheering on Celtic against Rangers in an enthralling 3-3 draw. So unprofessional. I should have gone to cheer on my own team, but a two-mile trip down the road to Parkhead for an Old Firm game seemed a much better option.

The season went well for me, there were a good few goals and plenty more assists as well as more silverware. I won another Young Player award. When my name was called this time and I had to go up on stage I was so astonished I was incapable of saying anything coherent. I don't think I was nervous or scared, just incredulous that I was standing there at that moment, it was all so alien to me. I wasn't thinking about the glory, just about being photographed wearing a dinner jacket and bow tie but not in an ironic way. What would my mates say!

I would have felt more comfortable in black jeans, Joy Division *Unknown Pleasures* T-shirt and a leather jacket. It felt all wrong, and deep down I was asking myself, 'Am I really going to allow myself to be dragged into this world?'

That night a bunch of the Clyde lads were going out and as a winner of an award I 'had' to go along. I really wanted nothing more than to go back to the east end and tell Alice what had just happened. She had giggled uncontrollably when she saw me in the tux beforehand, understandably. I was clearly hamming it up. So instead of my usual haunt of the student union on Level 8 at Strathclyde Uni or one of the clubs where I'd turn up with a hundred others to watch unknown up-and-coming bands of the time (such as The Fall, New Order, The Associates or early Simple Minds – the latter were particularly hated by most footballers back then for being too weird!), I was dragged into one of the nightclubs where the Spandau Ballet, Duran Duran and Wham! lovers hung out – the self-proclaimed beautiful people, known in Glasgow at the time as 'posers', with big hair, big shoulder pads and a big line in self-delusion about their reality as far as I could see.

They were far more glamorous than us scruffy, punky, indie-kid types, but this is where the real footballers hung out and tonight this apparently is where I had to be. I am sure the then young Celtic starlet Charlie Nicholas was in there that night and fitting in very well indeed!

One of my teammates, who had a rather blinding charm and wasn't a bad-looking lad either, said over the noise of George Michael asking to be woken up before he went, went, 'You know, because you're a footballer you could get any of these girls in here.' I tried to explain that I had a girlfriend already and wasn't interested but I felt he was talking rubbish anyway. I had a decent appreciation that I was far from one of the beautiful people.

He said, 'Honestly, I could get any girl in here and it's mostly because I am a footballer, even if it is just for Clyde.'

'OK then,' I said, 'I choose the girl and you have to have her in your arms within the hour?'

'No problem,' he replied, with disdainful confidence.

Intelligence was needed here. I scanned the room and there were plenty of totally unattainable, aloof and very pretty women in there, but I needed more of a challenge. Then I spotted a waitress who was as stunning as any other girl, not unlike Susanna Hoffs from The Bangles. She looked as unattainable as any but more importantly she was also working, so obviously my super-confident teammate had no chance. Half an hour later he was snogging the face off her and she seemed to be very happy with the situation. And he was only a Clyde player!

I was young, principled and this all seemed far too superficial to such a pure young soul. I was too earnest by far in retrospect, but at least it was honest. Instead of getting me more interested after winning my award, the entire night moved me further away from the idea of becoming a real footballer.

Out of the blue that was just about to change, however, and it was complicated.

I had been chosen for the Scotland Under-20s side to play in the 1983 FIFA World Youth Championship in Mexico. After the Euro-railing I had fallen in love with travel, and so an exotic trip combined with football was a huge temptation. The problem was the same as it was with the European Championships. They would be right in the middle of my end-of-year exams. If I went to Mexico I would have to miss all six of them. I could resit the exams in August but if I failed even one of them, then that was me out, I would be off the course and the chance of a degree would be gone.

And then Chelsea came back in trying to buy me with the offer of a two-year contract. Following a great deal of soul searching, I had a lightbulb moment.

My mum certainly didn't want me to leave a solid education to go to London, a place she only ever referred to as 'that den of iniquity'. My dad on the other hand was, very quietly, extremely keen on me going down to push my career. I decided to talk to the course organisers at the tech and ask if they would allow me a two-year sabbatical to sign for Chelsea. I could go to Mexico with Scotland and instead sit the resits at the end of the summer. If I failed one of the exams, I would still have a two-year football contract to fall back on. Plus, there was no reason why I couldn't do a course down in London while I was with Chelsea. I imagined I wouldn't be that busy because obviously getting into the first team would be a very long shot.

If I passed all the resits I could come back at any time to finish the final year of the degree. It was simple logic, with the only downside being that if I missed a year I wouldn't be rejoining my best friends on the course when I got back, but I would just have to deal with that, very much a first-world problem.

Just as importantly – and here was perhaps the clincher – I had by this time realised that I could go to even more great gigs in London than I could in Glasgow! I might even get to meet John Peel at a gig – you never know – and if that happened my life would be fulfilled.

Somewhere in the back of my mind was there a vague idea that I might actually succeed as a player down there? But that was such a long shot that it really wasn't worth dwelling on – the jump in standard was bound to be huge – but hey, there's only one way to find out.

And so I said, 'let's talk!'

The negotiations were interesting. I did all the talking on my own behalf as I have never had an agent in my life.* Ian McNeill was the assistant manager at Chelsea, and he was the guy hanging about outside the family home in the east end of Glasgow pushing to get me to sign on the dotted line.

It must have been difficult for him. He couldn't use all the usual lines – 'You could be a star, rich and famous, recognised on the street, you could be on the cover of magazines . . .' – as I didn't have the slightest interest in the fame and fortune side of it. Finally, a year on from his first efforts, he understood where I was coming from. It was all just about the love of playing. I think he and the manager John Neal liked that attitude when they finally accepted it wasn't a bargaining tool. They got the fact that, yes, I wanted to entertain, learn and enjoy football but I also worked incredibly hard too and was a winner at heart. It is a dichotomy that few people in the game understood at the time.

One of the final things I said to Ian before I signed was blunt and to the point: 'I don't know if this is a good contract or not but if you mess me about, I will take a tube to Euston station, get on a train and go straight home to carry on my studies. I couldn't care less about your profession if it is not ethical and honest with me. You have my word on that. If you are fair with me, then no one will work harder than me to help the team.'

It was another youthfully grand statement! But looking back now

---

* Other than for one day, the day I signed for Everton, and then over twenty-five years later I did finally get a real agent . . . for this book! Apart from that, I have always just talked to and listened to the people who were offering me contracts.

he would have said anything to get me to sign and he agreed to my conditions. Years later I discovered two things. First, that Ken Bates, the larger-than-life Chelsea chairman, had said to Ian, 'Would you bet your job on this skinny little kid?' Ian had said yes and Ken replied, 'I'll hold you to that.' That was a very big call by Ian but also, on that last trip north to see me, Ken had said to him, 'Don't bother to come back to the club unless you have his signature on a contract.'

The second thing I didn't know was that my dad was in the opposition camp! He knew how strong-willed I was, but he also knew that I was in danger of missing a great opportunity in my life. He ensured that Ian said the right things when I was having second thoughts. Both men wanted me down in London where they believed I was good enough to play for Chelsea. I didn't share their confidence, in either sense of the word…

Before that there was the small matter of the trip to Mexico. We had a fine team and little old Scotland felt it had a real chance of being world champions, as well as European champions, with this group of players. Had we learned nothing in Argentina in 1978?

We had Paul McStay from Celtic, a brilliant player; Brian McClair, who went on to play for Celtic and then Manchester United; Steve Clarke, who later became a Chelsea legend; Bryan Gunn, the Aberdeen and then Norwich City keeper; and Eric Black, who scored in a European Cup Winners' Cup final against Real Madrid for Aberdeen, managed then by Alex Ferguson. There was also Ally Dick, who was the wonderkid at Spurs and went to Ajax after that, though he never fulfilled his true potential due to injuries.

We really believed we could do it and we came impressively close. The heat was searing but it was the fact that we were playing at 7,500 feet above sea level that was most difficult to deal with. Nosebleeds, dizziness and fainting are not unusual for sportsmen there until you get truly acclimatised. We got through to the quarter-finals where we lost in the Azteca Stadium, Mexico City, 1-0 to Poland. In other circumstances we could have won that game but by then most of our lads just wanted to go home and get ready for the new season back in a sensible environment. That final game played at altitude in the searing heat was just a step too far mentally and physically after what had happened in the previous game. That was the most interesting one, as it was played against the home nation, again in the Azteca. Over 85,000Mexicans in that vast stadium were seriously displeased when I put in a corner from the left, it was flicked on at the near post and Stevie Clarke headed in the only goal from two yards to knock out the hosts.

Their fans went mad and I mean mad as in furious. They were rioting, throwing everything they had from the top of the crumbling old stadium down on us hundreds of feet below. They had three-litre water bottles made of thick green glass, which many had brought to help them hydrate in the 100-degree heat. They also served as fantastic missiles and when the game ended they were exploding like small bombs all around us as we tried to make a dash for the tunnel that would get us to safety in the bowels of the stadium.

There were two ways of getting through the glass bombs and shrapnel. First try to spot them hurtling down and dodge between them for fifty yards as you tried to get off – I personally went for that option. The other was to get your head down, sprint for safety at full speed and hope for the best. In front of me Paul McStay went for that ploy, which was nearly his downfall.

I could see one of those bottles heading straight for him from high up in the stands, but he was gloriously unaware as he sprinted. Fortunately, it missed, exploding just behind him, but I truly believe it could have killed him had it been a direct hit. After that I think some of the lads just wanted to get home to Scotland and safety.

It had been a long trip already, with altitude and heat acclimatisation in Colorado needed beforehand; we had experienced enough. But luckily there was no damage done to the players that a few glasses of alcohol, drunk not thrown, wouldn't resolve. The upside was that aged still only nineteen I would now never be fazed by any away support. Nothing could be more intimidating or extreme than this, even if it was Anfield, Old Trafford or Wembley.

By that time my room-mate on that tour, Brian McClair, had become my best friend in football. Like me he had exams to think about and he was another outsider, maybe seen as even more odd than me by the general football fraternity. He had been studying Maths at Glasgow University while playing for Motherwell but Celtic then Manchester United beckoned. An extremely principled guy with a humour drier than the Elysium plain on Mars, Brian underplayed his talent throughout his entire time in football and still does to this day, but he went on to have an incredible career. Despite our studies, fate had decided that a career in football was what we were going to have. By the time we eventually retired it turned out we had won all the same medals; he just got a better version of mine. Every. Single. Time.*

---

*

	Brian	**Me**
Scottish League Champions	Top division	Third tier
English League Champions	Top division	Second tier
FA Cup	Winner	Runner-up
European Trophy Winner	UEFA Cup Winner	Under-18s Champions
Scottish Player of the Year	Main prize	Under-21
Divisional Player of the Year	Top tier (Scotland)	Third tier (Scotland)
Club Player of the Year	Manchester United (twice)	Chelsea (twice)

PART TWO
LONDON

8/
LONDON CALLING

Chelsea had not been doing well.

They had very nearly fallen into the third tier of English football a few months before, famously saved by a late Clive Walker goal to win at Bolton. Ken Bates had taken over as chairman and it was clear some serious changes had to be made. Unknown to me at the time, I was a part of that revolution. Eddie Niedzwiecki, Joe McLaughlin, Nigel Spackman, Kerry Dixon and I were bought for a combined total of less than £500,000 – an astonishingly small amount of money, even back then – to rebuild the team. Unusually, all five were almost immediately to become stalwarts in the side. Getting five out of five right is an unusually good strike rate in this business, especially with limited funds. John Hollins came back to the club at the same time as player-coach and although he didn't stay in the side too long, he was the perfect man to take the training sessions.

The pre-season training was held in Aberystwyth in Wales, and we were based at the student accommodation at the university. At least I felt at home there but for the Chelsea players of today putting up with that same spartan existence is unimaginable. To say I had come with little fanfare is an understatement. The rest of the first team thought I was a new youth player and seemed quite surprised that I was allowed to train and run alongside them! I was still very young-looking and very skinny. All the talk was about the new golden boy, striker Kerry Dixon, who had been signed from Reading. I was very happy for him to be taking all the media attention.*

Three moments stood out in that pre-season that helped change the rest of the players' perceptions of me. The first was the morning training/torture sessions in the Welsh sand dunes. Training on sand is old-school – an incredibly hard but fast way to build your fitness. It was not unusual to see players vomiting after the sprints and slogs up and down those gigantic dunes. As ever I had neglected to mention that I was a distance runner, so those dunes were a piece of cake for me as I flew through the sand with negligible weight to carry compared with everyone else. At the end of the shift there was a distance run along the beach back to the town, probably about four or five miles. The new boys Joe McLaughlin, Nigel Spackman and myself hammered ahead, almost out of sight of most of the rest of them.

The manager was impressed but one or two of the other players were less so. This was a different, more modern, professional, athletic and dedicated group that had turned up en masse in their midst and it must have felt very threatening.

A few of last season's team did buy into the new work rate. John Bumstead seemed to love the idea of a load of players who would work as hard as him, and skipper Colin Pates similarly liked what he saw. They also became two of the best friends I ever had in the game, but then I was always going to get on with a couple of comic surrealists like those two. You didn't get many of them in football back then, but then again probably more than you get now.

---

* In the same week that I had slipped down quietly to join Chelsea from Clyde, Charlie Nicholas had gone from Celtic to Arsenal in a blaze of publicity. I was thankful to the media and to him that 'Champagne Charlie' had got and loved all the headlines. It was a blessing to be able to turn up in London with no expectations from anyone.

The next important moment involved manager John Neal. John was a lovely man and a fantastic coach too. He also had a quiet, no-nonsense, northern wisdom that you underestimated at your peril. On the second afternoon John decided, along with his assistant Ian McNeill, to organise some fun skill races with an *It's a Knockout* theme. This meant running and dribbling the ball through cones for thirty yards and back. Having done my 10,000 hours, much of them involving that very skill, with my dad all through my life, I would have backed myself to beat anyone. At that time, I could go through those cones with a ball about as fast as I could without a ball. If I could, I would have played my 'Joker' on this one! When the players first saw me doing it, there was an audible 'Wow!' It was clearly a set up by the manager to integrate me and change the lads' viewpoints on the quiet incomer they thought should be playing with the kids.

When I did open my mouth some of the southern players either couldn't understand a word I said or affected not to be able to understand my accent, so it was clear to me that there was a bit of work to be done on the integration side. In the end perhaps the same could be said for my entire career, accent or not.

The third moment in those first few days of pre-season was when I got the ball played up to me during a bounce game and I had the man-mountain, Chelsea legend and by then veteran defender Micky Droy coming from behind to tackle me. I threw an outrageous dummy and he bought it going five yards one way, while I went five the other. The big man reacted brilliantly, I could hear him laugh as I spun away and saying in his thick cockney accent, 'I'm too facking old for this game.' It was a seminal moment only two days into my time at the club when I dared to think once again, *You know what, I might just be able to manage this level.*

Although I'd come to the pre-season training, there was also the small matter of the financial details to be sorted out. I had agreed to the princely sum of £180 per week for the two-year deal. That was fine by me initially as I was only earning £30 at Clyde. I also had a promise that the club would source a rented flat in London – I had stated categorically that I wasn't staying in digs or with a family. Put simply, I felt mature enough to take care of myself and having bummed round Europe with a tent I knew I could manage. I wasn't someone who needed to be mothered or held by the hand. I did not expect to be treated like a child or indeed a youth footballer!

There was also the transfer fee to be hammered out. Clyde wanted £500,000 and Chelsea had suggested £35,000; both were ridiculous in their own way. It was taken to a transfer tribunal to decide a fair price. In fact, I believe it was one of the first tribunals in British football history.

Before going in I had the Clyde representatives taking me to one side and whispering, 'Do the right thing by us in there and we will make sure we take care of you, nudge, nudge, wink, wink.' A few minutes later the Chelsea chairman Ken Bates said conspiratorially in the corridor, 'Play your talent down in front of the tribunal and there might be something extra in it for you.' No direct promises were made, but I think I got their drift.

The clubs made their pitches to the panel, which was led by the sagacious Professor Sir John Wood. Clyde made me sound like Diego Maradona's younger but much more talented kid brother. Chelsea described me as an averagely skilled, scrawny, malnourished Scottish youth player who had no real chance of making it in England with the big boys. The prof got the clubs to vacate the room and asked me what I thought my value should be. I remembered what the clubs had said to me and answered smiling, 'I don't know, and I don't care. That's their problem and indeed your problem.' The prof laughed and said he liked my honesty. Instead of talking football we spent a pleasant ten minutes discussing education and literature before calling the clubs back in.

He settled on £95,000 and I turned and smiled at both clubs as we went out. Guess which one offered me a thank-you gift? Neither, unsurprisingly. They ought to have offered me something afterwards really – they wouldn't have lost out because I wouldn't have accepted it. The contract had been signed, agreements had been made and the deal had already been done, there was no need for anything more for me. Except, as I soon discovered, Chelsea didn't fancy keeping every promise!

There were a few friendly games building up to the opening day of the season, then the new lads were all going to be thrown in together to see how it went. All except me. By all accounts that first league game of the 1983–84 Division 2 season at Stamford Bridge was fantastic. Chelsea won 5-0 against Derby County, the new golden boy Kerry Dixon scored the first two of his astounding 193 goals for the club, but I wasn't even there to share in the glory.

I still had it in my mind to sit those resit exams I had missed while I was in Mexico. All six had been in Glasgow that week so, much to the surprise of the manager, I went back to sit them all. It made perfect sense as I absolutely expected to be back doing my final year of the degree in two years' time if not before. I passed all the exams, so on the Friday I got a train back to London content in the knowledge that I would be playing for the reserves at Luton instead of joining the first team on Saturday.

Even that journey down south didn't go smoothly. I was still being treated like a small child by some of the Chelsea staff and it was winding me up. I am very mild-mannered 99.9 per cent of the time but I can be righteously stubborn if I think I am being treated unfairly or, worse, dishonourably.

I had left my girlfriend Alice waving goodbye on Glasgow Central station to go to London like many young lovers have done before me. It was an incredibly poignant moment because we both knew it could be the beginning of the end of something very special. We were right, it didn't last; a short while later we were no longer 'going out' and it was no one's fault but mine! I knew I was too young to settle down and the distance didn't make it any easier either. Happily there was no falling-out, but there was a great sadness and she was a huge help to me in that first season when she came down to London to see me.

By the time I arrived at Euston there was a lot of emotion coursing through me. The journey down should have been filled with worries and concerns about a new city and a new life I knew nothing about. There should have been fears about not knowing anyone and fears of failure on the football field. Maybe there should have been huge excitement about the possibilities instead. The success I might have, the new people I might meet and the fabulous glory that might be waiting for me. I could dress the journey up like that, but it would be a lie. It was six hours thinking of the sadness and heartbreak of leaving someone I cared about, with little or no room for anything else. I tried to clear my mind by reading a book, but I couldn't concentrate. It was a big moment, but only in terms of the relationship. Worrying about everything else that lay ahead as soon as that train pulled into Euston would have to wait until I got there.

I arrived and made my way up the slope towards the concourse ready to start a new life, carrying nothing more than a big shoulder bag on one side, balanced out with a sports bag on the other, still not knowing who I should be looking out for. The Chelsea representative sent to meet me there was Gwyn Williams and though he spotted me right away, after he introduced himself the meeting went downhill pretty quickly.

'Right sonny,' he said, 'let's get you to your digs out of town, we have a nice family who will be taking care of you.' I was not in the frame of mind to hold back, having left so much behind in Glasgow that I loved and I certainly wasn't 100 per cent sure I was doing the right thing anyway. The idea of being treated like a child on top of that was always going to rile me in that moment.

'There has been a mistake, I will not be staying in digs, I have been promised a rented flat in town. I am happy to stay in a hotel for a while, but I made it crystal clear in the negotiations that I will not at any point be staying in digs, like some little kid.'

Gwyn mostly dealt with the younger kids at that time and maybe I did look like a young waif, but he made a mistake when he laughed at my suggestion.

'OK, that's fine. I have something I have to do just now, so it's been nice meeting you, Mr Williams, goodbye.'

He was confused. 'What are you doing, young man?'

'Well, there is a train over there on platform one which is going back to Glasgow in twenty minutes and I am going to be on it. I'll be back when you as a club are willing to fulfil your promises.' And off I tootled towards the train, kit bag thrown back over my shoulder.

He managed to stop me and a few calls later from the phone box in the station, a hotel was found. The result was that they never did pay for a flat because it wasn't actually written in the contract, so I had to pay for that myself. But I also did not spend one day in digs with a family. A lesson learned on both sides.

London can be an intimidating place but if you come from a busy city like Glasgow it is maybe a bit less scary at first viewing. I was fairly streetwise, and I had also travelled around Europe via London already. London as a city was somewhere to explore, get to know and understand more than fear from my youthful perspective.

I stayed for a short while in the Lily Hotel in West Brompton, one District Line stop on the tube away from Fulham Broadway and Stamford Bridge. It was basic, simple, friendly and clean with no airs or graces, and suited me well. Some of the same staff work there to this day and are still just as friendly!

In those very early days, there were logistical things to figure out, like how to get to training, which was held at Harlington near Heathrow. There was a minibus that took the training kit out every morning from Stamford Bridge, driven by a sharp wiry Scot called Jimmy Hendry, that had space for some youngsters to squeeze in. It was perfect for me as I couldn't drive or get close to affording a car. Jimmy helped me look for a flat and sort out things like utilities accounts, which in hindsight was a godsend. Scots have always looked after each other in London, especially when you are a new arrival; it's an unwritten law but accepted by us all.*

---

* It was also the accepted rule for the next few years that any college friends, or friends of those friends who arrived late at night in London on the bus from Glasgow and found themselves stuck with nowhere to stay that night, could call me and I would let them stay at my flat. I was happy to help but sometimes picking up a couple of bedraggled girls I hardly knew from Victoria station at 1am on a Friday night before a big London derby was pushing my helpfulness to the limit. Especially as I would then sleep on the couch cushions strewn across the floor and they had my bed. Nevertheless, it is a common Caledonian courtesy, at least that is what I was led to believe.

The Big City was to be survived at the start with the help of a few friends and I was prepared for that. Getting to know it would have to wait a little while.

After arriving I made it to the reserve game the next afternoon at Luton. I didn't know the players that well, but I made one major discovery that day: I quickly found out who thought the way I did, and who didn't.

Reserve players, unless they are youngsters on the way up, are a notoriously disgruntled bunch. Some if not most of the lads that day thought they should be in the first team playing against Derby at a packed Stamford Bridge instead of an echoing, empty little stadium in Luton. I was, however, startled by the reaction when news came through at full time that the first team had won 5-0. Two players jumped up shouting 'Yes, get in!' Those two were midfielder Tony McAndrew and me. The rest either said nothing or limited their comments to 'F**k!' or 'Bollocks'.

I couldn't get my head round the fact that any player with a half-decent attitude would want his own team to get beat. Yes, you want to be in the first team and maybe you stand a better chance if they are losing, but wouldn't it be far better if you just became a better player and made yourself too good to be left out of the first team? Any chance of a little serious introspection instead of blaming anyone but yourselves, lads? I hadn't come across such open antagonism to a club from within before. It was a culture and an ethos that was totally alien to me, but I soon discovered it wasn't that unusual in the professional game.

Tony Mac in contrast was my kind of guy and I respected him even more as in time he became the moral strength behind the first team. He was seven years older than me and a leader. He was made first-team captain and was the man who saw to it that anyone in the group who had the wrong self-indulgent attitude was told in no uncertain terms that he was a disgrace or indeed an arse.

The real shame was that he became the player the fans would turn on first. He wasn't flashy or showy, he just did the right thing on and off the park but sadly the fans had no way of knowing how important he was to the group. When he eventually left it was as big a blow, if not bigger, than any of the top stars leaving.

I settled into training and working hard to get near to a first-team place. At nineteen maybe I was being presumptuous but during training each day with the senior players I quickly began to think I could add something new. It still sounds arrogant saying that now, but by then I had realised you must have that total belief if you are going to stand a chance. It is still the antithesis of who I am off the field, but then appreciating your ordinariness is an easy perspective to have. After all it is only kicking a ball about, it isn't as if you are part of the push to cure a pandemic or cancer or even being a doctor or a teacher. So, to my mind, being a footballer shouldn't inflate your ego too much, although I accept that not everyone agrees with this hypothesis.

Where did I get this on-field confidence from?

I was totally awestruck as a kid watching talented footballers, but I was not particularly affected when I met them face to face – they were just guys after all. However, put me on a football field up against the best defender in the world and I absolutely believed that I was better than him and could beat him. I have no idea where that belief came from, but on the pitch it didn't matter if it was Stuart Pearce, Kenny Sansom or Andreas Brehme, who were the world-class defenders back then – I always fancied my chances.

It also helped that I never, or incredibly rarely, got nervous. Some players would struggle to perform at their best because of their nerves but I couldn't understand their problem because I had that innate total belief in my ability when I was on the field. It may be that I always had it on a football pitch from when I was a kid, but it certainly helped that I had a safety net as I got older. I knew I could afford to fail as I had an education to fall back on. Other players didn't have that and maybe that is why they were affected by the stresses more than I was. Fear of failure must have its negative side-effects.

Even though I had that confidence it was still a bit of a surprise when I found myself being moved towards the first team so quickly. After all

In the garden at Barlanark, Glasgow, *c*.1975.

The Blue Star Under-12s in 1976. We'd won every competition we entered that year, including the Scottish Cup. I hadn't realised how miffed everyone else was that I got to hold all the trophies though.

Signing on as an 'S' form for Celtic FC in 1977, aged 13. I am the one on the far right. This photo, printed in *The Celtic View,* blew my cover at school, where I'd previously kept my footballing on the quiet.

Practising my skills with Shandy in the garden
at Barlanark.

Football boots and pixie boots in the Clyde FC dressing room, 1982.

Chelsea v Newcastle United, November 1983. A pitch-length dribble that saw me beating Kevin Keegan (pictured), starting a love affair between me and the Chelsea fans that still persists.

Celebrating in the dressing room with the rest of the Chelsea team after winning the Second Division at Grimsby in May 1984 and going into the top flight as champions.

Pat senior and junior at home in Glasgow, January 1984.

I loved making goals for Kerry Dixon. I liked him a great deal, too, but was maybe not as besotted as this picture, taken at White Hart Lane in November 1984, makes me look.

Chelsea v Manchester United, September 1986. That's John ('Nugget') McNaught on the left. Norman Whiteside and Brian McClair are looking on at the dog, while Joe McLaughlin doubles over in the background.

David Speedie and I, 1984. We may have clashed off the field, but on it we had a fabulous understanding. He was a great player who feared no one.

In my MGB GT, summer 1986.

(Left) There were many photo shoots, but I enjoyed doing this one for the
August 1984 edition of *City Limits* because I used the magazine to find
things to do as a newcomer to London.
(Right) 'New Faces' for the *Sunday Express Magazine* in January 1984.

they were winning and there were some established players in front of me in the wide positions. There was Paul Canoville, Clive Walker, Peter Rhoades-Brown, and then Mickey Thomas joined soon after. Even so, with six games gone and still no defeats, John Neal named me among the substitutes for a League Cup match against Gillingham. I got off the bench there for a short cameo and by the Saturday I was starting for the first team. I must have done OK. That season I started every single game from then on.

9/
A NEW CAREER IN A NEW TOWN

John Neal, the manager, must have truly believed in me, in fact I know he did. I felt he wanted to understand my idiosyncrasies and push my boundaries. He just kept piling more trust on top of me when the more obvious thing would have been to shield the softly spoken youngster in the corner with his weird gear, the different interests, the different vocabulary and the different…well, everything. He clearly liked the way I was dedicated to the craft, always staying late after training or coming back in the afternoons to do extra on my own without mentioning it to anyone, including him. He also liked not only my work ethic but also the ethical stands I took: on almost anything that I felt was unfair or not for the benefit of the group, I would suddenly be heard.

I have admitted to being a bit over-earnest when I was younger – and I was – but it was from the sincere belief that there had to be integrity in life as well as in sport. It didn't stop me spending lots of time laughing and joking, I promise you. No one could be that self-righteous all of the time! But on the other hand, if I came across an injustice, I just couldn't accept it.

Getting in the first team solved one problem that had cropped up, through no fault of my own, and one that I hadn't foreseen. Despite initially seeming like a lot of money, my wages of £180 per week disappeared very quickly. The rent for my ground-floor bedsit in Earls Court was £100 per week, tax and subs were about £60, so I was left with the grand total of £20 per week to live on. I had some company in the form of my best mates who would come down from Scotland sometimes, which helped, but mostly I was in the flat on my own. For a short while I was worse off in almost every sense than I had been as a student in Glasgow! Back there I had my grant, I was staying with my mum and dad and I was getting paid by Clyde. I was minted and surrounded by company in comparison to this initial period in London.

The low points were when I found the flat had fleas in the carpet. I had no idea what they were and why I kept getting bites on my ankles, having come from a home spotlessly cleaned by my mum. At one point I also had to surreptitiously 'borrow' a knife and fork from Pizza Hut as I didn't have any cutlery in the flat. I took them back a month later when I could afford my own cutlery and got some very weird looks! I was mostly on my own but even though I came from a big family I surprised myself by coping quite well with my rather solitary existence. There were those regular visitors from Scotland and I still had the student attitude, that staying in watching *Cheers*, or listening to records or Peely on Radio 1 while reading serious literature, constituted an enjoyable way to spend an evening if I couldn't afford to do anything else. In fact I was perfectly happy, so you can cut the violins in the background right now! As Roddy Frame from Aztec Camera was helpfully singing at the time on 'Oblivious': 'They'll call us lonely when we're really just alone.'

Fortunately, my financial saviour came in the form of win bonuses. A win at the top of the league could earn me as much as £275, a veritable fortune! And as we were winning nearly every week, I didn't starve, in fact after a few weeks in the first team I found I had more money than I had ever had in my life. When we won I may well have earned more than my dad did back in Glasgow most weeks. I wasn't interested in wealth, just survival and maybe a little comfort, and suddenly it was comfortable. Just after I broke into the team, we had three away games in a week, against Huddersfield Town in the league on Saturday, Leicester City (including a fresh-faced Gary Lineker) in the League Cup on Wednesday and Fulham on the Saturday. We won all three and the record shops took a hammering from me the following week with those three win bonuses.

I liked going to Notting Hill Gate at the time for records, but Soho also still had a good vibe. Then there were the independent shops such as Rough Trade, where you were as likely to bump into bands hanging out as you were music nuts searching for that latest Japanese seven-inch import picture disc single they couldn't get anywhere else. I was very rarely recognised in these haunts, which was a bonus, but one day the aficionado behind the counter at Rough Trade clocked me but didn't seem particularly awestruck. When I asked if he had 'Kicker Conspiracy' by The Fall he was suddenly much more impressed.

Records, food and rent aside, I didn't have much else to spend my money on. Instead of things, I only wanted experiences and that meant time with friends, going to gigs, the theatre, movies, galleries and of course by now I was also hooked on travelling.

After just a few months in London my weekly copy of the *NME* could now be used to find those gigs in and around town. It was a magical time as now I could afford to go and there were some great bands around. A youthful New Order and The Fall were obviously always still caught when they were in town, but I was also seeing plenty of small bands that I loved: The Shop Assistants, The Jesus and Mary Chain, Orange Juice, Paul Haig, Strawberry Switchblade and even one or two bands that weren't Scottish!

Seeing Cocteau Twins live for the first time at the University of London around then was magical, one of the best concerts I had ever been to. In truth it probably still is my favourite. They played every track from their new album *Head over Heels* and each one was, and remains, some of the most perfect music I've ever heard. Liz Fraser's voice was far beyond any singer I had heard before or have heard since. That night it was captivating, mighty in its power, pure in its feeling, ethereal, soulful and other-worldly. There might even have been a few tracks from their EP *Sunburst and Snowblind* thrown in and each of them was of the same standard. Robin Guthrie's wall-of-noise guitar soared like nothing I had heard before. Even at the time I knew that this night would live with me for the rest of my life.

I still go to a lot of gigs where people get excited and even carried away at the big moments. There is a rare state beyond that when an audience just stands there as one at the end of a song, slack-jawed, in a trance-like state, dumbstruck, looking bewitched. This happened more than once that night and those were mind-expanding moments. It felt like that depth of emotion you get when you first fall in love with a girl, but then on top of that she presents you with the official soundtrack.

A gig by The Durutti Column was so beautiful and emotional that my eyes were still watering the next day at training (explained away to the players as just a bit of hay fever, obviously). A Certain Ratio were always great live too, but I wasn't a complete indie snob, I would happily go to see a show band like Kid Creole and the Coconuts. London was so diverting and with every kind of movie available too, it was an education for me as well as wonderful entertainment. Unlike today, it really felt like there were a number of 'scenes' in London, usually based around musical styles. You would often see many of the same people at a variety of gigs and certainly many of John Peel's listening fraternity would be on nodding terms.

It probably helped that the *NME* decided to interview me at the time and put it on a double-page spread with a very moody set of photos. For me this interview was much more important than one for any national newspaper – it was what I read to keep up with my passion. The writer Adrian Thrills had spotted somewhere that I had mentioned that Joy Division was my favourite band and immediately got in touch with me via the club. Footballers were rarely if ever allowed into the august pages of the *New Musical Express*, they were much too unstylish to be even considered in those days, so it felt like a great honour. I probably have had as much reaction to that interview over the years as I had for any other during my career.

Adrian was a good bloke and we got on famously. A while later when I had to move out of my Earls Court flat, he was looking for a new place too, so we became flatmates in Pimlico. It was very handy to have Adrian as a flatmate: as a record reviewer he got loads of free new releases to share. Gig-going was another part of his job and he introduced me to lots of interesting folk. All in all he was a great flatmate for me to have.

Adrian and I regularly went to the same gigs and more often than not I would be offered free guest list entry to go along with him. I always refused, reasoning that these little-known bands need every penny they could get as they battled through the industry. One afternoon we went up to Kilburn to interview a new band who were going to be playing there later that night. At the *NME*, Adrian was the biggest champion of the emergent Scottish music scene, so with them he had even more Caledonian clout than me, even though he was a southerner! As they were 'a bit' Scottish, he thought I might like to meet this new duo and maybe translate for him. They were great lads and I stayed to listen to Charlie and Craig from The Proclaimers do their afternoon sound check. I was blown away; I couldn't wait to hear more that night. The rest of the ex-pat audience were well ahead of me as they went down a storm.

This is what I loved: something different, they were not openly copying anyone else but confident in what they had to say and how they would say it. Oh yes, and they had some great tunes on that first album. At the time I loved going home on the tube after gigs, sometimes chatting with other folk who had been at the same event. People used to moan about how dirty the underground was, but I regarded it as a fantastic system that was brilliantly integrated, organised specifically to get me to any gig anywhere within an hour. I was quickly falling in love with London, its excitement, its culture, the anonymity it afforded and the interesting people that it allowed me to meet.

I usually felt more comfortable around people from the music world than the football fraternity – we just had more in common. Richard Jobson, formerly of the punk band The Skids, was a great mate from the day we met. He had an uninhibited passion for his work that I felt an affinity with as well as our shared love of Glasgow Celtic at the time.*

Most days around this time I would go for lunch in a cheap but friendly little restaurant I found called the Chelsea Kitchen on Kings Road. I often went there for dinner too. I had met and become great friends with Simon Raymonde, who had just joined Cocteau Twins, my new favourite band. It was a glorious time and we would meet and chat for hours on end almost every single day. You need friends in a new town and Simon, along with Richard, was a lifesaver for me.

I had also finally been introduced to Annabel at a party back in Glasgow's west end. My friend Julie was still telling me this was the girl I was going to marry even though it had taken quite a while for us to meet up. I was immediately spellbound and I mean immediately from the precise moment I saw her. Apart from being beautiful, intelligent and funny, she was also the sweetest girl I had ever met. She was studying English and Fine Art at Glasgow University and to my eyes she looked more like an ideal of a human being than a real one. I started going up at weekends after games to see her in Glasgow, then now and again to her family home near Coldstream in the Scottish Borders. She became a more regular visitor to London where I would sometimes try to take her to nicer restaurants than I usually frequented myself, though she didn't seem to mind where we went. We became very close, very quickly.

When Annabel wasn't around, if I wasn't eating at the Chelsea Kitchen you would often find me at another cheap café called Vince's at Fulham Broadway with another friend, John Millar, the new young Scottish full-back at Chelsea. I always tried to help and integrate the young players

---

* I was sitting in my flat one afternoon having a cup of tea when the doorbell rang downstairs. It was Richard and when I opened the door, he bounded upstairs and said, 'Shut up and listen to this.' He put a tape in the stereo and played his new Armoury Show single that he had finished in the studio in Notting Hill Gate just twenty minutes before. He had run all the way to the flat to play it to me and indeed sing along at the top of his voice. That exuberant excitement is one of the most joyous things to behold and people like that are fantastic to be around.

coming through, especially but not exclusively if they had come down from Scotland. In the café we started chatting about 'fitba' and 'Glesga' to a gruff, Rangers-supporting, six-foot-tall Glaswegian called Wullie who worked as a road sweeper. We started to see him regularly in the café and I suppose what follows tells you a lot about why I loved London so much.

A few months after we'd met him Wullie asked, 'So wit ur ye daein the night wee man?'

'Actually I am going down to the South Bank,' I sheepishly said. 'There's a retrospective on about the German film director Werner Herzog and he is doing a talk afterwards that I want to hear…' I tailed off expecting a torrent of abuse from the road sweeper for being a culture snob.

'Funny that,' says Wullie. 'So am I.'

After months of talking 'fitba', spouting nonsense and judging each other as rough 'Glesga boys' it turned out that among other things he had a deep love of the arts, had an encyclopaedic knowledge of Wagner's *Ring Cycle* and was also a friend of Sir Peter Hall!

One night all three of us went to the South Bank to see a play with an up-and-coming young actress called Joanne Whalley, who was brilliant and helpfully very beautiful too. Afterwards Wullie arranged for John and me to go backstage to meet the cast. After training the next day we went to lunch with Wullie for the debrief.

'Well, there's good news and bad news for you, John,' Wullie reported. 'The good news is that all the girls in the cast appear to be in love with you.'

'So, what's the bad news?' John asked.

'Well, most of the men in the cast feel the same.' Like me, John didn't have a homophobic bone in his body but he never did go backstage there again.*

---

* I was also into the new burgeoning alternative comedy scene. Adrian's then girlfriend Sophie was friends with these 'ordinary' guys who we met in a pub in north London one night, and I laughed so hard I was in pain. Within months Harry Enfield was on the TV every week and his mate Paul Whitehouse was writing some of the funniest lines on the box at the time.

I had a growing circle of good friends and was going to lots of gigs with them, so I reckoned it was only a matter of time before I bumped into my hero John Peel while out and about watching these bands. To say this was a dream of mine is no understatement, but I was far from the only one who thought that way in Britain's musical subculture. A simple shake of the hand would have sufficed and a couple of words from the great man would have been relayed to every single friend back home immediately.

Peely was the most important DJ that music has ever had. His shows were an education over the decades, and no one has ever come close to his ability to spot and promote brilliant young musicians. From Radio 1 in the evenings he spoke to and encouraged everyone from the flower-power generation to the punks and well beyond. Like so many others, much of my teenage life before I got to London had been spent tuning into Peel's late-night show on Radio 1, sometimes under the bedclothes on a transistor radio hoping to hear that brilliant new alternative track you would never hear anywhere else. Everyone who loved his shows thought of him as a close friend, just one they hadn't met yet.*

I will be honest and say that on the train journey down from Glasgow in the odd cheery moment, I would have had meeting John Peel as one of my top fantasies, well ahead of scoring a goal for Chelsea against Arsenal.

I loved going to see a Scottish comedian called Jerry Sadowitz, who was like Billy Connolly without the filter. I often went to see and became quite friendly with another Glaswegian who went by the name Bing Hitler. After a year with only a couple of dozen of us turning up at some of his gigs, Bing said he was fed up trying to break through and getting nowhere so he was leaving and 'going off to break America'. I said, 'I'll see you back in a couple of months then.'

He reverted to his own name, Craig Ferguson, and did indeed break America, eventually fronting his own ground-breaking programme *The Late Late Show* on CBS for a decade. He was arguably the most famous Scot on that continent for a while.

* When he died, BBC Radio 6 Music was eventually formed to basically cover what he did. Even though I like it and listen to it, an entire radio station still doesn't do as much for creative and interesting music as he did single-handedly.

So, after a while I came up with a plan that might actually make this happen.

Quite soon after my arrival, Chelsea asked if I wanted to write a column in the club newspaper, *The Bridge News*. Once I had made them accept that the deal was it wouldn't be ghosted, they agreed.*

They were, however, slightly surprised that I wanted to do a music column and not one about the day-to-day goings-on inside our team's dressing room. Bless them, but they went along with it and luckily for me, my 'Hooklines' column seemed to go down well. I'll admit now it was all part of a plan, and one day I made a suggestion…

'Why don't I interview John Peel? It would be a great interview; he likes football and music so that fits in perfectly with my page.' A stage whisper to the side adding, *'And more importantly I will actually get to meet him.'*

So as you did in those days, I wrote a letter to John saying, 'I write a column in a small west London publication called *Bridge News*. I wonder if I could meet you for an interview for it?'

The reply came back very quickly in the post. 'I am sorry, but I am very busy at the moment with my radio show and going to see new bands, maybe we could do it sometime in the future.'

It was a brush-off, a very polite one, but a brush-off, nonetheless. So, I tried once again and to my eternal shame I wrote the following:

Hi John, thanks for your recent letter regarding the interview with *Bridge News*. It would however be better to do it sooner rather than later because the team I play for, Chelsea, are playing your team Liverpool in a few weeks, and I wanted to incorporate it into the build-up to the game. So, you will understand that if we could do it sooner it would be better.

---

* Nothing I have ever written has been ghosted, as you can doubtless tell from the standard of this tosh, specifically this clumsily composed sentence.

Not that subtle I grant you, but John phoned a couple of days later, admonished me for not saying that I was a football player in the initial letter and we arranged to meet up.

The finished article was more a rant aimed at the BBC because there was some suggestion that Peely was going to be removed to make way for the next bright young thing, who didn't have 2 per cent of his knowledge, none of his incredible instinct for emerging genius or indeed even a true love of the music. Sacrilege!

In that week's 'Hooklines' page I had a story about meeting Boy George from Culture Club before the previous week's game at Stamford Bridge – he was making a video there. There was also a plug for the latest This Mortal Coil release from 4AD records in there as well and I did get one very decent story from Peely in this extract from the column:

Peel came across as a very humble man, but also probably the most interesting guy I have ever met. I asked about the big names he must have met over the years and this prompted a memory about John Lennon.

'I'd never met him before, but got a call from someone purporting to be John Lennon. Thinking it was a mate winding me up, it took a bit of time to convince me. What happened was that Yoko had been taken ill and needed five pints of blood. She told her husband to get five people whose blood he would like her to have, and I was one. It was incredibly touching.'

We did the interview, got on extremely well and in a totally comfortable way, shared stories for hours about the people we had met. It didn't feel like we were showing off about who we knew, just sharing interesting tales. We were clearly two outsiders who just happened to have the inside track in our industries.

In fact, we got on so well, that soon we started to arrange to meet up at gigs and sometimes go for a curry. Standing at the back of a gig by someone like The Men They Couldn't Hang while John listened on was like having Lionel Messi coming to watch an Under-14s match. Everybody wanted to say hello, but few had the courage to do more than thrust a cassette tape into his hands and slink off.

Soon – and incredible when you think about it – he started to invite me fairly regularly into the studio during his evening shows, just as a mate to keep him company and to help log the tracks for payments to the weird and wonderful obscure bands and labels, ensuring they got their small broadcast payment for being played on the BBC. Needless to say, this was heaven for me.

There were some other young people there, who would now be called interns but then we were just considered friends. Paget, who worked for Peely at the time, became one of my closest friends throughout my life, though she still probably secretly sniggers at my limited musical knowledge in comparison to hers.

The BBC building at Broadcasting House was a warren back then. John would always have us come in through the big main doors before going on a long and winding route through the bowels of the building. Down we went through a maze of what looked like dimly lit tunnels instead of corridors before eventually emerging in a different wing of the building altogether. I really had the feeling that apart from John, Paget and a couple of friends of theirs, no one else in the entire organisation knew about these hidden depths.

I loved going into the studio, it was so relaxed, and he was so keen to chat while the tracks were playing, mostly to extol the brilliance of some mad noise merchants from Germany, folksters from Ukraine, jangling guitar Glaswegians or glowering Mancunians. It was mostly vinyl that Peely played that he had carted down from his office beforehand. The office looked pretty shambolic to the untrained eye, and certainly could have done with a filing system that was easier to understand. The studio itself was similarly strewn with records ten minutes into the show, many confusingly had white labels with little or nothing written on them. There was an anarchic but establishment feeling kept in perfect balance about the entire show. If we did too much chatting, John would play the next record at the wrong speed by mistake before proclaiming he liked it better that way.

There was one night with a couple of Japanese girls, going by the name of Frank Chickens, that got so weird and funny that I thought I might have to take over the decks as John laughed so much at their delightfully madcap attitudes. From their perspective, it was imperative that I get on their plane the next morning and go to Japan with them; they didn't quite see the importance of me going back in for training at Chelsea instead.

I became and stayed friends with John Peel for the rest of his life. Apart from the gigs and curry we would meet up now and again in the afternoon if I was around the BBC's Broadcasting House and he was there too. He was very shy by nature, sometimes painfully so, but I liked him all the more for that. He was constantly concerned that the BBC were desperate to get rid of him and that insecurity wasn't misplaced: there were plenty within the organisation who didn't understand his value. Happily, they kept him on and near the end of his life I think they actually began to understand his importance and indeed his great talents.

What made it special over and above everything else was that very few other people had been invited into this inner sanctum, particularly from the 'celebrity' world. He once told me how badly he had been hurt when he thought that Marc Bolan from T. Rex, a huge star in the 1970s whom John had done more than anyone else to catapult into stardom, had dropped his friendship completely the moment he hit the big time. He wasn't angry, he was crushed, and it deeply affected him. This uncertainty and distrust about people liking us because of what we did as a job, as opposed to who we were as people, was something we both felt at the core of our personalities back then. It was probably an even bigger bond than our shared love of football, film and music.

I didn't miss many games for Chelsea, but one was a midweek away game at Carrow Road against Norwich City. I remember it because of the reason. I had gone out to a gig and then for a curry with John Peel two nights before and came down with food poisoning. Not my most professional moment.* After drawing the game 0-0, the manager John Neal said to the press that the team had missed my creativity. Cue Colin Pates half-joking to me the next week: 'For God's sake, you get man of the match from the gaffer even when you aren't playing, bloody teacher's pet!'

This was living the dream for me, far more than the idea of being a footballer. I had found a way of being welcomed into London, I had met a lot of new and interesting people, the music scene was fabulous and, incredibly, I had become friends with my hero, who turned out to be the sweetest but also most interesting guy. And while it was understood that he would never mention me by name, as I sat in on those radio shows, diligently writing down the names of bands and tracks, John would occasionally lean in to the microphone and say conspiratorially to his listeners, 'I have the famous footballer in tonight.'

I was in seventh heaven.

---

* I mean the curry not the gig was unprofessional. Going to see the kind of bands I went to see the night before a game was fine. I wouldn't have anything alcoholic to drink, there was never trouble, I didn't stay too late and I was very rarely recognised. The people who did recognise me wouldn't shop me to the football club anyway and even so, the manager would have understood it was my way of relaxing pre-match. It is hard to imagine a Strawberry Switchblade concert at the ICA turning dangerous!

10/
EIGHTIES FAN

My first goal for Chelsea was at Fulham in a 5-3 win, which was great, fun even if, as ever, I enjoyed my assist for Colin Lee more than my own goal. That game was a perfect example of the exciting new style we were developing. It certainly helped that the game was played near the start of the season: the pitch was lush and flat, giving us a chance to use our skills to the maximum.

Most of the teams were to my mind playing an unsophisticated style but then try playing tiki-taka football on the dreadful pitches from November back then and you wouldn't get very far. It was to some degree the British way and certainly it was much rougher back then as well. Fans sometimes forget that intricate, thoughtful play was often despised by the majority on the terraces – well, it sounded that way anyway, with the cry to get it in the box/mixer/to the striker as soon as possible being the norm. Not all teams were like that but sometimes it was hard to be one of the few who were trying to be different. English football still had a strong base in the long-ball game that Charles Hughes had promoted from within the English FA's coaching structure. It was well respected in England but considered grotesque and simplistic by the rest of the football world, including back in Scotland.

I had been brought up on a diet of watching Celtic's brilliantly skilful, attacking European Cup winners who had been league champions nine times in a row. At the same time I was hooked not only by the Brazil 1970 squad including Pelé but also Ajax and Holland with Johan Cruyff developing their total football. Watching English football's addiction to the physical long-ball game, even to my young eyes, seemed regressive at best.

It didn't help that in the previous decade of English football many of the flair players were seen as untrustworthy, laddish, big drinkers who didn't fancy working hard and were basically luxuries that couldn't be fully trusted. From Frank Worthington and Alan Hudson to Stan Bowles and of course George Best, their genius wasn't denied, but their commitment was. The hangover from this outlook was still there in the early 1980s even if the skilful players were now getting much more professional in their approaches.

One of the players I felt was my contemporary in style and attitude was Chris Waddle of Newcastle United and early in that first season he was playing against us down at Stamford Bridge. We won 4-0 and I suspect that was the day when the Chelsea fans really took me to their hearts.

Newcastle had a very good team; alongside Waddle there was Peter Beardsley, Terry McDermott and the legendary former Liverpool and England player Kevin Keegan all in their ranks. Even so we thumped them but I had two other things going on in my mind that day; personal, private arrangements I had first with my dad and secondly with the manager John Neal.

Dad was still coming to every game home and away, even though he was a hardworking man who had a day job with long hours and he and Mum were still living in Glasgow. His journey down each Saturday meant getting up at 5am, catching the 6am train, getting to the ground just before kick-off, with no time to meet me as I was already warming up. With five minutes to go he had to leave to miss the crowds so he could catch the last train from Euston back to Glasgow at 6pm, and he wouldn't arrive home until the early hours. This was his day off and he did this every weekend and got to most midweek games too, by hook or by crook. The midweek games were even more demanding. He had to get the overnight train back up to Scotland and then go straight to work in the morning from Glasgow Central station with little or no sleep. I don't know how he did it.

I was acutely aware of his sacrifices and dedication, so it was torture that I couldn't get to see him even for a moment at the games considering he had travelled so far. Instead we developed a signal that would mean 'Hi Dad' from me during every game. At some point in the match I would do at least one 'mad mazy dribble', as Dad called it. There was no need to create a chance or try to score a goal at the end of it. It was just for the sheer exhilaration of beating players, and because I could do it, and to entertain the fans, and to remember all those hours training together working on my skills, and crucially to say, 'Hi Dad.'

That is why against Newcastle when I picked the ball up in my own penalty box and went around Kevin Keegan, I kept dribbling and dribbling, past player after player until I got to the other penalty box, just failing to then find Kerry Dixon with the through pass. That was simply 'Hi Dad'.

The Chelsea fans who were there have never let me forget that moment and it seemed to fix in their minds that I was trying to entertain them as well as trying to win the games.

It was far from the most important thing that happened to me on the day though. As we cruised to a 4-0 win and I could seemingly do no wrong,* I couldn't help noticing that Kevin Keegan was working harder than anyone else on the field, even when getting hammered with a minute to go. His attitude was exemplary for a world-class player, indeed a European Player of the Year in his time, but at 33 years of age he still gave everything he had for every single minute.

He congratulated me as we walked off and told the press afterwards

---

* There were plenty of days when I did lots wrong or was just, as they say in the game, bang average.

that he thought I was an 'incredible' player. 'Young Nevin had the ball tied to his boots, we couldn't get it off him.' I did also manage to tell him at the end of the game that I was totally inspired by him and his attitude.

The other secret agreement was one I had with the manager. If we were three goals up in any game, only then was I allowed to enjoy myself completely and just beat players for the pure fun of it. I could do as much as I liked as long as the victory was assured. It didn't often happen but when it did, I loved my playtime. Any of my former teammates reading this now might think, 'Oh, so that's what he was doing.' In reality they seemed to enjoy it too, because our hard-working midfielders Nigel Spackman and Johnny Bumstead in particular would often say, 'Just give it to Pat and we can have a little rest as he keeps the ball for a while.'

These days a player showing a specific trick or unusual skill is applauded, back then it was frowned upon and sometimes it was even dangerous. I had a few special tricks I had copied from the Celtic players I had watched but I also developed a few new ones of my own. If they were considered too elaborate or showy, I would be considered fair game to be attacked/assaulted by the opposition. Back then even some of your own players would think it wasn't 'a good show old boy' because it was considered disrespectful. There was even one referee who said to me:

'You deserved that [a clattering tackle at about waist height] because you had beaten him three times in a row and gone back to beat him again just to show you could. You can't blame him really, can you?'

For a moment I thought he was going to book me for getting fouled! I never felt it was being disrespectful, especially if the skill worked and I kept the ball or got past the defender, even if it was admittedly over-elaborate or a bit tricksy.

We were a very attack-minded side during this time at Chelsea, with some huge characters helping the spirit. I adored the Welsh duo of Mickey Thomas and Joey Jones, who shared some of the carefree 'we are normal people' Celtic attitudes that I had. It took me and everyone else years to discover that they hadn't moved to London from their beloved North Wales but were in fact commuting the 400-mile round trip to London.

They were also in the habit of foregoing the cost of a cheap hotel and instead kipping in the referee's room the night before games. Mickey is still a great friend and maybe the bubbliest human being I have ever met. There have been brushes with the law and even time inside after using fake bank notes but he still manages to be the most lovable rogue, in the nicest sense, you could ever meet.

Many years later I met John Terry walking out of the new Chelsea training ground at Cobham. He loves the club and collects valuable memorabilia from its history. This day I saw him appear with a framed Chelsea shirt from the 1983–84 season. The originals are very rare, though I still have my own number 7 at home. 'Is it an original, John?' I asked.

'Yes, it is, I got it from Mickey Thomas.' I think I managed to keep a relatively straight face before I had a closer look (and it didn't look like an original to me). I think JT could afford to take the financial hit from Mickey's little scam if it was not actually the real deal though.

The experience and attitudes of both Mickey and Joey were invaluable as the season gathered pace, and after Christmas we were vying for promotion and the title itself along with the other sleeping giants Newcastle United, Sheffield Wednesday and Manchester City. The crunch game with City came near the end of the season one Friday night at Maine Road and it was to be shown live on BBC TV, a very unusual occurrence in those days. There were many millions watching and fortunately for me I had a pretty good game, getting the Man of the Match award and scoring the opening goal in a 2-0 win. Jimmy Hill, the legendary presenter, spoke about the team in glowing terms and the pundit, the even more legendary Bobby Charlton, was extraordinarily kind about my skills, likening them at one point to those of Stanley Matthews and Tom Finney! It was a real announcement to the football public in England that Chelsea as a top club were back. Or so I was told later. I had other things to concentrate on after the game.

This was Manchester in the early eighties and I had only one thought in mind: after a quick shower I was going straight to the mecca of the northern music I liked, the Haçienda Club. I didn't like nightclubs generally but I loved Factory Records. They had Joy Division, New Order, A Certain Ratio as well as Vini Reilly and his band The Durutti Column on their label. This was before the 'Madchester' rave scene and I was aware this club didn't yet have a great atmosphere – indeed, on that night, *any* atmosphere, as it was almost empty with maybe only a couple of dozen people in. I didn't care, I wanted to see the design, the architecture, hear the music in that environment and simply experience the place almost as a pilgrimage.

It was an incredible place. It seemed huge, but that might have been because it was so empty. The music was already morphing well away from what Factory Records themselves were mostly producing. The dance tracks were being played, the audience just hadn't turned up yet; the club was ready and waiting long before the Madchester scene was.

Tony Wilson, who was the impresario behind Factory Records, was already telling me over the thumping beats what an incredible place this was going to be and how it was going to change the whole idea of clubbing. I must admit it had the same effect as a used car salesman trying to sell me a 1960s Mercedes 280SL with 250,000 miles on the clock. It looks great but it just isn't going to work, is it?

I loved the place and its Factory chic décor. The cover artwork for Factory's releases was designed by the label's co-founder Peter Saville and sometimes was as impressive as the music itself. I was already a collector. (The Haçienda itself was considered part of the Saville design ethos and numbered FAC 51.) I owned most of the records including FAC 2 (the compilation EP *A Factory Sample*) through to FAC 73 (New Order's single 'Blue Monday'), which was utterly perfect for the ambience of the place and played at least twice that night. The first Happy Mondays EP (FAC 129), however, was still a year away. The club might have looked finished but little did we know then that they had only just laid the musical and cultural foundations. Tony Wilson was right, but not for the first or indeed the last time he was there long before everyone else when it came to the cultural zeitgeist.

So instead of hopping on the team bus back to London I went to the 'Hac' – I knew where my priorities lay! I had met both Vini Reilly and Tony Wilson and had a wonderful evening.* After leaving the club at 3am I wandered down to Piccadilly station and slept on a bench on the platform before getting the early train back down to London. The thing is, even though the night before I had been starring in a match between Man City and Chelsea with a sell-out crowd and millions watching on telly, I didn't find it at all odd that I was sleeping on a bench waiting for the milk train. My dad had done it often enough to come and watch me, so why shouldn't I do the same? I accept that this behaviour does sound a bit incredible when you compare it to a modern-day Premier League footballer, but I would underline that even back then it would have been considered unusual behaviour from within the game.

I didn't take the press coverage or indeed the press very seriously either. They were generally very nice to me back then, but they did think I was a bit of a curio. One red top took the rip because of my preference for Oxfam and thrift shops instead of trendy expensive stores. It is now considered a very eco-friendly way to shop, but back then they were laughing at me, so I had to get them back.

When asked for my favourite 'weirdo' band, I said I loved 'Joy Davidson', which they put in a headline. Oh, how the other indie kids must have laughed. Probably only a couple of hundred people got the joke as Joy *Division* were almost unknown back then, but the journo himself was less amused.

---

* I kept in touch with Tony on and off for the rest of his life. Vini and I became close friends and there is even a song he wrote for me when I was at Everton called 'Shirt Number 7', and it is very nice I reckon.

11/
BIGMOUTH STRIKES AGAIN

Before that Man City game there was another that was even more important to me and maybe in some respects was the most important of my career. We were playing Crystal Palace at Selhurst Park and battled to a 1-0 win. It was an important win but as I walked off, I couldn't have cared less about the game, the points, the league table or even the fact that I had scored the winner. I was angry, I was livid.

I am slow to anger but on this occasion I was more furious than I had ever been before, during or after any other football match in my life. Our other winger Paul Canoville was getting an increasing amount of racial abuse, which was bad enough, but what was worse is that some, if not most of it, was coming from our own (alleged) fans.

Having spent my late teens being an anti-apartheid activist in Glasgow and having been on many an anti-racism protest as a student, it was bound to set me off. We didn't do racial, religious or any kind of hatred in our family. My best friend for many years when I was very young was the only kid of colour at the school, Paul Clemence.* To then be confronted by this vile abuse was so alien and so unacceptable that I just couldn't understand why everyone else around me was putting up with it. Why weren't we, the players, the clubs, the media doing something? Yes, the past is another country but it was time to act and I not only knew what to do but felt I had no option but to do it.

Afterwards I refused to speak about the game or my goal to the waiting reporters huddled outside the players' entrance. There were no post-match press conferences in those days, so backed up against a wall, I tried very hard to stay outwardly calm.

'I am disgusted by the way the so-called supporters, even many of our own, abused Paul Canoville for no other reason than the colour of his skin,' I explained.

I tried not to rant but I probably failed. At the time football probably thought it was a societal problem, but I felt that football could also do something to change it, or at least try to change the narrative instead of meekly accepting it. Happily, that outburst seemed to have more effect than all my previous activism put together.

The newspapers duly and kindly produced the desired copy and the headlines. Early the next week Chelsea called me in for a little chat.

'Did you think that was sensible?' I was asked. 'Do you really think it is a footballer's place to get involved in this sort of problem? Do you think it is the right thing to do to have a go at your own fans? Do you think you can have even the smallest effect by saying these things, particularly

---

* Paul Clemence, who later changed his name to Wylie, his original family name, was adopted and lived in the next street. He was a very good goalkeeper and we formed a real bond travelling together as kids to represent Glasgow Schools. The weird thing is that I can't even remember thinking of his colour. I am not sure I really noticed, he was just my mate. Unfortunately, Paul couldn't be blind to it. We lost touch over the years then I met his sister a couple of years back and she told me Paul had recently died after a difficult life which she felt was accentuated, maybe even directly caused, by the racial discrimination he came up against after he left school.

about some of your own fans? Do you think you could tone it down a bit or preferably not speak about it again?'

I was amazed on one level and had a simple answer: 'Yes, yes, yes, yes and no. We could and should do the right thing.'

My first thought was, *Why would anyone even think to ask those questions?* The answer is obvious in hindsight, I suppose. From their perspective it was simply the done thing. There was a culture of casual racism widespread throughout the country, not just in football, and abuse was almost completely ignored, with little more than a disappointed shrug suggesting, 'What can we do?'

There was also the danger associated with my comments. The hooligan culture that was rampant in a small section of the fan bases at many clubs was wrapped up in the problem. The far-right National Front were using football to advertise and forward their own political beliefs and I felt they were getting a clear run, at least they were from those inside the game they were destroying. The clubs sometimes made the odd comment, but from my perspective they needed to be more proactive. It was one time when my youthful earnestness, even in hindsight, wasn't misplaced.

At some level I accepted that the club also had my welfare at heart. To get to Chelsea games I either got the tube from my flat in Earls Court or just walked there and back – it took little more than fifteen minutes. I didn't have a car, so I could see their concern about the danger, but I felt their worries at the time were overblown.

There was no chance of me backing down or becoming more timid. I wasn't a loudmouth in any way, but I felt there was a deal. If those so-called fans brought their political viewpoints to my workplace then I had every right to respond with mine. I also thought that this small percentage, but still very significant in number, were not representative of the vast majority of Chelsea fans, who were embarrassed and angered to be tainted by association. I also strongly believed it would drive away many more decent fans, real football supporters who would love to come to the club – and that wasn't just people of colour either.

I was doing well on the pitch and even though it was my first season

I didn't feel any threat of being disciplined or left out of the team. There were also the usual comments, 'That's just oddball Pat', but I honestly thought, not for the first time, I was the normal one and it was their attitudes that were strange, out of place and increasingly outdated. Apart from anything else I was so committed to my beliefs that if they thought it was too problematic, I was happy to leave and go somewhere else or more likely go back home to Glasgow and pick up on my old life.

The next game was against Shrewsbury Town at Stamford Bridge and I was clear in my mind what I wanted to do and I wasn't telling the club. When I went out onto the pitch, I was going to manipulate it so that I walked out alongside Paul Canoville and I made sure I had Kerry Dixon beside us too. I wanted to make sure Canner's walk out there was met with the best possible reception from the fans. It was also a signal from Kerry and me, a show of support. It worked out far better than I could have expected. As the three of us reached the pitch the fans started singing Paul's name before ours, they sang for a long time and it was very pointed. For me it was a magical moment; the previously silent majority were able to make a very public point and if I ever had slight concerns that I was misreading how most true Chelsea fans felt, they were crushed there and then. Having said that, even if I had been misreading the majority's attitudes, it wouldn't have made a blind bit of difference to me.*

---

* To this day when I am in London walking the streets or travelling on the underground, I meet black guys of my age who come up to me to say thanks. Sometimes it's a cool handshake or a fist bump and a smile. Now and again it is a nod across the carriage and one word: 'Respect'. It is never overdone, it is almost like a secret little club, but it happens regularly. I know it is not for what I did as a player on the field, but for what I started that day at Selhurst Park and continued doing in football for the rest of my career. I don't mind when fans ask for an autograph or a selfie or a quick chat. It's fine, I can cope now, and it is usually quite nice. However, when the secret club members give me that knowing smile, I secretly glow inside. It is nothing to do with minor celebrity, it is something much better than that.

Over the next few years Gordon Taylor at the PFA got in touch and a variety of anti-racist campaigns began to be set in motion. It was small and haphazard at first but over time it morphed into more organised groups. The Commission for Racial Equality got involved in football and Show Racism the Red Card also sprang up in the game. From there the FA, UEFA and FIFA eventually got on board too, but it took many years. There were very few of us speaking out at the start and I hugely admired the black players who joined in – they had to be far braver than me in that climate.

There were several fabulous, very driven and brave people who worked very hard in those early years and sadly are not credited the way they should be. Gordon Taylor, Brendon Batson and others at the PFA were pioneers and are often erased in discussions about the genesis of the anti-racism campaigns in football. The game is in a far better place now because of them. Hundreds, sometimes thousands, breezily singing racist or sectarian chants from the terraces and stands in the UK is all but a thing of the past, except for in one or two particular places.

There were many letters in support of my comments at Selhurst Park and there were a small number of irate messages in the post as well. I was even invited to meet a couple of men from the National Front, who also claimed to be in the Chelsea Firm of hooligans. I certainly didn't tell the club that I decided to go and meet them, listen to them and give them my point of view face to face. But that's just what I did.

I am not the biggest fan of no-platforming and although I disagreed with their point of view, I will always listen, consider, debate and argue for my ideas on a way to move forward or just to aid understanding of each other's position. You should be ready to change and adapt; after all, who thinks they know everything other than the truly ignorant person? It is my opinion that no specific political or pseudo-political group should be allowed to hand down dictums on who should and shouldn't be allowed to speak and debate.

We met in a cheap restaurant in the Fulham Road in the afternoon – I thought that would be the safest venue. The far-right guys behaved pleasantly when we met, they spoke passionately and even listened to my point of view. At least to me they had the decency not to be threatening in any way, though I understood that being a player for 'their' team would obviously influence their demeanour, as would the colour of my skin. They even suggested I bring along one of the black players to meet them next time so they could underline that it wasn't personal, that there was a considered argument that led to their wish for foreign nationals to 'go home'. But I didn't think I'd take them up on that offer. The truth was, we hardly managed to find a single thing we agreed on other than a love of reggae and ska music. I did, however, understand their point of view better afterwards and what their base thinking was, which I think made my future arguments stronger.*

In those days horrible hooligan elements still attached themselves to the clubs and although as regards those people anger was the go-to emotion that I battled to restrain, there was fear too, but never for myself. At an evening midweek game away to Cardiff City when it was seriously kicking off in the stands, it got particularly violent. I was out on the right wing (physically not politically), nearest to where the trouble was. I knew that my dad was somewhere in that stand. He could take care of himself and I knew he was streetwise enough to absent himself from the trouble, but I still had concerns for him and the other people who might get caught up in the crossfire. There was one point when I got the ball, stopped and turned to that area hands outstretched pleading, but the hooligans weren't watching – they weren't even vaguely interested in the game, surprise, surprise. It turned out to be a great game that the idiots were missing, we

---

* There wasn't a second meeting, but I did come across another of their number in a hairdresser's in the King's Road a while later. He was huge, stereotypically bovver-booted, with the regulation skinhead and red Harrington jacket. He was more threatening in his stance, but I stood my ground and he eventually just sat growling in the corner while I got my 'Mac from Echo and The Bunnymen' haircut renovated. I personally think their politics is born from a position of ignorance and hatred. But I do not want to meet their intolerance with a blank, unyielding intolerance of my own, so I listen and I debate.

came back from 3-0 down to get the draw and a vital point, but it was spoiled for me and a vast majority of the decent fans there.

In yet another game, at Stamford Bridge against West Ham, those so-called supporters were fighting again, this time between the old away end and the west stand at Chelsea where a lot of families with children would go. I turned around to say something to the much-loved and, even then, venerable Billy Bonds, the full-back who I was directly up against. When I looked at him he seemed to be choking back the tears. The good name of his beloved Hammers was also being besmirched by their thugs and it hurt him deeply, much more than the 3-0 defeat we inflicted on them.

My teammates rarely if ever mentioned my political comments and that didn't surprise me. For many in our society at the time, it was the norm to understand that racism was there and if you weren't interested you just ignored it. I wasn't campaigning inside the dressing room, but I could sense who was on my side, who wasn't and the vast majority who just didn't really seem to care as it wasn't their problem. In fact, even for the guys whose problem it definitely was, I can never recall any of the young black players at Chelsea ever talking to me about the subject either. Many years later most have by now told me that they admired my stance at the time, but back then it just wasn't the culture inside a dressing room to, as they saw it, open up that particular can of worms.

There have been many books and even films made about that period romanticising those casual hooligan days. They disgust me generally; the people who were involved nearly destroyed the game and those still reminiscing should be spending their time apologising to real football people instead of glorifying an ugly, self-serving, skewed history.

I never considered the majority of them football fans and I just wished the media and authorities, including the government of the time, understood this. The hard core often travelled, fought, then went home and didn't even bother to go into the games. They were using football and football clubs as vehicles to get their political message across to a wider audience than they had any right to, considering their numbers. Yes, I accept other 'sheep' who weren't from the far right were drawn into the brawls, maybe because of the excitement, but it was still a minority and all the while the players and the clubs themselves despised them and did all they could to rid the sport of their presence. They disgusted me and I still think they have too many apologists out there. Many still pin the blame squarely on 'the sport', a sport that always relentlessly made it clear it wanted nothing to do with them.

12/
THIS IS THE DAY

That first season at Chelsea was magical for true travelling fans and those at the home games too. Promotion back to the top flight was within our grasp. It finally came when we beat Barnsley in front of a large and excited crowd at Stamford Bridge. For once I could understand and accept a pitch invasion. With five minutes to go and 3-1 up, I had scored a couple of them, thousands were on the touchline preparing to celebrate. I have an idea the linesman was able to do his job only by running five yards inside the pitch.

After the match I sat on the edge of the main stand sharing the moment with those fans. Surrounded by friends and teammates, knowing that in this moment there was pure joy to be savoured – we had succeeded.

In football and in all elite sport, most of the time you are looking forward to the next game or the next challenge. Celebrating for any longer than a moment is a guilty pleasure; there is always another battle ahead. But in that brief moment I felt total contentment. It was fleeting, and it was rare, but it was wonderful. How many moments in life are really like that? In retrospect one of the delights of being a footballer is that these moments are often caught on camera, be it still or moving. I can still look at that picture and feel the warm glow of that perfect moment.

After one of the games near the end of the season I was walking out of the Bridge back up towards my rented flat in Earls Court. An elderly gentleman fell in step with me and started chatting.

'You're young Nevin, aren't you?'

'Yes,' I replied. 'Were you at the game, did you enjoy it?'

He took a moment and said quietly:

'I did enjoy the game and I specifically came to see you. I don't get out much these days, but someone suggested I might like watching you and your skills. You entertained me from forty-five minutes before the game and all the way up to the final minute of the game itself, thank you.'*

I was about to breezily say something else but he turned and ambled slowly away in the other direction. By the time I reached home fifteen minutes later I realised, that was it, that was the reason why I played football. To me it is an entertainment over and above everything else. He had got out of his house, had a good day and I had been part of the reason for that. That was the real crystallised reason why I would never give less than everything during any game. My dad had made an 800-mile round

---

* My pre-match warm-ups were a rather unusual sight. I needed my touch to be perfect, but how to achieve this? I would go out early, fifteen minutes before everyone else, and dribble round cones (or even football boots) the way I did with my dad. I then did keepy-ups and tricks to help me feel at one with the ball.

My favourite, however, was to get a group of the young ball boys and girls to come on to the pitch and say to them, 'Try to get the ball off me.' It was fun for them, helpful and fun for me and the few people who were in the ground watching got entertained into the bargain. After ten minutes of seven or eight youngsters chasing me around trying to get the ball off me, I was warmed up and my touch was perfect. In the intervening years fans have said that they started coming to the games an hour early just to see that warm-up.

On one occasion I went out to do some of those pre-match skill drills and got carried away with my juggling, forgetting about everything else around me. When I finished a roar went up behind me and only then did I realise, I had been inadvertently entertaining about 200 bored police officers waiting to be deployed around the ground. It turns out they are human too.

trip anyway, but so many others had spent their time and money to be there, and their effort deserved my respect. They had invested emotionally and even if they had just come out for that one day, then they deserved every effort on my part to entertain them with every bit of skill and energy I possessed.

There was still one game left that season. We had battled all the way with our mortal rivals Sheffield Wednesday and now found that if we won away from home against Grimsby Town on the last day of the season we would go up as champions. The travelling hordes of real Chelsea fans turned up and the stadium was bursting at the seams. Clearly there was massive overcrowding, and many told me later it was dangerous, with crushing a constant fear, but it made for an incredible atmosphere. The spring sun blazed and we played well but struggled to break them down. Eventually we got a penalty and at this point I was the designated taker. Here was a chance to win the league and be the player who scored the winning goal.

Naturally the keeper saved it. The twenty-year-old me was still nowhere near as good at penalties as my eleven-year-old self. I had to make up for it and fortunately did by creating the only goal for Kerry Dixon and on reflection it was much more fitting that he should score the vital goal, he had already scored 34 that season. David Speedie got 13, I pitched in with 14 in the league campaign. Together we had become a very productive triumvirate with well over 60 goals between us in all competitions.

The celebrations afterwards and on the coach back down south were fantastic, the fans' cars passing the bus with scarves and honks all the way home. There were a few bottles of champagne produced but there were mostly beers by the barrel load. The beer was a bit useless for me as I simply don't like the stuff. Before you think I am too much of a goody two shoes, I do love malt whisky and decent wine, so yes I did have a few glasses of the champagne generously provided by Ken Bates.

Although this was the day we had been dreaming of, there was one downside: for once my dad didn't make the game. My sister had the audacity to get married that same day and my dad was double booked. To many it would be an obvious decision and needless to say he honourably did the right thing, but it must have been torture for him. After the huge amount of travelling he had done and how much time he had invested in my football over the years, this was the biggest moment so far and it was a shame he wasn't there to see it and share it.

Ken Bates was so happy he jumped in the team bath with us afterwards. We were now champions, promoted to the big time and the big money, so Ken could finally let his hair down a bit with the boys. In fact he was so excited he gave us all a present for winning the league...a pen.

I preferred the champagne.

That season I was voted Chelsea's Player of the Year. I hadn't even considered it a possibility even at the awards event. The 1-2-3 was me, Kerry Dixon and David Speedie but it meant very little to me at the time. I was entirely focused on the importance of the team over and above any individual glory. Had you asked me then I would have said, and probably did say, 'It was nice but unimportant in the bigger scheme of things.'

If I am completely honest, I think I wanted to be spending the time with my new girlfriend Annabel, who was there that night, but I chatted more to the fans instead. I felt a confused guilt then and it continued throughout my life. In company I never wanted to let the fans down by not talking to them, but neither did I want to let Annabel down by not spending time with her while we were out together.*

It was only years after I retired that I looked at the names of the players who had won that trophy that I felt differently about it: from Peter Bonetti and Charlie Cooke to Didier Drogba, Frank Lampard, John Terry, Gianfranco Zola and Eden Hazard. I would not for a moment put

---

* I don't think I have ever managed to square that circle satisfactorily, but my wife and close friends were, and always have been, understanding. It doesn't happen as much these days fortunately!

myself in their bracket as a player, but it is pleasant to be on the list.*

Being Player of the Year should have helped my upcoming contract negotiations with Ken Bates. I now had a year left on my contract and believe it or not I was still not convinced I should stay on as a footballer. I still naively thought I could go back to Glasgow in a year's time after a season in the top flight and re-enter that happy, devil-may-care life I previously had. It was more of a temptation than most people would believe. It certainly seemed to surprise the chairman when I explained that it was still on my mind.

Ken Bates was a huge character back then and liked to use his position of power and importance. There was a story that had made it down to the dressing room that summed it up for the players. Someone had asked him why the players were never allowed into the directors' suite upstairs after the games. His possibly apocryphal answer was, 'If you ran a large company would you let the cleaning staff eat and drink with you?'

Whether true or not I have no idea, but it wouldn't have surprised me. He asked me to come to see him in his office at the end of the season and said he wanted to offer me a new contract. The money would be handy obviously and it would be good to have some options, so I asked what he was offering.

'That's not how it works,' he explained. 'You have to make demands and then we can come to an agreement after that.'

'But you just said you wanted to *offer* me a contract.'

After a bit of to and fro about semantics it was agreed I would come back the next day with my 'wishes', as I didn't like the word 'demands'. I didn't have an agent, so I had to consider how to approach this myself.

So off I trotted and asked a few of the players for advice. Micky Droy

---

* On the list a couple of times as I won the award again a few years later. If I ever do try to impress youngsters who ask me who I played for, I will maybe mention that I was twice Chelsea Player of the Year. I leave it a moment before adding the caveat that the club in the last couple of decades might just be of a bit better standard than my team was! Maybe a bit of an understatement there.

was incredibly helpful and along with his friend Geoff had become very protective of me. So, the next day, having printed out my 'wishes' on a single A4 sheet of paper (different times!), I walked into Ken's office at Stamford Bridge.

I sat in the low chair that was clearly deliberately positioned so you had to look up to him behind his huge desk in his elevated chair. This was basic Reggie Perrin cod psychology to make you feel intimidated and it was having absolutely no effect on me. In fact, I was once again stifling laughter at such an obvious power play. I also knew perfectly well that I was holding a few strong cards. If I left to go back to my studies then Ken would get none of my now increasing value and he definitely thought (correctly) that I was weird enough to do it.

I laid the sheet on the desk with the following written on it:

Two year contract, I will not discuss a third year!

£450 per week for year one.

£500 per week for year two.

£5,000 signing on fee per annum.

5 return flights home to Scotland per season.

20% increase in wages if I become a full Scottish International.

Ken picked up the paper, perused it briefly, stood up without looking at me, scrunched up the paper and threw it in the bin as he walked to the door. He opened the door, walked out and slammed it angrily behind him. His gold Rolls-Royce Corniche was parked outside the window of the ground-floor office behind the Shed End; he jumped into it and drove off at speed. I thought to myself, *Well, that didn't go too well. He didn't even say hello.*

Even at that seemingly stressful moment I thought it was unfair, that it was just an attempt to intimidate a very young man. He had, however, failed to consider one part of my background. Although I was quietly spoken and used the odd polysyllabic word I was still originally from Glasgow's east end and did what I suspect many from that area would have done in the same situation. Instead of meekly walking out, I rifled through the drawers in his huge desk.

In there I found a list of the other players' contract values. I went back to my flat in Earls Court, did a mean, median and mode average of the contracts and was well prepared when he called me back into his office the next day. I explained that 'I am only asking for the average for the team.' Micky Droy had got it just about spot on with his suggestions. 'So I am not being greedy considering I am the current Player of the Year.'

'You can't know what the average is,' he said.

I shot back with, 'Yes I can, I rifled through your drawers when you walked out yesterday and I found all the contracts.'

There was a moment of fury, but it quickly turned into an almost respectful smile and seconds later he was laughing. 'Brilliant, it's yours, we have a deal.' So that was how to impress Ken: play him at his own game. From that moment we got on very well even if we were never going to be bosom buddies hanging out together – our outlooks on life were far too divergent for that to be the case.

There was a further small problem with the contract after it was drawn up the very next day. I was literally just about to put pen to paper when I stopped above the documents.

'I want one more thing,' I said. 'I do not want to play in the second half of the friendly at Brentford tomorrow.'

The manager was confused and Ken fuming yet again. I always wanted to play and trained more than anyone else. What was the problem now?

I gave what I thought was a perfectly reasonable explanation. I was very fit and had nothing more to gain with that extra 45 minutes at the end of the season in a friendly game. If I got off at half-time, I would have time to get down to the South Bank and see New Order playing. I am pretty sure it is the only time going to see an indie band was part of a contractual negotiation. There were resigned looks all round and then it was quickly agreed.

John Neal said, 'Leave it, it's fine.' For some reason he knew that I was committed and not frivolous. If I was doing it, it was because it was something I deeply cared about. If I wasn't in good enough shape and needed that extra 45 minutes, I wouldn't have considered it. He seemed to know that my judgement was to be trusted, however odd it sounded.

During that season on more than one occasion John Neal had given the entire team talk without mentioning me before ending it with the line, 'And if you give enough of the ball to wee Pat we will win.' That could have put huge pressure on me to perform, but he instinctively knew it would have a positive effect. As the youngest in the team it could also have led to resentment, but he had now pulled together a group that was fine with that to a degree. At least there was no overt resentment, but maybe some was being stoked up in one or two minds for the future. It meant, however, that I had to perform.

How on earth did he know so much about my personality? He was a great manager and seemed to have a very good understanding of players' different characters, but even so, very few people in the game were able to read me so well. A year or so later I found out part of his secret. He had finished his team talk before a game and gone back to his office down the corridor. I then remembered that I had to tell him that I was being called up for the Scotland Under-21 team. On my way out to the pitch for the warm-up I popped my head around his office door to mention it. Sitting there talking to John Neal the manager and Ian McNeill his assistant was my dad!

'What's going on?'

John answered nonchalantly, 'Oh, your dad comes into our office for a wee whisky and a chat before every game.'

None of the three had bothered to tell me that had been happening for the past year. But they weren't just milking (or 'whiskying') my dad for information, they were also just three friends who liked each other and enjoyed each other's company. It was clear then and there why they knew so much about my personality.

13/
BLACK STAR

This felt like the moment when we would find out if we really were good enough for the top level.

We were playing the first game of the season in glorious sunshine away to Arsenal at Highbury, a very good team at the time and football royalty compared to us upstarts. Most of us hadn't played in the top division and now here we were – so this was it.

The 1-1 draw with Kerry scoring yet again was enough to give us belief that we probably wouldn't be relegation fodder but the real stars that day were our fans. They turned up in such huge numbers and made such an amazing noise and spectacle throughout that they all but drowned out the home support.

It felt like the start to a great year.*

---

* At the first home game that season I was startled as I was calmly walking out onto the pitch before the game. I looked up to see Chelsea fan Sebastian Coe six yards away, walking off the pitch directly towards me, while milking applause from all around the ground. He had just won the Olympic 1500m Gold in Los Angeles and was holding it up. I had admired him as a runner for many years and went to move out of the way of this global sports star, but he deviated and came straight towards me.

During that summer the manager John Neal had asked if we could meet when I was in Scotland.

He wanted me to join him in a game of golf at St Andrews and we arranged to meet at the first tee at 10 o'clock one fine sunny morning. Now I had never played a round of golf on a real course but had a few clubs as a kid, like most Scots. My brother Michael and I would go over to the local park and smash a few golf balls around now and again, so I knew I could hit the thing. However, your first ever drive on a real golf course being from the first tee at the Old Course at St Andrews, that *is* unusual.

John knew the starter and we walked over, with me carrying a borrowed set of clubs. 'Are we teeing off at ten then?' I asked. Apparently not: we were teeing off at midday. What on earth were we going to do for the next two hours?

John explained. 'We're going to stand here and watch everyone teeing off before us.'

I struggled to see the point of this, but I respected him and stood there dutifully watching. Now most people with even the faintest knowledge of golf will know that the fairway on the first at St Andrews is one of the widest in golf. Even a novice hacker under normal circumstances would have to try hard to miss it. Time and again, however, these very professional-looking men who obviously played a bit, were coming up and either duffing it twenty yards, missing it altogether or slicing it wildly out of bounds to the right.

Finally it was my turn. I popped one up the middle and casually

---

'Hi, Pat, how are you doing?' he said.

Slightly stuttering, as I could not believe Seb Coe actually recognised me, I said, 'Oh, fine.'

I wasn't really going to be driving this conversation, so he said, 'Are you feeling fit?'

Before I blurted out, yes, I was fabulously fit, I stopped myself. I realised I was talking to the best middle-distance runner on the planet – OK, along with the lovely Steve Ovett – and one of the greatest athletes in history. I think I got the right answer for once: 'Well, I was until I met you.'

walked on. John explained why we were there walking up the first fairway.

> Most of those guys you were watching are good golfers. There are American and Japanese millionaires who run multinational businesses and make huge decisions every day of their lives with no fear. But put them on that tee, at the home of golf, a moment they have dreamt about most of their lives, and you see them turn into nervous shaking wrecks.
>
> Never lose that fearlessness you have. Some people say that nerves are a good thing for them, but they don't know if that is really the case because they are always nervous before games. Maybe they would be far better if they could be as calm and controlled as you are. You are still able to care enough to give everything. It is a special gift that not many have. Cherish it and know how lucky you are. I've had lots of footballers who were crippled by nerves and never maximised their potential because of it. Most importantly, do not take it for granted, it is a great advantage to have.

That confident attitude when on a football field was a huge help with every step up in standard and it never failed me. What sometimes failed me was an ability to understand why everyone didn't have the same attitude. I was an individualist on the ball but was still a team player at heart. It made sense to me. There was a great spirit among the group of players in that side that I shared but also accepted that when you scratched the surface there was quite a lot of aggro going on too. The truth was that physical fights between players in training were not uncommon. When I consider the coverage now and how the tiniest little spat or disagreement gets picked apart and its importance exaggerated, I almost always shake my head and sigh. You have twenty to thirty men working closely together, in a physical environment, being ultra-competitive and in many cases fighting for each other's jobs and livelihoods. Clearly, there are going to be some flash points.

The press almost always read too much into these clashes, suggesting it reflects the atmosphere throughout the entire club and that any breakdown of relationships means that the manager has 'lost the dressing room', but it is often tosh. Most players are mature enough to be laughing it off later the same day. Maybe some modern players are less able to cope with these scenarios, but I suspect most still can and do recover quickly from a fracas.

But having said that, in my time there were plenty of fist fights at Chelsea during training and travelling. I can clearly recall David Speedie fighting with Colin Lee, David Speedie fighting with Kerry Dixon, David Speedie fighting with Joe McLaughlin, David Speedie fighting with Paul Canoville – you will notice there is a bit of a pattern developing here. David was usually part of it and he usually ended up losing, but he was incapable of backing down, even though he was generally six inches shorter and two or three stones lighter than his opponent. He would drive me mad as well, but he was an excellent player and though we had no understanding off the field, on the pitch we had a brilliant telepathic relationship in those early days.

Speedo's fight with Joe McLaughlin during a bounce game at training was a particularly vivid example of how things have changed. David nagged and nagged at Joe, who snapped, but snapped in a very slow and deliberate manner. During the training game, Joe, our good-looking, smooth Paul Young lookalike,* walked all the way from centre-half up to the centre-forward area where Speedo was still asking, 'What are you going to do then?' Joe showed him instead of explaining. Our big, usually mild-mannered centre-back delivered a well-timed haymaker to settle the matter before calmly walking back down the field to his customary position. We just all shrugged our shoulders and carried on, playing one-twos around Speedo as he lay groggy on the soggy ground. Could you imagine what the media would make of that today? Two hours later they were the best of mates again. I am not saying it is healthy for team spirit, but I did notice throughout my career that the tensions sometimes

---

* Paul Young was a star pop singer at the time.

needed breaking, and a scrap would often seem to lance the boil and release the poison.

One of the most ridiculous fights, in retrospect, was after a pre-season training session back down at the university campus in Aberystwyth. The final run of the day was one of those five-mile slogs along the beach all the way back to the campus. The great prize for the first eight home was to have their own single-person bath. Outside the top eight and you had to make do with a dribbling shower or wait an eternity for a bath to become free as the rooms themselves didn't have any.* Paul Canoville and I were as ever in the first eight to get back. I didn't care for the baths as much, a shower would do me fine. I knew some of the older players needed the bath to soak their now aching, ageing muscles far more than I did. Paul ran his bath and then ambled off to his room to fetch his various oils and unctions but by the time he got back in there, Kerry Dixon was in his bath quoting that ancient legal case law, 'finders keepers'. And so I found myself in the shower a few yards away confronted by the site of a naked white guy of six foot one and a six-foot totally starkers black guy battering lumps out of each other standing in a tiny enamel bath. It was moments like that when I really thought I was in the wrong profession. That sort of thing didn't happen in my student life back in Glasgow. What had I done getting involved in this world? And they called *me* weird?

The very worst fight was the one between Paul Canoville and another player at the club. It upset and angered me as much as anything that happened in my time at the club. In fact, I was so infuriated I went to the manager's office to hand in a transfer request because I thought it had

---

* Once again something current pros probably don't have to worry too much about. Along with driving ageing, clapped-out cars that wouldn't start in the morning; the number 22 bus to the ground along the King's Road being stuck in traffic; pitches so rutted or boggy the ball wouldn't run straight; the stinking kit and towels that hadn't been washed since training, not yesterday, but last week; sitting at the back of the plane behind the smoking journalists in cheap little seats while the club officials sat in business or first class up front...I could go on but I might begin to sound a little bitter.

been so unfairly dealt with. This one did destabilise the team spirit and got way out of hand.

On the last night of pre-season, again in Aberystwyth, the players were given some well-deserved time off. There is usually one evening when the lads can have a 'few' drinks after working extremely hard for a week and abstaining from the booze. It is stressful at the best of times because players are vying for positions and they have been cooped up together day and night, but in pre-season when the big decisions are being made about team selection it is even more tense. Like many men, they weren't always the greatest group at verbalising their feelings, so on this particular night there was a tinderbox feel in the air.

This player came back from town and clearly had drunk far too much. A few hadn't gone down into the thriving metropolis that was Aberystwyth town on a Friday night, including 'Canners', along with two other up-and-coming black kids in the team, Keith Jones and Keith Dublin. Mr Goody Two Shoes here would never have considered going out drinking during pre-season, so I was with those lads. They were closer to my age anyway and I got on very well with them, each were perfect professionals and likeable guys.

Heavily inebriated, the staggering player decided to use some very inappropriate slurs towards the two Keiths. They had been there before and treated the language with disdain, but Canners butted in and said in a conciliatory tone, '*Leave the brothers alone mate.*' The perpetrator then turned his invective on to Canners, which was a big mistake. It escalated and he came a distant second in the battle, before staggering off to bed with a very sore and badly marked face. That should have been that but next morning, having sobered up, he decided he wanted retribution at breakfast. He launched himself across the room with tables and chairs flying everywhere. It looked like he had a metal bar or something in his hand as he lunged towards Paul, who fortunately managed to get out of the way. Everyone jumped in to restrain them but it still wasn't finished there. Canners was transported in a car back to London while his assailant was parked on the team coach – the wrong way around in my opinion.

Paul was sold a while later but the other player was kept on and I had a real moral problem with that. I thought it was preposterous and came close to walking away there and then. Maybe Paul was going to be sold anyway and I cannot know for sure. Either way it is worth reading Paul Canoville's brilliant autobiography, *Black and Blue,* to discover the long-term cruel consequences of those grotesque twenty-four hours.*

I missed Paul or to give him one of his other names, the King. There was a fabulous appearance as sub against Sheffield Wednesday in a cup game at Hillsborough. When he came on at half-time, we were 3-0 down against our arch rivals. Paul scored seconds after his introduction and turned the game. His celebration on the TV pictures after the first goal is now seen as an iconic moment in Chelsea's history. It also makes it clear how stupid his attacker in Aberystwyth was to think he could take on this fabulous figure of a man in a fight, Paul could have been a professional boxer with that physique.

He was so charming as well as being a dude. He was also a trailblazer, an incredibly brave man and a great friend. We bonded over a shared devotion to music: both of us have been DJs but we have very different tastes. There was one moment of mutual enjoyment when I played him Lou Reed's 'Walk on the Wild Side' for the first time. We both loved the song but for different reasons. He loved it for the girl backing singers and when he first heard it, he was having feelings that were bordering on sexual.

Canners was a red-blooded male anyway and he once gave me some advice on seduction techniques. Picture the scene: we are downstairs in the entry hall of the student accommodation at Aberystwyth, the walls are

---

* Paul left the club soon after for Reading. He was crushed, got some injuries, had to retire very early, ended up becoming a crack addict, survived cancer and was almost lost to us on a number of occasions. He has turned it around since then, beaten his addiction and now does inspirational talks to kids and adults on anti-racism and helps with drug educational programmes. His story in the book is extraordinary.

hospital green, the floor is linoleum and it still feels cold in the middle of summer. I'm feeding coins into the payphone, finishing a call to Annabel back in Scotland. We were a sweet young fey indie-type couple, so the final tentative words were 'Bye bye darling, missing you, can't wait to see you, bye…bye…bye', tailing off to a twee whisper.

I put the phone down and there is Paul behind me. 'Watcha doin' man, that ain't how you talk to the chicks, man. Listen here and learrrnn.' He dials up, puts the coins in and says in a drawling deep voice that John Shaft or Barry White would have been proud of:

'Hey babe, it's the King. How ya doin'. I'm lyin' here on ma bed playin' with ma big thing.'

About this time I started to get a fair bit of what might very loosely be called fan mail. I thought the polite thing would be to write back personally to every single person who wrote to me, which after a while started to take up quite a bit of my time. For whatever reason I received many funny, intelligent and interesting letters, quite a few of which I have kept. Some of them became regular correspondents and a few from around that time still get in touch now and again.

I count Katie and her husband Peter as very good friends. Katie originally wrote to me every week with a recipe once I'd revealed in an interview that I couldn't cook. As long as there was no fan worship from their side, and it was just two people communicating, that was fine with me. There was one young girl who wrote to me regularly who had the genius writing style and surreal humour of Spike Milligan – high praise coming from me. Maybe I shouldn't be surprised that she ended up becoming a GP.

There were also now and again some (not many) girls who would send pictures that were a little too revealing. Clearly, they should have been writing to some of the other players not me. I was much too honourable, serious-minded and, as some back then would have said, boring and weird, to abuse my position and take advantage of this situation. OK, there was a bit of the 'St Patrick' going down here again, but that was who

I was and to some degree who I am, though thankfully I am much less judgemental towards others these days. The day I read P J O'Rourke's line, 'Earnest is just stupidity gone to college' I knew I had got many things wrong. He had me pegged.

It was quite nice in the old ego department to suddenly get hundreds of birthday cards and then the same number of valentines instead of one or two. I knew it wasn't me but the media persona that intrigued them, but it was briefly quite flattering.*

Of those 'fans' who contacted me, most were unusual outsiders who saw a bit of themselves in me, and I loved hearing from them. I spent a large amount of time writing back, especially if I thought they had something to say of interest or if I could help them understand that even us outsiders can have a place in this society and that conforming isn't always the only answer.

I could never take any of the day-to-day fan worship seriously for more than a few seconds though. It was too superficial, and I really thought that if they knew me personally they certainly wouldn't be nearly as impressed! The Sunday supplements were keen to get the story of this oddity and for a short time, there were even young girls' magazines printing pictures of me. A great friend, the actor Gerard Kelly, put me in my place around about that time. 'You are quite good-looking in a pretty-ish sort of way,' he said helpfully, 'but one harsh winter will see to that.'

He wasn't wrong.

---

* A favourite was one Valentine's night a girl called me – I have no idea how she got my number – and sang a gorgeously breathy, a cappella rendition of Sam Cooke's 'Cupid' ('draw back your bow'). She would not tell me who she was or even speak after the final words, but it was deliciously good and stunningly cool. I never did find out who it was.

14/
ALL TOGETHER NOW

There were many moments that now seem questionable at best in these more enlightened times, but back then were placed in the category of lads' humour. When we played West Ham United at the old Upton Park ground, their passionate supporters were only yards from you on the touchline, which, being a winger, is usually where I was positioned. The common shout of 'F*** Off You Little Scotch Poof' was considered restrained, maybe even polite. I got plenty of that and probably didn't help my cause by surreptitiously winking and then blowing the odd kiss in their direction when the referee wasn't looking. The joys of not having twenty-five TV cameras at every game meant that you could have a little fun with the fans.

Generally, most football fans enjoyed that bit of repartee but there is a large rump who are deeply unimpressed with whatever you do if you happen to be wearing the wrong colour shirt. 'C'est la vie' was my attitude. I had annoyed the Hammers' fans down there even more when I scored the winning goal with a towering back-post header in the 1985–86 season – no honestly, I did – from a Kerry Dixon cross! I never gave it another thought but many West Ham fans over the years have said to me how important it was to them and how annoyed they were with me. It was near the end of the season and they were riding high in the league with Tony Cottee and Frank McAvennie scoring freely. Some felt they may have become champions had they not lost that game to that goal. Sorry guys, I had no idea, I was only thinking about my own team.

What it led to was that a group of their fans always seemed to feel the need to call me gay throughout my career. Back then, if you were in any way different in football – be it an interest in music, the arts, reading, alternative style, not using laddish language and so on – then the fans' first port of call was to shout, 'You're gay.' I couldn't have cared less about their ignorant abuse, but the idea of turning around and saying, 'I happen not to be gay, but so what if I was?' would certainly have annoyed them even more. It did annoy them because that was my standard reply when I was close enough to be heard.

Even though I was sometimes asked about my sexuality it never troubled me. It was a perfectly reasonable question to ask, if a bit personal, but it gave me the opportunity to say how upsetting it was that it should concern anyone either way. I knew I was straight, and I didn't happen to know of any 'out' players back then with the exception of Justin Fashanu,* but there probably were a few other gay men dotted around the game…so what? What has that got to do with the ability to play football or indeed your ability to be a decent human being generally? Times had to change, people had to be educated and I thought talking openly was the only way. The thing is, I knew it was easier for me to be outspoken because not actually being gay I was unlikely to get persecuted in the game. But could others who were gay or bisexual be as certain? The answer was clearly no. They couldn't confidently trust all the players, the fans on the terraces or society in general not to persecute them.

There is the vexed question even now, why are there no 'out' gay

---

* Back then Justin Fashanu did come out and he felt his career was made difficult because of his sexuality. I would have loved to have talked to him about it but never did get the chance before he tragically took his own life. Even his own brother disowned him back then!

players in the game? Especially if some estimates suggest between 2 and 5 per cent of men are either gay or bisexual. Surely there must have been dozens if not hundreds of closeted gay pro footballers over the years in the UK?

Even though I am sure they are there, I am not sure the numbers are that large. There are some professions where the numbers are way higher than 10 per cent, say in ballet for example. My friends Fiona Chadwick and Antony Dowson, principals at the Royal Ballet at the time, were clear about that, and never said it in a pejorative way, just as a statement of fact. I suspect some professions are more welcoming to the gay community or at least seem more welcoming from the outside. Clearly these days there would still be abuse online and even some from the stands, but inside the actual game, I am convinced that a top-level gay player would not now have an insurmountable problem coming out in this country. Yes, you would have those players who might grumble a bit, but then there are still some closet racists around as well. They just know that their stance is unacceptable right now because of the campaigns, so they keep quiet about their bigotry. The same would happen to the homophobes. If the player was good enough, I believe he would now be accepted and more people would be ready to stand up and be supportive with a concerted campaign.

Throughout my entire career, I know of only one other gay player I played alongside, and I didn't discover he was until I was in my fifties. I was in the company of three of his former teammates when we were told at the same time and the conversation was enlightening about their attitudes.

'Do you know that XX XX is gay and out with his friends?'

First player: 'No I didn't, but now you say it, it does make sense. He did say he lived with his mum even when he was in his thirties. Maybe he didn't feel he could tell us the truth?'

Second player: 'Shame that. I just hope he is happy now. I wish he had felt that he could have told us back then instead of hiding it. It would have been fine after a bit of light piss-taking to normalise the situation.

That must have been tough for him.'

Third player: 'Yeah, right enough, now that you say it, it makes perfect sense, he did dress a lot better than us, didn't he?'

No homophobia, just a little bit of a laugh among the caring sentiments. I wouldn't be surprised if those three guys were representative of most players, because they, like large sections of our society, have been educated and have evolved. The modern young player would in general be even more understanding.

That said, I know that coming out as a top Premier League player would not be an easy decision to make. There would still be the fear of fan abuse, of online abuse, of lack of acceptance from some teammates and opponents. Would he also ever know the real reason why that top team didn't buy him – was it because he was not good enough as a player or was it because he was gay? Then there is the danger of becoming a cause célèbre as opposed to just a player. It is demanded that top footballers be role models now, even if they do not seek that position. If you were a prominent gay player, the expectation would be for you to become a trailblazing spokesman and campaigner; maybe you would fancy just being a player first and foremost, as that's how most others feel. I will admit that there were times when even I didn't initially discuss some of my passions with my teammates, not just because they didn't share those passions, but sometimes because I couldn't be bothered with the tiresome hassle from one or two less open-minded people about what they considered a 'suspect' interest.

Two of my best friends at the time were the above-mentioned Antony Dowson and Fiona Chadwick.* On one occasion Fiona invited me to watch from the wings at the Royal Opera House – being a principal, she could get away with that sort of thing. She danced the lead in *Swan Lake* that night and I stood there entranced to be in the middle of this

---

* I first met Fiona on a bizarre photoshoot alongside John Parrott, the snooker player and top Evertonian, and the singer Marilyn. Apparently, we were to be the faces of 1984. George Orwell would have been very disappointed.

magical world, the entire corps de ballet squeezing past me to make their perfect elegant entrances. Afterwards in Fiona's dressing room the flowers and presents arrived from the besotted older men, exactly like the classic Hollywood movie versions of the theatre stars after their performances.

I was desperate to go into work the next morning and share the experience with someone, but I suspected I knew what the response would be from at least some of the knuckle-draggers on the playing staff. 'Ballet, are you queer?' My reticence only lasted for a short time though because my willingness to push the fun of certain situations got the better of me and after a while I started to tell the players about my love of the ballet just to see their reactions. As I'd guessed, most were rarely that shocked and hardly any were offensive enough to use the 'poof' word with intent towards me. Even the most blokeish ones quickly got bored trying to wind me up because I clearly didn't give a stuff about their efforts. Sometimes, in fact most of the time to be honest, the ribbing was humorous and good fun, which was fine by me.

Any attempts to make me conform were pointless. We just accepted we didn't share the same interests and happily got on with life and work. That's why I have always wanted a gay player to come out. I expect it will not be that bad, particularly in the dressing room and on the pitch itself, but I accept that you can never be totally sure of anything until it actually happens.

The players would try to wind me up about anything, but at a certain level I knew it was usually a test. You could not be seen to be too self-absorbed or too precious in that company. There was a running gag for a while on the team coach to away games when someone would steal my copy of the *NME* and shred it. Very funny, but I always bought a second copy and kept it hidden at the bottom of my bag.

The reality is that when it came down to it most players weren't overtly homophobic or even against me liking music and the arts. My instinct is that this was really just the way many working-class lads with limited interaction with gay culture, who'd spent their lives focusing on football in their own little bubble, talked to each other. Confronted by an openly gay man in the dressing room – and yes, even in the showers – I reckon most would be perfectly cool about it.

There were, however, some limits to what I was willing to share. We were at Stamford Bridge, doing some light training one Friday before a game, and one of the letters in my mail contained a full-length picture of a guy wearing a leather biker's jacket. Nothing unusual there except he wasn't wearing anything else! How did he get that one through the developers at Boots? You have no idea how quickly I stuffed that photo back in the envelope before any of the players caught a glimpse.

Thinking back about that moment, I realised that the idea of letting them see this picture was unthinkable. It wasn't worth the hassle of them winding me up mercilessly and doubtless pinning the picture up on the dressing room board with a sign saying 'Pat's Pal'. This would have been unfair on the sender, who had unfortunately misread me just a little bit. I sometimes wondered what would have happened had he sent the fruity photo to one of the unreconstructed players: would he have received an angry visit rather than a polite reply from me saying, 'Thanks for the note, but I have a girlfriend and be careful what you send in future, not all players would react so benignly'?*

I admit there were one or two players, just as in all sections of general society, who were openly and offensively homophobic. There was one rare night when Annabel and I were dragged out with the lads to a club called Browns. It was definitely not my scene, far too swish. But I was impressed when Alice Cooper walked by and then Elton John came over for a chat with Annabel and me. Elton wasn't totally 'out' at the time and just wanted to talk some football, though I obviously wanted to talk music. I managed to move the conversation on to an old Peel session he had recorded around 1973. I knew he had played some of his huge early hits such as 'Daniel' and 'Your Song' in a fun pub-piano style. Like me, he

---

* It is worth underlining here that photos of semi-clad women would have been stuffed back in the envelope just as quickly by me and returned to the sender with a polite note.

was and is a fanatical music collector and we had Peely in common too. We were having a great discussion and he was genuinely lovely until one of our players walked by and at the top of his voice shouted, 'Hey lads, watch your arses, Elton's around!'

It ruined the conversation and indeed the night. Annabel and I left immediately after saying goodbye to Elton and he himself looked very upset by it, though his reply, 'I heard that ducky', was an impressively brave and calm throwaway response in the circumstances.

Even back then, however, the player with the gross comment didn't get the reaction he expected. Despite being thirty years ago it was still considered gauche and offensive by most of the players and their wives in the company.

In football the reality is that not everybody was accepted or was able to fit in, even if you were just a bit effete in comparison to the group. It wasn't actually always an anti-gay thing, sometimes otherness just confused some of the lads. There was a young guy who managed to get far enough in the game to be able to train with the Chelsea first team for a while, but he was what was then called a 'Sloane Ranger' or a 'Hooray Henry'. He looked like David Bowie only taller and better-looking but he had a penchant for saying 'OK yah' at the end of every sentence with a voice that was way too genteel for the earthier football folk. One freezing day he was asked to take a turn in goal as the keepers could not work in those conditions. 'OK yah, but my hands are cold yah, so I may be a shade inexpert you guys, OK yah.'

I really liked him, he was talented, intelligent, but sadly there was no way in the world he was going to be accepted by the others, even though I tried my best to help him integrate. This time I failed. He couldn't tone it down and was hounded out of the training ground that day never to be seen at Harlington again. I met up with him a few times for a chat at his restaurant (that Daddy had provided) and years later I could swear it was him in a TV deodorant advert chasing a girl to give her flowers after getting a waft of her aroma. If it was him, I think he found his calling as an actor–model.

I had this habit, not only at the club, of looking after and befriending the waifs, strays and the outsiders in any situation. I helped as much as I could but sometimes it wasn't enough.

Another waif soon turned up. I always needed help in the lone afternoon training sessions as no other first-team players would stay behind to help with my technique and skills work. What a weirdo, wanting to do more work! I would go to the youth-team coach and agree to have his left full-back work with me. The first one was John Millar, who did well, became a friend but eventually left for Hearts, so I was forced to go and ask who was the next left full-back in the youth team I could use for my extra sessions. A wan-looking youngster was pointed out and was probably quite pleased to be chosen. The chance of one-to-one training with a first-team player instead of doing chores such as cleaning boots, washing strips or painting the stand had to be an improvement on the day. He also didn't look, dress or sound like the other kids: he was a kind, sweet-natured kid, so a break from the 'banter' being aimed at him might have been a relief.

One of my regular regimes was to box off an area and then try to dribble past the youngster as he tried to tackle me. I would then let him drive at me with the ball so I could improve my tackling and general defending. It would help him improve as well because he was getting the very same benefits as I was. The problem was that this kid was improving alarmingly quickly. Was I losing it? I was a first-team 'star' but after a couple of months I was finding it difficult to get past this youth-team player. What on earth was going on?

How was I supposed to know that the youngster I had chosen randomly was going to play not only 300 times for Chelsea but also 36 times at left-back and left wing-back for England? I like to think those sessions helped Graeme Le Saux improve as a player, especially as an attacking full-back. I don't think I can claim to have made him the player he was but hopefully I was even more useful to him in a deeper sense.

Graeme was different from most of the other youngsters coming through at Chelsea and I knew exactly how it felt to be an outsider.

The nice, well-spoken, middle-class boy from the Channel Islands wasn't a comfortable fit among some of the young, streetwise London kids around him. His interests were different from theirs too. I took him out a few times and he would come to my flat to see me and my friends as well. I knew he had to be shown that it was all right to have alternative interests, to be yourself and still be able to become a footballer.* It was a joy to think I might have had a little positive influence on him along the way.

I realised eventually that it was much easier for me than it was for Graeme. I hadn't left a protective home life to go through that whole intense, insensitive, male, youth-team pressure-cooker experience alone at a professional club. Any weakness or difference there was mercilessly exposed, whatever it was. In contrast, when I was seventeen I was still living at home but, more importantly, I was a streetwise Glaswegian. I could not be psyched out or be routinely bullied by gang mentality and all the while I was surrounded by like-minded, enlightened students who would validate my principles.

Over the years Graeme and I have stayed friends, but it was painful to watch when he went through a period of being called out as gay not only by fans, but also by some players. There was a particularly awful moment when Robbie Fowler made what looked like homophobic gestures towards Graeme on the field in a Chelsea v Liverpool game. It was beneath Robbie, who has since grown up and I hope he is embarrassed by what he considered then to be banter but looked a lot more like ignorant homophobia.

The problem was that Graeme got very upset by it for a while and at the time I couldn't understand why. I knew that like me he wasn't gay, but why did he feel it was such an offensive slur? He is an intelligent guy and I thought that like me he should just have laughed at the ignorance and the stupidity of these comments and maybe even used it to promote a better

---

* I decided not to take Graeme down to the last night of the GLC where I was a guest on the terrace of the South Bank building as Ken Livingstone's flag was lowered for the last time. It was a case of little steps to start with.

message, instead of getting angry and retaliating.

We did talk about it and there was a variety of problems. He simply didn't like the fact that anything that was said about him was untrue, whatever it was. He did get this 'stick' at a much more extreme level than me, he played for England not Scotland like me, the game had a bigger media machine around it by the time this was happening to him and maybe the fact that he reacted so strongly egged on some of the worst parts of our society and indeed the fourth estate.

Graeme has been less positive than me on whether or not it would be a good idea for a Premier League player to come out, suggesting that he will need to have a strong character and put up with a lot of abuse. I said to Graeme, 'You just have to laugh at it. You're standing on top of the giant mound of moral superiority, why jump off to attack these idiots?' He correctly but forcefully reminded me that although I had it first, I hadn't had it to quite the same level as him for quite as long. It was a fair point.* We will only see if the expected trolling lasts for a long time when it finally happens.

For over three decades I and, increasingly, others have consistently tried to get the anti-racism message across. There is still a long way to go but these days all the players wear the T-shirts, hold the banners and take the knee. It is finally mainstream at last. Football and footballers can just as easily now be in the vanguard of educating society in showing acceptance for LGBTQ life and culture too. The PFA has always offered support, most clubs not only have mission statements but also have well-promoted inclusivity programmes. Even the Rainbow Laces campaign was well supported if sadly much less well promoted in some areas of the media.

When I played some players were homophobic, but I don't think it

---

* As the years went by Graeme's career flourished and his ability blossomed. His fame grew and his ability to cope with the stresses improved. My acquired position as the go-to semi-intelligent, arty footballer was usurped by the acolyte. He could have go that status; I didn't want the fame anyway.

was any better or worse than the general levels in young male society at the time. I'm convinced, however, that now, if a player comes out in the UK he will get strong support from the vast majority of other players.

It is time to be positive. I have always looked at the women's game and found it incredibly heartening that they seem to have no problem whatsoever with some of their teammates being gay; it is just fully accepted and scarcely even discussed. I have been to many women's games and covered the 2018 World Cup and can't recall, at any point, anyone caring a jot about which players are straight and which gay. The men's game can certainly learn from their attitudes.

I have watched black players become integral to the game and racism become unacceptable in football grounds. I have witnessed Glasgow Rangers sign Catholics after over 100 years of resistance. The acceptance and promotion of openly gay players is the next, most obvious and most necessary barrier to be dragged down. It can be and I believe will be normalised in the men's game, just as it should be. But it will need a strong character, maybe one loud, proud and brave man to be the first to step forward. I hope it will happen very soon.

By the time you read this, it might even have happened; I hope so. If not, I promise that when that first gay player steps forward, if he wants I will stand shoulder to shoulder beside him and we will not be alone.

15/
KNIVES OUT

Like a lot of young people, especially the annoyingly high-minded, I was interested in wading my way through classic literature. So reading that intense stuff was one of my favourite pastimes on Chelsea's team bus for away games. The choice was either that, hours of card games or staring blankly out of the window. Nowadays I am more likely to read P G Wodehouse than Camus or Dostoevsky, but I enjoyed going through that phase. One day I was reading the collected short stories of Anton Chekhov on the coach en route to Newcastle. Yes, I know it sounds pretentious!

Suddenly one of the players, the lovely but now departed Dale Jasper, said in his thick 'cockerny' accent, 'Patsy, I can't believe it, I know one of your authors.'

Dale was a true friend, along with his comrades Pates and Bumstead, but he was also definitely, 100 per cent the very last person I expected to be interested in Russian literature. But how dare I judge him? How arrogant of me. I was obviously too much of a snob to have noticed Dale's hidden depths.

'Sit down, Dale, and please tell me how you discovered Chekhov.'

'Well, I've just always liked *Star Trek* but I didn't think it would be your sort of thing, Pat.'

I didn't have the heart to tell him it was the wrong Chekov, so we had a nice chat about Kirk, Spock, Sulu and Pavel Chekov for a while.*

Even though I was playing for the first team, scoring the odd goal and receiving fan mail, I was just being my normal self and bumbling along. After all, why shouldn't I? I had moved to a rented one-bedroom flat in Pimlico, one without fleas! I steadfastly refused to do the expected footballer things just to fit in. My flatmate Adrian slept in the bedroom one night while I kipped in the sitting room on the sofa cushions; the next night we would switch it round. I always had the bedroom the night before a game though. I was still travelling by bus or tube around London and on reflection this was perhaps a bit too naive. One night it nearly had serious consequences for me.

In my first season with Chelsea we had been in the second tier of English football and because of that we'd had no games on European nights. Adrian was a Tottenham Hotspur fan. Now and again on those European nights he and I would go to see Spurs. Being from out of town, I was not in any way aware of the animosity that Chelsea and Spurs fans had towards each other.

The reason I went and even stood on 'The Shelf' watching Spurs was simply because I really liked some of their players – they were the type that entertained me and that I could learn from. The likes of Glenn Hoddle, Ossie Ardiles and Micky Hazard were a delight but the idea of a Chelsea Player of the Year hanging out on the terraces at White Hart Lane does now, I admit, sound a bit surreal and maybe even stupid. Ignorance was, however, bliss on those occasions.

---

* On the coach during those journeys, there were perfect opportunities to be an enthusiastic voyeur and eavesdropper. Trivial Pursuit was suddenly all the rage on the bus with pairs of players playing against each other. I loved the answer given by one of the players to the following question. How many spots are there on a pair of dice? Quick as a flash: 'Right, Joe, you count one and I'll count the other, then we'll add them up.' Oh dear.

By my second season things had changed but I was still blissfully ignorant. We played against Spurs at White Hart Lane and this time I was on the pitch. I had a decent game, we managed a draw and afterwards I didn't fancy waiting for the team coach back to Stamford Bridge, as it would take ages. So being a regular at the Lane I decided I would just take my usual journey home, by tube on the Victoria Line straight to the flat in Pimlico. I met Adrian outside but he was going to see a band. I had to get back quickly as I was off to play in a representative game the next day, my football boots in my bag.

When Adrian got off after a couple of stops a Spurs fan stood up and positioned himself between me and the door of the tube as it sped along.

'You're facking Nevin, aren't ya?'

Three things were obvious. First of all, he wasn't saying it in a friendly way. Second, he was a hefty, thick-set beast of a man. And third, the knife he had in his hand looked bloody big and pretty sharp from my angle.

Quick as a flash I replied in my best mockney accent, 'Ooze Nevin? Whatcha talkin' abaht?'

'You're Chelsea intcha?'

'Nah, I'm Spurs.'

This flummoxed him for a moment then I quickly realised a fourth thing about him: if brains were dynamite, he couldn't ruffle his own hair. He tried to catch me out.

'Awright, who's your favourite Spurs player then?'

I thought, *Really? If I was 'Nevin' and had just played 90 minutes against Spurs I could probably, at a push, name a Spurs player.* I had to go along with it even though there was a temptation to underline the obvious flaw in his prosecution technique.

'Aw, definitely Micky 'Azard, mate.'

He still wasn't fully convinced and blocked my way to the door as the train crawled into Warren Street station. I looked at my bag. If he checked inside, then the dirty football boots would have been a bit of a giveaway. As the tube stopped some old training kicked in from a previous life in Scotland. I pointed up and behind his left ear and in my best, hardest, loudest and gruffest Glasgow accent I shouted:

'What the f*** is that?'

As he turned around to look, I thumped him with a right hook and gave him an over-the-top, definite-red-card, straight-leg, bone-crunching 'tackle' to his knee. He crumpled and I legged it down the platform. I have never been so happy to see a couple of policemen step out in front of me.

I bought a cheap Datsun 160Y the next day, got some L plates and learned to drive in it.

Once I was in the top division, it seemed there was a certain type of person who thought it was open season when it came to threatening small, Scottish wingers. There was a gig by The Clash in Brixton, and somehow, I had still never managed to see one of the greatest bands of the age live. It was as brilliant as I had hoped it would be and I totally lost myself in the throng moshing around at the front of the stage. For some reason near the end I looked around and just then saw a particularly thuggish bloke eyeing me up. Having spotted me he pulled a knife from his pocket and headed in my direction. I made it smartly through the seething crowd and outside before wheel-spinning the car back up north of the river, to hell with the encore! Those jinky winger's skills came in handy just when I needed them.

In retrospect maybe I should have been more spooked by this sort of incident, but it had very little effect on me in terms of fear as soon as it was over. I put this down to growing up in the east end of Glasgow, where gang culture, beatings ('getting jumped' as we called it) and fights with knives and the like were just part of everyday life. It was always there around you in the background but you learned how to avoid it most of the time and if you didn't and you got a hiding you just got on with it afterwards, having learnt a lesson on where to go and who to be wary of. In an odd way, I blamed myself if I got into tricky situations and hadn't seen the danger coming. By the time I got back to civilisation north of the Thames that night I would have been thinking more about 'London Calling' blaring through the car speakers, with me ecstatically shouting along.

It didn't affect my love of London and specifically west central London. I felt comfortable there if maybe slightly less so when I travelled further afield, but that didn't and still wouldn't stop me exploring the city. When I first moved down I let that little flea-ridden place in Earls Court, then moved to Pimlico, had a six-month stint in Gloucester Road, before finally buying a flat on a quiet road just behind the very fancy Kensington Church Street. So there goes any vestige of street cred right there. My excuse for the up-market address was that it was logical. We trained at Harlington in those days, which is just beside Heathrow. If I wanted to do extra work on technique (which I did most days), I went back to Stamford Bridge and trained on the pitch on my own without telling the staff. So, living round the corner from the Bridge was handy.

I have never been the materialistic type, with one or two very specific exceptions, such as my first real car, which was an old MGB GT in British racing green. (The car was named Green, not after the colour of the car but after Green Gartside, the singer from Scritti Politti.) It wasn't hugely expensive at £2,000, but it was indulgent and maybe the flashiest thing I ever had. My excuse was that it was a 'classic sports car' as opposed to a Porsche or a Ferrari showpiece. I argued that it was a work of art as well as a car. Total nonsense of course but I did love it. Most MG fanatics feel the same and never forget their first love on four wheels.

Living in that part of London made the journey to training every morning easier when I had learned to drive. While most of my teammates had nightmare journeys through awful rush-hour traffic, I cruised along the M4 every morning at a steady 70mph directly against the flow, it was a pleasure. I have fabulous memories of warm weather, the driver's window rolled down, elbow resting on the door of my little MG, listening to The The singing 'This is the Day' or if I was in an unusually 'poptastic' mood, Tears For Fears proclaiming that 'Everybody Wants to Rule the World'. London on a sunny morning has its own special exciting beauty which I still love.

Training right beside Heathrow had an added bonus. On Tuesday I could get on a cheap standby flight home to Scotland and be in Glasgow by 3pm. With Wednesday our day off I could stay until Thursday morning before getting the red-eye back in time for training. I sometimes ventured much further afield, too. I once flew to Paris, got a train down to Bourges in the middle of France, caught a Cocteau Twins gig and flew back on the Thursday morning with no one any the wiser. The only sleep I got was on a bed with no blankets, but I was covered by my big black 'gloom boom' coat as usual – it had its uses other than the style. It was also worth it because Liz Fraser dedicated the encore to me and my efforts in getting there. These days a player would just get a private jet there and back. Where is the fun or the adventure in that?

Sometimes there was a little too much adventure, such as after a game against Newcastle United at chilly St James' Park in November 1985. I was being marked by left-back Kenny Wharton, who appeared to have some anger management issues on the pitch or at the very least he had when I was in the vicinity. He was booked for scything me down and then thought it perfectly reasonable to pick up the ball and smash it into my face with the aid of a perfectly timed half-volley. These days you would get a ten-game ban for that; back then the referee gave him a yellow card, a stern warning and even waggled his finger in his general direction. He must have thought it was serious.

As far as the Newcastle fans were concerned, it was clearly totally my fault that their hero had been booked. I couldn't follow the logic but that wasn't important, I got dog's abuse for the rest of the game. Nothing new there and it didn't bother me one bit as we had won 3-1, except for the fact that my student mates from Glasgow had made a rare trip to see me play and we had arranged to go out on 'the toon' that night. Again, in retrospect this was not a very clever or well-thought-out move.

As the four of us were walking into the city centre after the game a group of around twenty Newcastle fans started following us about thirty yards behind. I could hear the grumbles growing.

'It's him, it's that little shit Nevin, let's show him what we do to anyone who takes the piss out of the Geordie lads.'

There was no time to waste. I said to my mates, 'Turn left here and then we sprint but split up and let me go alone. There is no point in you staying with me and getting a hiding.'

Just as importantly, my mates would slow me down! Off I flew and the Newcastle fans were soon after me. Not many people would be able to catch me even after 90 gruelling minutes of football, but they had the advantage of knowing the streets. After a while it was clear they were going to get me because they had cleverly split up to cut me off.

Once again the Glaswegian east end experience kicked in. In those situations, if there are no police around you head into a restaurant. It confuses the enemy, it is busy, it is cluttered and, importantly, there are chairs you can pick up to use in self-defence. Pretty street smart, eh? I sprinted into the Wimpy and went to pick up a chair, which like all Wimpy Bars had every seat securely nailed to the floor, so not quite so smart after all. Happily, they stood outside banging on the windows like zombies at the end of the Will Smith movie *I Am Legend* and I legged it through the back kitchens and off to safety.

That was a crazy weekend. During the game, in the opening minutes I went on a dribble (Hi Dad!) and beat a few men but after a ricochet it went out for a goal kick to them. As I jogged back one of their players, some young newcomer called Paul Gascoigne ran past me the other way and said in a thick Geordie accent, 'Hey, Ah can dee that, watch.' He got the ball off his keeper and went on an even better mazy dribble than I had. When he eventually lost the ball, he ran past again and said, 'Told ye Ah could dee that.' I had never heard of this young lad they called Gazza before, I thought he must be off his head, but could see he was extremely talented and I warmed to his madness immediately.

Each time during the game when I did something skilful, from wherever he was on the pitch he would catch my eye, grin hugely and give a thumbs-up. I found myself reciprocating in what quickly became a game within a game.

With moments to go he was down in the corner and we were directly up against each other. He tried a dummy on me but I got the ball off him.

I tried a more outrageous one in return, but he got the ball back from me and tricked his way past. As he went away, he turned around and deliberately elbowed me in the face nearly breaking my nose. Moments later the referee blew the final whistle and as I got up groggily from the turf he came over and said, 'That was great, Ah loved what ye were deein' the day.' He seemed to have no knowledge, control, memory or understanding of what he had just done. This was a very strange character who ran on pure adrenaline and joy. But it was impossible not to warm to him even when he had nearly broken my already unpleasantly large nose.

It was very physical on the pitch in that era and I seemed to come up against a certain type of head case, week in, week out. I had a chat recently with former England internationals John Barnes (Watford and Liverpool) and Chris Waddle (Newcastle and Spurs), who were wide-playing contemporaries of mine back then. Chris surprised me with an interesting concept: he said he thought it was harder for me than it was for them in those days.

'Why? Is it because I was smaller or something like that?' I was intrigued to know and well on the road to being offended – well, as offended as I ever get.

'Back then all the real psychos in the game were left-backs, the players you played against as a right-winger,' he explained. Chrissy and John were predominantly left-wingers and playing up against right-backs who, for some obscure reason, were a much more sensible breed by and large. I managed to play an entire career without noticing this anomaly.

Mark Dennis of Southampton turned football into an extreme sport. You had to have your wits about you and be ready, a couple of times in every game, to ride a tackle aimed at your waist, or worse still, a couple of inches below. West Ham had a good run of professional hitmen at left-back, Julian Dicks being the pick of the bunch. Francis Benali at Southampton would leave a bit on you and Pat Van Den Hauwe at Everton was rumoured to be totally unhinged, something his tackling style did nothing to repudiate. I think Chris had a point.

The most famous was Psycho himself, Stuart Pearce, then of Nottingham Forest and England. I didn't think he was a dirty player at all, just extremely hard and uncompromising. He was also a very good footballer and improved throughout a career where we faced each other many times over a fifteen-year period.

In the early days with me at Chelsea and him at Forest I had a good deal of success. He was rash and impulsive, I scored a few, and got a few penalties against him. But as time went by and the rules about rough-house tackling slowly became stricter, he stopped lunging in as much and thus became harder to beat. I always tried to lure defenders into tackles, believing I had quicker feet, more skill and could get by them that way. Being 'jockeyed' or shepherded towards safety was not as easy to beat quickly. Stuart was by then the best in that position and a fine attacker too, but unlike a lot of wingers I loved playing against him because on every level he was a worthy opponent.

He would try to psyche out and intimidate every player he played against and some lightweight 'chicken' wingers were easy prey. I managed to play against him throughout most of my domestic career and even once for Scotland against England without having or more importantly showing any anxiety. To show that I wasn't intimidated, if he managed to 'mistime' a tackle on me or follow through far more forcefully than was absolutely necessary, I would never make a fuss or complain to the referee. I would just get up, show no pain, get the ball back and go straight at him again.*

This felt innately like the right thing to do but I guess somewhere in my past I had watched others, specifically Jimmy 'Jinky' Johnstone at Celtic, doing a similar thing. Watching him I immediately knew that showing any fear was unacceptable and it was the quickest way to lose the battle. Jinky was much smaller even than me but he was fearless and had

---

* Modern players rolling around as if shot by a high-powered rifle when they aren't hurt at all revolt me. Is that harsh? Tough, it is how I feel about the practice. I cannot warm to any player who does that, whoever he plays for.

ball skills that would rival Lionel Messi, he really was that brilliant at his best. But that fearlessness was crucial, and I learned from watching him being assaulted on a weekly basis. Even if I would never be close to Jinky's standard as a player, I felt I had to try to learn from the best. There was also that nagging voice from a young Davie Moyes still in my head from the Boys Club many years before.

I played directly against Stuart Pearce for all of those years but we never once exchanged a single word or even shook hands at the end of a game. There was absolutely no sledging, just those deathly shark eyes which I suspected were meant to strike fear by being mysterious and lacking in any vestige of empathy. Wingers would be trying to swap wings within minutes to get away from his biting tackles.

My answer was to ask the manager before the game to play me on the other wing to start with and then I would shout over to the gaffer after a few minutes, 'Can I swap wings and play on the right?' I.e., against Psycho. There is more than one way to intimidate and suggesting that you find him an easier opponent than the other full-back was one way of attempting to get inside his head, just as he was trying to get inside mine.

Sometimes he won the day and if I got a penalty, scored or made a goal then I considered I had got the better of him. I never backed off and never shirked the duel until one fateful day at Everton a few years hence, more of which later.

For all the violence of many of the tackles in those days in England, they paled in comparison to some by players from other countries. In one Under-21 Scotland match against Mexico, whose Under-21s wouldn't have passed for Under-31s, it was far worse than anything I had come across before. The game was at Fir Park, Motherwell, and long before half-time my shirt was soaked, but it wasn't raining and I wasn't sweating that much, it was just the sheer volume of spit from my opponents.

Before the first half ended I was minding my own business in the six-yard box, waiting for a corner to be delivered. The player who had been marking me – well, attempting to assault me at every opportunity – then ran at full speed from ten yards away and head-butted me square in the face with the referee standing right there watching it happen. I went down covered in blood with a broken nose. As I looked up the referee was sending him off but also ushering a furious policeman away who had been at the side of the pitch and was clearly intent on arresting him for GBH before he got to the dressing room.

I enjoyed playing for the Under-21s from my introduction in 1984. And from day one, the beauty of playing abroad with the team was always the prospect of playing against someone who had never come up against my specific skill set before. One such case was in a game against Spain in Cádiz in February 1985. There was a large Spanish crowd that night and we knew this would be a serious test. Just as important as pulling on the blue jersey that night was the fact that Jock Stein, then the Scotland national team manager, was in the stadium to check us kids out. Jock Stein, the same legendary figure who managed Celtic's fabulous European Cup-winning side, who also won nine league titles in a row and had god-like status with all Celtic fans. Twenty minutes in and I knew I was in for a tough night. First, the kid I was playing against was the same height as me; I hated that. If my opponent was tall, and preferably much taller than me, I could use my tricks, twists, turns and tighter turning circle to my advantage more easily. Secondly, he was very good; he was quick and not lacking in skill. All the advantages I usually had weren't of much use. I tried just about every trick I had. It didn't seem to matter that he hadn't checked out my style before, so at that point I had to shift to Plan B.

Plan B was to run the legs off any marker. If I could run almost constantly at three-quarter pace and with a load of sprints thrown in, then by 60 or 70 minutes his legs should start to go and I should then be able to beat him pretty easily. It is no surprise that many managers choose this time to make their substitutions; every player gets tired, you just have to be the one who tires last and then the advantage is yours. So, I ran this kid and by half-time I had given him a test that Mo Farah would have been proud of. It was 0-0 at the break when we went back into the changing rooms. I knew I had worked incredibly hard and though I hadn't played brilliantly I knew what I was doing. Our then Under-21 coach Andy Roxburgh was just starting the team talk when the dressing room door burst open. In marched the imposing figure of Stein, all six foot of him, and he made a beeline straight towards me.

He didn't even reach me before firing off both barrels at the top of his voice.

'You useless, arrogant, hopeless wee bastard. Who the hell do you think you are? That was an embarrassment of a display, you should be bloody ashamed of yourself. Just because you play for Chelsea you think you can swan about for Scotland. You are miles off being good enough to wear that shirt, in fact you are an embarrassment to that shirt...' On and on he went for what felt like an eternity.

There was a liberal use of expletives in there that I haven't included here, and he was screaming so loud and so close to me that the spit was landing on my face. He turned and stormed out, slamming the door furiously behind him. It seemed to last for ever even if it was probably only a minute or two.

I was shell-shocked – I thought I had done OK. I certainly didn't think I had an ounce of arrogance about me or my play. I was also convinced that I had worked bloody hard and not 'swanned about' like he said. All that was unimportant, however, because Jock Stein thought I was useless. I was crushed, or could have been.

The rest of the half-time break was a blur. Andy Roxburgh said nothing to me other than 'Go get a cup of tea,' but as I walked out the fog lifted. *I'll bloody well show him, I'll make him see the real player I am. I am not being destroyed by anyone, not even Jock Stein.* For all the negatives that have surrounded his acolyte Frank Cairney from the Celtic Boys Club days, I must be brutally honest and say that he had prepared me well for that moment. Over the next 45 minutes I worked and ran as hard as at any point in my entire life. I tried everything I could think of, fuelled with anger at his unfair outburst. At the end I just about crawled off and was so wrecked I was checked out by Doc Hillis for exhaustion.

Soon we were on the team coach heading for the airport after the game when Big Jock walked up the aisle. My head was down still recovering, but I was also not in the mood to take another verbal volley. He breezed past, ruffled my hair and said, 'Great wee man, superb from start to finish, well done.'

'What?!'

What the hell was going on? It took me a while to figure it out. What had he seen in his few previous dealings with me back in Scotland? In his eyes I was a quiet, slightly introspective, maybe overly sensitive little guy who said things like 'If I gave up professional football tomorrow I wouldn't care, I just play for the love of it and I can do that anywhere in any park game.' Or 'I like winning, but it is secondary to the creative side of playing.'

He simply had to find out if I had the strength of personality to cope with pressure. How could he trust me in the full national team if I was the kind of delicate flower that would wilt with the first hint of frostiness? In short, did I have the balls to fight back? I passed the test, I fought back and wasn't cowed but I also realised what a genius he was. He set up that entire situation, just to learn about my character and my reactions. He was a natural and brilliant psychologist.*

Over the years I heard stories about how Stein had played mind games on many other players from Jimmy Johnstone all the way to Kenny Dalglish. He was the master – I suspect even Sir Alex Ferguson would agree with that. Sir Alex once said of his time alongside Big Jock with the Scottish national team, 'I am working with someone who has won the European Cup and nine championships in a row. It was a boost for me at

---

* Psychology is such a big part of any sport, but surprisingly few took much notice of its benefits up until relatively recently. Gamesmanship has always been used conspicuously by the best; tennis great John McEnroe's outbursts in his heyday were not all just his lack of control. Muhammad Ali was not a loud-mouthed big-head; he was a genius as a boxer but also a master manipulator of his opponent's psyche. These days sports psychologists are in post at every football club and players have access to them whenever they like. That was unthinkable during my career, so the best manipulators stood out.

that time in my career. I was basically learning all the time and keen to do so. It was an honour first of all. But what an opportunity, the chance to learn from someone like Jock Stein.'

Those were the only harsh words Mr Stein ever said to me. After that day he was always supportive and helpful but mostly he liked to interrogate you. He never tired of analysing people, especially the players he worked with, to uncover their strengths and weaknesses and what motivated them.

As Scotland were qualifying for the 1986 World Cup by drawing with Wales at Ninian Park he suffered a fatal heart attack after collapsing near the dugout. If ever there was a 'JFK moment' in Scottish football that was it, September 1985. Scotland lost one of its greatest sons and a man who was also a father figure to many of us.

In the mid-eighties while I was at Chelsea there were many awful times for the English game. I was in Glasgow when the Heysel Stadium disaster happened following violent clashes between Liverpool fans and Juventus fans at the Champions League final. I hated the entire game of football at that point. My anger and grief were mirrored by the whole of our society's fury at what the hooligans had done and the fact that they would probably get away with it again. It didn't matter a jot which club's supposed fans had caused the trouble that led to the deaths of thirty-nine innocent people and the maiming or injuring of up to six hundred others. There were more disasters to come and it was a bleak time for the game, before most of those morons were eventually ousted from it.

The Heysel disaster led to a ban on English clubs playing in European competitions, which denied me and those of my age group any chance of playing in those competitions during the peak of our careers. It is an insignificant point alongside the deaths and I didn't argue against the ban for a second, but it is yet another reason why I feel so infuriated when that period of fighting and hooliganism is glorified by these now sad old men – and it is always men – who have the gall to talk about it wistfully.

Another disaster was at Valley Parade, the infamous Bradford City stadium fire in May 1985, where fifty-six fans were killed in a stand that was clearly not fit for purpose. The game rallied round and raised a great deal of money for the cause, which was the right way to react. It also ushered in the dawn of stadium safety finally being taken more seriously.

After the worst of the violence there was a movement that came from the terraces that deserves more credit than it has been given. Great efforts were made by the clubs and it is impossible to say what was the single most important game-changer in the efforts to rid ourselves of most of these thugs, but I liked this supporters' movement.

It may have started at Manchester City, but over a short period football fans started turning up at grounds with silly inflatables. Be it bananas, sheep, sharks, blow-up dolls or whatever, it was consciously ridiculous and fun. It felt like fans were saying to the world, 'We are not like those other morons; we don't accept their presence, that is not what we are and we certainly do not all deserve to be tarred with the same brush.' It is hard to organise a serious fight in a ground when you are surrounded by hundreds of people having fun and holding up daft inflatable kids' toys.

The fanzine culture also had an effect. After the punk revolution in the late seventies there were countless music fanzines that positively affected various areas of youth culture, but the movement scarcely touched football for years. Then suddenly football seemed to develop its own taste for fanzines, some of them even covering music with football. These homemade magazines were not emanating from any large publishing corporations, just from people who truly loved football and their clubs. They were among the groups of people who were trying to recover football's reputation from where it had been dragged by the hooligans. It is hard to know how important they were in saving the game, but those who tell you it was down to Sky TV and the Premier League for changing the atmosphere are way off the mark.

The fans were already doing it for themselves years before the big boys arrived on the scene.

16/
BACK TO BLACK

In among the ugliness of the sport, the 1984–85 season had been a great one for Chelsea, and it was also fun on and off the field for me. We played an exciting, positive brand of football; we had a manager who saw the game the way I did; and our cavalier style was loved by our fans as well as being admired by the media. We finished in sixth place in Division 1 and it really felt like we were at the start of something very special.

We wanted to gauge ourselves against the best and at the time that meant Manchester United, who we managed to get a creditable draw with at Old Trafford in the fourth league game of the season. Everton, the eventual champions, were beaten 4-3 at Goodison Park and though Liverpool beat us 4-3 at Anfield we saw them off 3-1 in the home tie. Games like these allowed us to believe we could stand toe to toe with the best and there was a general fearlessness about the group.

In the space of two seasons we had gone from being inches away from dropping into the third tier to being serious competitors for the top prize. The impressive thing on top of that is that we seemed to be doing it in style by playing attacking football and scoring a lot of goals. Well, Kerry Dixon scored a huge amount of goals and the rest of us chipped in.

We were desperate to do well against the other London clubs and it could be argued that the two league draws against Arsenal and the two against Spurs were as important as any other games. From nowhere, suddenly we were on a level footing with them, even finishing above the Gunners in the league, albeit by goal difference. Nobody had seen this coming. Even with our other neighbours, famously tough games, we didn't lose in the derby games in the league against West Ham or QPR either that season.

A highlight for me was scoring a free kick from 20 yards against Spurs at the Bridge with Ray Clemence the legendary England keeper between the sticks. I hope the guy who had pulled a knife on me on the tube four months earlier enjoyed that goal!

Not that this is the piece of action from that era you would find if you Googled my name now.

In the last minute of a League Cup game against Manchester City in November, I won us a penalty. We were 4-1 up and it was the perfect opportunity to try a new style of spot kick, one I had been practising. There was no run-up, just one or two steps and that in theory didn't give the keeper a chance to move. It was rare then, but many have tried versions of it and indeed perfected it since (check out Eden Hazard for proof). I clearly hadn't perfected it as well as the Belgian has.

I had scored twenty out of twenty the day before in training, but the day before hadn't been muddy. I think I managed to just about reach the goalkeeper with the kick, but a three-year-old could have saved it. The commentator Barry Davies said, rather kindly I thought, 'I don't want to be harsh on a player of undoubted quality but that must be the worst penalty kick I have ever seen at this level.' Cue for me to be embarrassed? No chance.

As I walked away trying my best to look disconsolate, the manager John Neal spotted that I was giggling away at myself. I'd had a good game, there was one piece of skill on the wing to set up a goal for Kerry I was pleased with, so really, 5-1 or 4-1, who cares? It was a cup tie and we were through. That was surely the time to try things and it was also undoubtedly very funny. The manager said in the dressing room afterwards that he was fining me for that reaction, which I thought was a little harsh. I never did pay the fine.*

Two of my favourite people I have ever met were my teammates at that time, Colin Pates and John Bumstead. Along with their slightly younger and just as funny sidekick, the late Dale Jasper, we were often outdoing each other with surreal stupidity. But even Patesy, who was also by now the skipper, would sometimes shake his head when I was unknowingly more peculiar than either of them. He generally wore number 6 and I was number 7, so we usually changed next to each other on matchdays. In our first season back up in the top division I leaned over to him just before the team talk and asked with complete honesty and ignorance, 'So, who is it we are playing today?' Eyes to heaven, then over to Bumstead and then back to me, he then sighed, 'That would be Manchester United, Pat, a little team from up north, you needn't worry about them too much, just do your usual thing.'†

---

* Still, am I embarrassed by it now? Well, no. I was asked about it a lot over the last decade because Colin Murray and I had a running joke for years about that commentary on a Radio 5 Live show we did. So, maybe surprisingly it was me who asked someone to put it up on YouTube. In fact I'm now slightly jealous if anyone says they have seen a worse penalty. I do think that if you take yourself or your image too seriously and cannot laugh at yourself, it is dangerous for your sanity.

† Maybe I should have paid some attention, particularly to Bryan Robson – he was an incredible opponent. There was one game when he seemed to be everywhere, so much so I thought there must be two of him on the pitch. On one occasion he was at the back post winning a header and nearly scoring against us. Eddie Niedzwiecki our keeper saved it, turned and immediately threw it to me on the right wing towards the halfway line. I managed to trick my way past the full-back only to find Bryan Robson tackling me, and not just any old tackle. As he won the ball clean with his left foot, his right came through and mangled my knee. Even as the pain hit, I was amazed by his reading of the play as he knew where the danger would be. I was bewildered that he got there so quickly and even secretly impressed by his skulduggery. I don't think I even got a foul!

The odd thing is that I had always studied players with my dad, but that was specifically to learn things that I could use to beat defenders. I tried to learn everyone's special tricks even as a kid; most players have their go-to skills. From the start of my career in England, I also got the videos of our games and analysed them, purely to iron out my own weaknesses and develop my strengths – I wasn't that concerned with the opposition initially. I suspect the manager and I were the only two people who watched those VHS tapes. Back then clubs might send one scout along to watch next week's opponents and report back. It was all a long way away from the deep knowledge and endless data that is out there now. It is not uncommon nowadays for players to have a specific recording, edited together by the club, sent to them to give all the information they need about the next opponent.

We had by now a phenomenal following behind us when we travelled which helped our away form and there was no better example than at our League Cup classic against Sheffield Wednesday. A serious rivalry had been built between the clubs the previous season when we pipped them for the league and this cup saga kept the pot at boiling point.

We drew 1-1 at Stamford Bridge and had to go to a heaving Hillsborough on a Wednesday night in late January to try to get through to the semi-final. It was a nightmarish first half for us in front of nearly 40,000 frothing fans and we found ourselves 3-0 down with what looked like no chance whatsoever. The manager juggled the team at half-time, moved me into a more central area, which I preferred, and brought on Paul Canoville on the wing. He scored 10 seconds after the break and we battered them with an incredible display of fast, inventive, skilful, committed football. Kerry Dixon got another, I laid on Mickey Thomas to get the equaliser and then Canners incredibly scored to make it 4-3 to us. It was more like a transcendental religious experience for the Chelsea fans at that point than a midweek away game in Yorkshire. They got an equaliser from the penalty spot and after no further scores in extra time it was back down to Stamford Bridge for a second replay.

Our fans were as excited as I had ever known them. With Sunderland now waiting in the semi-final, the road to Wembley was tantalisingly opening up. Again nearly 40,000 turned up that night and the highlights on TV later showed a great game. We went a goal down but I managed to create the equaliser with one of the best assists of my career. The entire Wednesday team charged me like a herd of elephants after a blocked free kick but I scooped it over them all, went past the keeper and cut it across for Speedie to nod in. Mickey Thomas scored the winner and our progression seemed unstoppable.

In the semi-final played over two legs we would have been expected to beat Sunderland, but the entire tie became an ugly farce. The first leg was played on an ice-bound, rock-hard pitch at Roker Park. Football boots were impossible, so most of us wore trainers – it wasn't even close to being playable. Our centre-back Joe McLaughlin fell, dislocating his shoulder, and our makeshift defence couldn't cope. We lost 2-0.

Still, the second leg would be at the Bridge and we were a free-scoring side so the tie certainly wasn't over. However, on their side they had our former player Clive Walker, the man whose goal had saved Chelsea from the third tier, the man whose position I had taken. He was brilliant that night in the second leg, scoring two goals. Some so-called fans couldn't cope with the irony and got on to the pitch and tried to attack Clive.

As the game drew to a close and we were going out, there were fans on the pitch fighting, attempting to get at the away support and generally there was pandemonium.*

It summed up our side in many ways; we were pretty good but not quite good enough. Chelsea did not have enough money for top-quality

---

* In the dying seconds I got on to a through ball and lobbed the keeper for a consolation goal which had no bearing or interest – except for the fact that there was a horse galloping in the other direction in the same penalty box just beside me. It was one of, if not the most surreal moment of my career. I am pretty sure the police horse was offside but the officials, who were in shock, didn't call it, so the goal stood.

back-up throughout the squad and it was our downfall time and again.

I was creating plenty of chances, but Kerry Dixon rightly was getting the headlines almost every week. In his first season in the top flight, he finished joint top goalscorer with Gary Lineker.

It was an impressive outfit built by John Neal, a far cry from the side that had almost been relegated to the third tier just before I arrived, and there was still a good atmosphere in the group. Most of the fans were excited and well behaved the majority of the time but the ugly minority were still there on the periphery ready to embarrass the club.

Chelsea invited Rangers down from Glasgow to Stamford Bridge for a fund-raising game to help the families of those who had suffered in the Bradford City stadium disaster. The Gers fans turned up in huge numbers in south-west London and the Chelsea fans were not only appreciative but also very impressed. Chelsea fans had always travelled in huge numbers themselves and for many they saw kindred spirits in the distant away end. The Scots also sang all night long, just as the Chelsea away fans always did. But there were other, more complex and some darker undertones as well: yes, Rangers wore blue too but they also had a penchant for flying Union flags and even St George's Crosses, some with red hands in the middle, as opposed to the St Andrew's Crosses and Lions Rampant that some might have expected from Scotsmen.

My name was being sung by the Rangers fans throughout but not exactly in a friendly way. As a well-known 'Tim' (i.e. Celtic fan), I was getting plenty of stick, the most pleasant chant being 'Dirty Fenian bastard'. To be fair I had grown up around this sort of stuff on both sides of the Old Firm divide and didn't take it too personally or seriously. As I walked off at the end, however, our manager, who wasn't really catching the subtle nuances of the Glaswegian accents, said to me:

'Pat, get over and wave to the Rangers fans, they've been singing your name all night.'

I think it was the first and only time I told the manager I respected massively to 'Piss off'.

Much to my dismay it was considered so successful that a return game was organised at Ibrox Park. The Rangers fans and now the travelling Chelsea contingent turned out in huge numbers and another love-in ensued. Once again at the start of the match I was getting the regulation abuse, but I was back in Glasgow and could see my friends and family afterwards, so I just got on with it. I wasn't even particularly offended; it was just on the darker edge of banter if you understood the city's sectarian dynamic.

However, it did get uglier quite quickly. Our young up-and-coming black midfield player Keith Jones was having a very good game and slowly the attention started turning towards him. He was on fire and even started throwing in a few flicks and tricks – after all, it was only a friendly to raise money wasn't it? The Bears (Rangers fans) didn't appreciate it and the few shouts of 'bloody black bas***d' and 'f***ing darkie' began to rise to a crescendo. There were few if any black players in Scotland and many clubs had pockets who made similar racial chants in the coming years. Just ask Mark Walters and Paul Elliott about what they had to put up with at various grounds.

I was by now getting very upset for Keith and embarrassed by the behaviour of my fellow countrymen. I went over to the manager during a break in play and suggested he substitute Keith. He shouldn't have to put up with this disgraceful and offensive abuse and by now it was beginning to feel a little bit dangerous too as Keith was winding them up. Accepting my local knowledge was probably better than his, the manager made the change.

As Jonesy ran off applauding the 'Bears' sarcastically, the shouts became even louder and more indignant: 'Get the darkie aff, get the f***ing darkie aff.' I cringed until he got out of sight and into the dressing room.

Moments later the announcement came over the loudspeaker system: 'Number 10 Keith Jones has been replaced by number 14 Phil Priest.' There was a moment's pause before they shouted as one, 'Get the darkie back oan again!' Poor Phil, a young lad from Birmingham, who had a shock of ginger hair just to make it worse, had absolutely no idea why he was being slaughtered for the rest of the game. Being a 'Priest' was obviously a more heinous crime to them than being black.*

The club's next bright idea was to go abroad to get the benefit of some warm weather training with a game thrown in to keep our fitness levels up while the country was in the grip of a freeze and no games could be played. Where would chairman Ken Bates organise our little fun trip? Barcelona, maybe Florida? No, he decided the Middle East would be a fun place to visit instead. I loved the idea; it was a chance to visit another country and see another culture, but the lads were less impressed and some even refused to go.

It didn't start well. Ken thought those five days away from home would be covered by the grand total of £30 expenses each. The team thought otherwise; surely the club was making a fair wedge out of this trip? We weren't that well paid and £6 per day meant that it would cost us to go out there. Ken thought it was our job and even the £6 he was offering was generous. There was a stand-off and other unrelated grievances arose. We couldn't get wives and girlfriends into our grotty little players' bar (I rarely used it anyway) and so on. There was talk of striking, refusing to speak to the club newspaper and, my favourite one for comedy purposes, ignoring Ken Bates when he walked into a room any of us were in.

There weren't many trips abroad with Chelsea probably due to the

---

* The Chelsea–Rangers love-in grew, much to my chagrin. We played one cold winter's day at Anfield, memorably standing toe to toe with a great Liverpool team, leaving with a point from a 1-1 draw. It was also the only time in my Chelsea career when I was booed from start to finish by most of the fans in the Chelsea end! Unbeknown to me, the Rangers game was cancelled that weekend, so thousands of Gers fans came down to rekindle their relationship with Chelsea. They gave us fantastic support throughout, except for yours truly who got the usual constant stick. I was a bit miffed at the time, but it had the effect of making me play with a bit more anger than usual. It worked and I scored our equaliser. For once my celebration wasn't with the Chelsea fans but at them.

costs involved. There was, however, a club sponsorship with Gulf Air that season and maybe that was the real reason we were flying to some random city in the Middle East for a game. It was one of the weirdest build-ups to a match I have ever had.

On the day of the match itself, when we took to the pitch we hardly needed to warm up as it was 100°F out there in the relentless sunshine. It didn't seem to affect our opponents at all as they went through an intensive full-blast warm-up in the other half. The crowd was in and it was a full house, the referee and his assistants were in place, the opposition were lined up and ready to go, as we were, when three o'clock came…and then went. Five past three, ten past and then quarter past, still no start to the game.

By this point we were getting a bit confused. What on earth was going on apart from us getting sunburnt as we awaited instruction or even just the odd nugget of information? There was no point in jogging about; we were boiled anyway and that would just sap our strength for the 90 minutes to come. So, we sat down there on the pitch with I guess 20,000 people in the stands equally bemused, but strangely they were not getting particularly restless. At one point quite a lot of the local fan base went on their knees in the stadium and started performing their ritual prayers. It is actually quite difficult to know what the correct etiquette is in that particular situation. Do we kneel too? Do we have our own Christian moment? We certainly didn't pass the ball around as a mark of respect, because at that moment it felt more like a mosque than a football stadium.

Eventually word got out that we were waiting for the guest of honour to arrive. Eventually he turned up and we were allowed to start the game after what seemed like an eternity but was 'only' 45 minutes. Now if that guest of honour had been Nelson Mandela I would have accepted it, but it wasn't: we were in Iraq, playing against their national side and our guest of honour was some guy called Saddam Hussein.

Back in those days he was seen as Britain's ally and he wasn't a well-known figure outside the Middle East, so to be fair none of us, including me, knew much about him or indeed his son Uday. Hussein junior was involved in coaching the national football team and the story goes that if they lost he had the soles of his players' feet beaten. So that's why they were intent on a serious warm-up for this friendly.

All this mucking about aside, personally I was extremely excited to be in Baghdad and was determined to see everything I could while I was there. Before the game I saw less than I should have because I had a heavy cold and fell asleep in my hotel room with my headphones on. I slept so well I missed the team bus to get to the game by eight minutes. I rushed downstairs and my heart sank – apart from anything else it was likely to lead to a huge fine and it also looked like disgraceful unprofessionalism. Except for the fact that the hotel clock was ten minutes wrong and I was in fact on time, but that didn't matter – they had all gone.

Then I noticed two shady guys standing in the corner wearing military fatigues, aviator shades and smoking cigarettes with one hand while gently tapping their guns with the other. *Definitely our security,* I thought, and had an idea.

'Excuse me, could you get me to the football stadium? I've missed the bus and have to get there, preferably before the bus does.'

'Of course, is no problem,' drawled the first heavy with his thick Levantine accent.

He then turned to his mate, slouched back against the wall and carried on with the conversation in Arabic. I left it a few minutes but was beginning to wonder whether they'd understood me and more importantly the time pressure I was under.

I asked again and again they said, 'No problem, we just finish cigarettes.'

This they did slowly and eventually motioned me to come with them to their car, a white Mercedes with blacked-out windows. They strolled over, laughing and joking, at a snail's pace, fired up the engine of the car, then the G-force slammed me deep into the back seat. Like an American movie, the driver slapped a blue light on the roof of the car, put his foot to the floor, put the heel of his hand on the steering wheel horn and didn't move it. We screamed through traffic, carts, livestock and traffic lights at suicidal speed. As I crouched in the back seat, they looked like they were out for a casual Sunday afternoon drive in the countryside. For a moment I thought, *I don't know who these people are, they could be taking me anywhere. I could be in real danger.* The thought didn't last long – I had to focus on surviving the car journey first.

We arrived at the stadium, straight through all the roadblocks outside without stopping. And suddenly there I was, sitting seemingly relaxed in the dressing room ten minutes before the team arrived. I casually explained to the manager that I obviously hadn't missed the bus but had gone out exploring and decided to meet them here. It was one of the benefits of being seen as a weirdo or semi-intelligent outsider; they just accepted situations like that as me being a bit different.

The game itself ended 1-1 and the next day was to be a day of rest. Clearly, we were expected to do a bit of lounging in the sunshine but the lads had obviously decided that hanging out drinking free booze in the basement of the hotel was the more sensible thing to do. I wasn't up for that; it's not often you get the chance to go to Baghdad and see this historic city, one that hadn't at that time had the crap bombed out of it by quite so many different armies.

I had two problems: how to get into the middle of the bazaar area from our plush hotel just out of town, and who I could take with me. There was only one guy I could talk into it: John Millar, the young Scottish left-back who had become a great friend. We had limousines and drivers at our beck and call, I just had to talk them into taking us into that admittedly rather dangerous-looking area. They weren't keen but I eventually talked one guy round.

Now, as a seasoned traveller, or so I thought, I explained to John that it would be best if we didn't stand out. He was already at a disadvantage in that he was tall, blond and dashingly handsome, unlike me, his small, swarthy friend. No matter. As long as we dressed down and looked as scruffy as possible with jeans and an old T-shirt, we would be fine.

The driver sped us towards the heaving mass of humanity that was pure Indiana Jones territory – there would be no Golden Arches here. He dropped us off on the dusty road beside the ancient low-rise buildings, he then spun round and with wheels screeching – all Saddam's mates obviously went to the same driving school – he drove off into the distance, leaving a cloud of dust around us. The dust slowly settled to reveal a small crowd of people staring at us as if we were aliens. Our attempts to dress down had failed miserably, even with a covering of dust. We were as inconspicuous as a couple of members of Duran Duran swanning about on a third world video shoot.

We were there now and walked into what looked like an impenetrable maze of tiny streets, which still somehow didn't manage to give any shade from the scorching heat. On the corner of every street there was a soldier in the obligatory military fatigues and sunglasses with an AK-47 in hand. Obviously in retrospect, I realise these were Saddam's Ba'ath Party henchmen, but I couldn't have told you that at the time – they just looked mean and humourless. This lot didn't look like they were ready to give us directions, which was a shame really because we were soon hopelessly lost.

After a while we got hungry, so imagining myself the intrepid explorer type, I suggested some street food. There was an elderly woman stirring what looked like a witch's cauldron; she was having a decent go at the witch's look as well just to help the moment. But the smell was delicious, so I used the international sign language for eating and produced some local bank notes. She smiled, obviously with no teeth, and gave the pot a stir for us to look at it and maybe develop the aroma a little more. All I could see when she stirred were dozens of eyes staring up from beneath the brown runny stew. It is amazing how quickly you can lose your appetite.*

It was an extraordinary thing to be able to do though; it was such an utterly different world to anything I had known. Instead of having any negative effect it just made me promise myself that I would never be tempted by the easy route of sitting in a Hilton somewhere and missing

---

* I made a not dissimilar schoolboy error years later in South Korea. This time it was a huge pig's head with eyes intact that was disturbed by the stirring ladle.

out on some adventure. I couldn't understand why the rest of the lads showed no interest in seeing other cultures, but to a greater or lesser extent it was a feature of every team I played with.

As we explored the warren of alleyways we were followed inexpertly at various points by soldiers, then plain clothes police who stood out more obviously than us, and even in the end a small group of women in full hijab. Right in the middle of all these houses and stores I looked carefully into one, to see if I could find anything either interesting or local within to take home as a present. I also fancied trying a bit of haggling just for the fun of it. In the entire three-hour period I found only one thing, clearly of Western origin: a second-hand football bag from the 1970s with Chelsea FC emblazoned on the side.

We finally got back to the hotel ready to prep for an early start and our flight home via Jordan. As I walked out there were a few hotel staff waiting to see us off and one commiserated with me about being beaten 2-1 by their national side.

'What? Who said it was 2-1? We were there and I can assure you it was 1-1.'

'It was on the radio this morning and the newspaper also said it was 2-1 to Iraq.'

It had seemed a bit odd after the game when we went up into the stand to meet Mr Hussein and to collect our commemorative medals, we were given a trophy the size of a beer can. When they went up to get their trophy it was as big as me! And they say fake news is a modern phenomenon.

Years later I asked Ken Bates what on earth that trip was all about. He didn't give me a clear answer, so I tried again, 'Was it to give you a chance to meet your old soulmate Saddam Hussein?'

His reply was unrepeatable.

17 /
FAME

No, I will not go into central London to appear on *Wogan*. Yes, it might be the top-rated TV chat show of the day, with millions tuning in for every broadcast, but why should I? I am here to play football not to play the fame game!

But OK, yes, I will go on a random youngster's music TV show with Muriel Gray all the way up in Carlisle, obviously.

Asked by Puma to be pictured in their national advertising campaign, I declined even though I was sponsored by them. 'I'll just wear the boots if that's all the same with you. And you can keep sending the boxes of sports kit, but I'll just keep giving them away to the youth team players.' It was still important for me to be doing a job, not just selling myself as a celebrity or being a walking advertising board.

I would also give my time for interviews with little indie music fanzines for free, that was not a problem. National newspapers, though, were generally avoided if possible unless they ambushed me after the match. Lads' mags? No, thank you. *NME*, that's fine.

When it came to the fame game, I did what I wanted to do and what suited me. To me it seemed obvious what was right and safe and what wasn't. If you play by their rules there is a cost, if you chase mainstream fame you give away the right to privacy, in the mass media's eyes anyway. I preferred to keep that world at arm's length, dealing mostly with my own subculture, where I felt comfortable. The media initially didn't seem to have a clear place to pigeonhole me and I liked the idea of my anti-celebrity status position.

The perfect role models for me seemed to be Joy Division and New Order: they didn't do interviews, didn't even put their pictures on the singles or albums, they just let their work speak for itself. The problem is that by default this makes you all the more interesting. It looks like you are being obscure and mysterious either for effect, because you have something to hide, or are very deep because you eschew the superficiality of fame and its trappings, so you get more publicity. You can't win!

I scored an equalising goal against Liverpool one Saturday at Anfield and openly admit that the nice lines in the newspapers were of limited interest. I was much keener to know how John Peel would react on his Monday night programme.

'I might be forced to tape over that *Ripping Yarns* video that Nevin loaned me last week,' he said in his usual drawl, 'probably with some Open University course in Yak Maintenance, if he does that sort of thing again.'

Getting a droll mention from Peely, for scoring against his team, was far better than a headline in any national newspaper for me.

I had been asked to go on *A Question of Sport* but I knew my knowledge of sport was inadequate. I played sport but I didn't really watch a great deal of it and I certainly wasn't an aficionado, not even in my own game. I liked the technical side of football and other sports but delving deep into the names, the personalities and the histories didn't interest me greatly.

When I was asked to do an art version of the same show called *Gallery*, I was well up for it! It was to be filmed in Bristol on a Wednesday, our day off, so it was perfect. The team captains were Maggi Hambling, an exceptional artist, and the unique jazz singer and bon viveur George Melly. It was an eye-opening experience and if I thought footballers were

Premier League-level drinkers then George was in a league of his own, way beyond the Champions League. He managed to drink solidly for two days while I was there and stay just nicely sauced for the entire time – that must take years of practice. He did the show half-cut but was brilliantly funny and knowledgeable even though there was clearly very little blood running in his alcohol stream. If I was going to do TV, this was much more up my street than *A Question of Sport*.

I would only do things that interested me, so when the Hayward Gallery on the South Bank asked me to be one of the curators of an exhibition called 'Introducing With Pleasure', I jumped at it. Among the other curators were Sir David Attenborough, Kate Adie, Roald Dahl, Jean Muir, Bruce Oldfield and Greta Scacchi. Getting to meet then talk to them at the launch dinner was a joy. The exhibition was considered quite a success. I chose works by Julian Cooper and Sir George Clausen as well as Adrian Berg, describing his painting as having 'the intimidation I was looking for but [it] remains a work of beauty and feeling…even though the figure is sleeping and the colours are cold, it remains alive with an inner strength.' To be fair it was the language needed for the moment and for those coming to see it; it probably didn't seem as pretentious then as it does now!

Having broken into the football scene, I was inevitably also being regularly asked to do things that I wasn't as comfortable with. There were dozens of magazines that wanted interviews. I always had it in my mind that if I did agree, it would always be for free, but also that I should always do it for a good reason, to get a message across. It might have been the anti-racism line, a political comment, to thank people who had helped me or even just to promote some little band I liked. In the earliest days I actually tried to keep myself out of the interviews about me – it just felt self-indulgent – but the journalists sussed that pretty quickly so I had to give up on that angle.

I grudgingly did the interviews with *Shoot* magazine, but was far more interested in doing a video interview with the world-renowned Scottish sculptor David Mach down at the Tate Gallery for their visitors to enjoy.

How much more fun is that!

There were front covers on the *Sunday Express Magazine, City Limits* and a few others around that time. Each was set up with no agent and me not trying to sell myself. I was usually given a very easy ride and even the ultra-positive promotion that a good agent would have dreamed of. It always surprised them that I didn't try or even want to monetise my growing notoriety. I still wasn't willing to play the game and give up the normality of my life.

The club asked me to model for the release of the new kit, alongside the then-famous actor Dennis Waterman and two very beautiful female models. This was very uncomfortable stuff for me. As ever, I explained I would only pose in positions that would be normal and natural in my life or in my job, and, as usual, the photographers said that would be fine. They then lasted about ten minutes before suggesting it would make a great pic if one of the girls could stand legs astride and I could go behind her and poke my head up and through her legs for the next shot. They seemed surprised when I took a leaf out of the tabloid journos' own book and immediately 'made my excuses and left.'

Many photographers from the red tops in those days thought it was a good idea to get players to dress up for their shots and that the players should be grateful for the privilege. I despised these more than just about any other requests. My mantra was the same: 'I'll only do it if it reflects my day or my daily work.' So, when they turned up with a tartan 'See You Jimmy' bunnet, and a heart-shaped 'I love Scotland' cushion with a mini Loch Ness monster to boot, I politely but firmly told them where to go.

In the build-up to a Scotland game at Pittodrie, a snapper appeared with a bowler hat, a black brolly and a briefcase, expecting me to put them on. This was because I was an 'Anglo' Scottish player and that is clearly how all English people dressed. Instead of my usual disdainful reaction I politely said, 'I can't do it today guys, but I know someone who would love to.' I went back to the dressing room and told Brian McClair there was a 'snapper' waiting outside for him. Brian didn't hold back with his dour exasperation when he spotted the snapper's props, much to the delight of the lads who I had gathered to watch the spectacle. 'Don't be so bloody stupid you imbecilic moron,' was the gist of the one-way conversation.

I will admit to getting roped into dressing up for the cameras just once. There was a local theatre that needed some promotion and as the profits were going to charity, some of us Chelsea lads were asked to dress up in the pantomime costumes. Obviously, Kerry Dixon would be the handsome Prince Charming but as I was the smallest, and the tiny actress Bonnie Langford was playing Cinderella, guess who was expected to be Cinders and wear her dress?

I refused at first, but they insisted as it was for charity. I agreed but only if the pictures were solely for the local paper, just as they had always promised anyway. After all, the club owned the pictures: surely, I could trust them not to flog them on? They agreed it would only be for the local rag and I believed them! To be fair it was a very funny picture and the *Sun* must have agreed because they plastered it all over their back page.

As a (too) serious-minded chap who liked intense music, one who would rather be pictured at *Medea* down at the South Bank or nipping along to catch *The Three Sisters* at the Riverside Studios, this wasn't exactly fitting in with the image. On this occasion in retrospect I probably deserved it.

The club thought it was just a big laugh, but I was seriously displeased. I then agreed it was funny after all and it would also be very funny if I refused to speak to the club newspaper for a year and stopped writing the music column that I had been doing for free.

The lesson from St Patrick today is 'Don't lie to me!'

So yes, there was a level of celebrity, but wherever possible, it was deliberately small-scale counterculture by design on my part. The TV appearances were smaller affairs with George Melly on *Gallery* not David Coleman on *A Question of Sport*. You might see me at a gig but never on a red carpet for an opening night, however often I was asked. The media I dealt with most of the time was smaller and, yes, there was a sports car, but it was an ancient MG not a flashy new Porsche! I could hang out with that other anti-celebrity John Peel but never a brash 'Smashie and Nicey' daytime Radio 1-type DJ. In my mind it not only made sense, it was blindingly obvious that that was the only way to be.

You could say – and some did – that I was now living in Kensington, going to see challenging plays at the Royal Court in Sloane Square, while being a media darling pontificating about liberal causes. At the same time I was driving a sports car and playing for Chelsea, so had as such lost any grip on reality, certainly the reality of the student from a few years back. Not surprisingly I didn't agree with what I felt was a superficial reading, but what I also thought was inverted snobbery. Just because you play football and are working class it doesn't mean you can't be interested in the arts, social causes, educating yourself and having your own style.

The 'celebrity' world was, however, creeping in a little and my answer was to do something anti-celebrity. I agreed to appear in a video for a band where I actually danced, albeit briefly. It wasn't some shiny big-name pop act but Vindaloo Summer Special featuring The Nightingales, my friend Ted Chippington and the band We've Got a Fuzzbox and We're Gonna Use It. That was exactly the sort of thing I liked to do. It was anti-celebrity, it wasn't adding to my nationwide profile, there was no publicity, it wasn't a huge band, it was just my way of having a bit of fun with people I liked, at the level I liked.

Nobody ever gets it right all the time and I certainly made some mistakes, but one seemingly small one above many others haunted me and taught me a lesson. I was asked to review the singles for a music magazine. There was the odd smart alec line about how good the new Associates single was, and how it would be single of the year had they put the John Peel session version on the B-side. They released it with that track on the B-side a couple of weeks later – I was proud of that. I was less proud of my review of the latest Depeche Mode single. I didn't particularly like it but my comments were snide and uncalled for. Even as I sent it in, I felt uncomfortable and annoyed with myself because it wasn't the person I was. I couldn't call it back on time and when I read it in print, I was furious with myself.

To make things worse it turned out one of the band had a liking for Chelsea, the emphasis being on the past tense. I had spoiled it for him. I learned a painful lesson and apologised when I got the chance but have never since been so self-servingly arrogant and cheaply smug towards any artist. Apart from anything else, I was just plain wrong. It never happened again but it was a lesson I needed to learn, and I learned it the hard way.*

It is very hard to think about those times and not wonder, was I doing too much, was I trying to fit too much in? On balance I don't think I was, and although my head was turned a bit, it never swivelled out of control. I was almost always keeping a good balance between having fun, going out, meeting people but also being a dedicated and disciplined professional. As long as I was doing this job, I told myself, it was worth doing it to the best of my ability and not screwing it up, so I tried my best to keep it all in balance.

My personal circumstances had changed. I had been seeing Annabel for quite some time, but we had parted even though I was still totally mad about her. It was purely because I felt too young to be married and it had become very serious between us. It didn't make sense then and doesn't in retrospect.

I did see a couple of other girls over the period of a year but then I had a moment of clarity. I finally knew I had to settle down, my age was right, the time was right and anyway I was emotionally destroyed when I finished with any of the girls I went out with. I thought I was too young before then and in retrospect I was absolutely right. You can't, however, keep breaking your own heart or, more importantly, the hearts of others because it will harden you as well as hurt them and I didn't want that to happen any more.

I stayed friends with Annabel and she later invited me to a wedding.

---

* It is one of the few things that makes my toes curl to this day. So again, sorry guys and I do play the odd 'Mode' track when I DJ these days.

All the time Julie was still insisting I would end up marrying her friend. Annabel was a bridesmaid for her sister Jane who was marrying Tim. I parked my car, walked around the corner of her parents' house near the Borders town of Coldstream to see her standing outside being photographed. She had no idea as she stood glowing in that yellow dress that I decided there and then I would marry her, if she would have me back of course. Fortunately for me she did.

One afternoon, a trusted friend arranged to meet up with me for dinner but made it plain to me that it had to be right away, that evening – tomorrow would be too late. Even though Kate Hoey went on to become an MP, I still trusted her, she was a good friend. During dinner the reason for the rushed meeting was made clear.

'I am only the messenger and have nothing to do with this,' she said, 'but Spurs want to buy you. Could you let me know if you are interested and I will pass it on?'

The animosity between Spurs and Chelsea fans is well known – even I appreciated it by that point. It would have been a very divisive thing to do at the time, but there was no chance of it happening because I was still very happy at Chelsea. Had they come a year later it would have been a much more difficult decision for me. They had brilliant players and they played my type of football, that's to say, they actually passed it along the ground sometimes.

There was also apparently serious interest from Inter Milan around the same time. Chelsea even informed me that the Italian giants had come to watch me at one midweek game. Serie A was the biggest, best and wealthiest league in the world at that time and all the top players were gravitating towards it. Chelsea must have hoped for a very big pay day indeed. With the 'only three foreigners allowed' rule still in force, it probably wouldn't have interested me that much, as I might have had limited game time. It was diverting nevertheless and maybe I could have linked up well with Irish genius Liam Brady and German star Karl-Heinz Rummenigge after all.

During the summer Celtic also made their interest known just when I was in a delicate situation. At the end of that season I spent the last two weeks sofa-surfing. The lease on my flat in Pimlico had expired, and I had nowhere to live, so there I was in London with all my belongings stuffed in the back and in the boot of my car. I couldn't afford a hotel for that long and the biggest fear I had was losing my vinyl and my hi-fi if thieves spotted my gear under the duvet that was covering it. Friends and teammates helped me out. I even stayed with first-team coach John Hollins and his delightful family for one night. I was still under contract and Celtic wouldn't have seriously tempted me at that precise moment, but it was satisfying that the club who got rid of me wanted me back again!

Looking back, this was an exciting, hectic and quite intense period. Suddenly everybody wanted me, but it was a feeling I was never comfortable with. Fame is a curious thing and despite my best efforts I was clearly being noticed by more and more people.

Despite feeling discomfort from some of the attention I was receiving, I recall those times at Chelsea with a warm glow and, having lasted a few years there, I saw no reason why they shouldn't continue for a good deal longer. Still, why shouldn't I try to make the situation even better? What if I could get my best mate from Scotland to sign for us at Chelsea? On my recommendation, along with others, John Neal came close to buying my friend Brian McClair from Celtic, just as Celtic were chasing me. But Chelsea dithered too long.

Brian went on to become a fabulous player and prolific goalscorer for Celtic and Manchester United for years to come, so I am pretty sure it would have been a good call to get him down to London. I openly admit, though, I wanted my mate around, and I knew he could be a good influence on me, as well as a certain success for the club.

In hindsight the biggest reason for the deal stalling was because John Neal's heart stalled right at the same time. He had been a heavy smoker and, with the stress of management maybe, a heart attack shouldn't have been that much of a surprise, but we were shocked and very worried when we heard the news. John Hollins had been taking training anyway since the day he arrived and he replaced John Neal, who was moved 'upstairs' during his recovery, ostensibly to help and oversee the new young gaffer.

Sadly, there wasn't the easy trusting relationship between them that all of us would have hoped for and that exceptional period of exponential improvement at the club was to slow down dramatically as John Neal faded, or some might say was pushed, out of the picture.

I was incredibly fond of John Neal – he was not far off being 'another' father figure to me – but I liked Holly too and I genuinely expected things to go on relatively smoothly. The older man's wisdom and knowledge looked like being a perfect foil for the rookie manager's exuberance and warmth, but the chemistry just wasn't there. I find it hard to pin the blame quite as easily, as most people did later, on John Hollins being totally at fault.

In football there has to be total trust between a manager and all of his coaching staff. There also has to be something deeper – more than a friendship, a willingness to see, if not the world, then at least football in a similar way. The bond must also be strong enough within their relationships to deal with disagreements – not every relationship has that. I have come across too many 'dream tickets' in life not to know that some things that look superficially great from the outside can be totally incompatible up close.

In my youthful naivety I didn't even consider that this change in management might affect me radically. I missed seeing John Neal around the place, but he had survived, and I thought he would be back in harness soon enough. It was simple: if I kept on playing well along with the rest of the team, then things would be hunky-dory. I would love to say I was thinking only of John Neal's health, but in day-to-day reality I, like the rest of the players, was just as focused as ever on the football itself. The game needs that level of commitment and single-mindedness. So although we were concerned about the gaffer's health, we kept calm and carried on with the business of being his team, even if he wasn't in the dressing room or at the training ground.

John Neal recovered his health eventually but never recovered his place at the club, which was a blow to me mostly on a personal level, because I liked him as a person as well as admiring him as a manager. His good practices would carry on for a while but without his influence at the helm eventually they would fade, and the new regime would have to prove their mettle. John Neal was spotted around now and again for a while and we had a few chats. He wouldn't openly bad-mouth the new regime, but I could sense he was clearly less than impressed with what they were doing, who they were trying to buy and how they started to change the team's style. He left soon after, and a man who was universally revered by Chelsea fans would not set foot in Stamford Bridge again for going on twenty years.

18/
CRASH

John Hollins had played for the team the season before and after his retirement his enthusiasm on the training pitch made him an obvious candidate to be the new 'trainer' on a day-to-day basis while manager John Neal was still healthy. Holly was definitely one of the boys, always up for a laugh and a superb mimic to boot. His parodies were never malicious but they were well observed and pointedly accurate. Even when affecting anger as the manager, you kind of knew there might be a laugh bubbling up under the surface. Reading the riot act because a couple of the players missed a game with food poisoning, after eating some dodgy out-of-date sandwiches from the corner shop near the Bridge, Holly cracked again. As the ten-minute rant about the importance of knowing the difference between good and bad sandwiches finished, his last line entirely ruined the gravity of the moment.

'Next time, don't be so bloody stupid, use your loaf.'

He started sniggering even before we did.

I can still remember him holding a ground-floor hotel window open while 'the escape committee' organised a breakout for some of the lads to go for a drink after curfew. A short while later he was our new manager and of course he could no longer be one of the lads or be your best mate, or have a laugh or indeed help the lads out of the hotel on an escape mission for beers after a curfew he now imposed. It is a very tough gig, stepping up from player to manager at the same club. Few people do it well and even fewer enjoy the experience. That previous incarnation of Holly clearly had a latent effect on just how much managerial respect he was going to be able to count on going forward from some of his former teammates.*

Fans always think players talk about nothing else other than what is happening at the club, in the team and with the tactics, but it isn't the case; they all have their own lives and their own relationships to get on with at the same time. I always got on well with Kerry Dixon and was aware he was dealing with some personal problems, though he never spoke about them at the time. It was tragic that the golden boy – who scored for fun, was one of the most iconic players in Chelsea's history, who would become England's centre-forward for a time – would also have to tackle these addictions throughout his life. He has been open about those difficulties and even with my headphones on, Walkman blaring, while reading a book on the team bus I couldn't help being aware that Kerry had the beginnings of a gambling problem. Once he asked to borrow £100 from me, money I could scarcely afford to lose. I said I would go to the bank to get it, knowing that it might be a long time before I saw it again, if ever,

---

* Wherever we happened to be, Holly often walked the corridors last thing at night in the hotel before away games. He might have been checking up on the lads, but it felt more like he was taking care of his players, making sure they were all right and not uptight. I am sure that because he was so gregarious, he also just fancied a chat and a laugh before bed. One night he knocked on my door and as he walked in the room, he asked why I was 'hooverin' at that time of night. He then looked around for the offending vacuum cleaner, but there wasn't one. I loved the look on his face when he realised that the only electrical appliance was my tape player and it was playing the first Jesus and Mary Chain single, 'Upside Down'. Listening to it again now, I can absolutely understand his mistake.

but he was clearly in dire need if he had to ask me. By the time I brought it back, he wouldn't take it. For someone with an addiction, even I knew then, that this must have taken a lot of willpower. The true kindness was not mine, it was his. There was a caring, considerate personality hidden below the problems and I could see that, in fact everyone who knows Kerry Dixon can see it. Happily those problems all vanished temporarily on the field and I never played with another player for whom it was easier or indeed more enjoyable to create goalscoring chances. He was lightning quick, a natural finisher, greedy in the box, lived for that moment in the limelight when the ball hit the net, not at all interested in the tactics other than how they got the ball to him in front of goal and totally, obsessively single-minded about what his job was. So just the perfect psyche for a top-class striker.

David Speedie on the other hand came as close as anyone in my career to making me stop playing football altogether. He was forever moaning and complaining when he didn't get the ball and I felt he was bullying other players, by demanding everything was done his way in training and in the games. He was slowly driving me mad, to the point where it was actually making me fed up. I stopped enjoying training, especially if I had to be in his team, because of this incessant belligerence and berating. I felt that if everything wasn't done for his benefit alone, he was a nightmare to work with. He was a fabulously committed player and a very good one too, but at the time I felt it was all for himself and little to do with the team. Any pass not made to him was a bad pass in his eyes. Previously anyone with those attitudes would have them curbed by the old regime, but the new staff seemed to accentuate his many positives without trying to eliminate the negatives.

The problems were quietly welling up for a few months, ready to destroy the team, before the damn finally burst mid-season. What I realised then was that the former manager had the wisdom and experience to know when to step in and keep those selfish attitudes in check. I liked John Hollins a great deal, I still do, but that particular expertise takes years to learn and even longer to know how to implement. He needed time and he needed to make some good decisions in the meantime but at the start of the season he appointed a new assistant coach in Ernie Walley. My diary entry after his very first session was to the point:

'This man is dangerous for the team. Everything he believes about football, I feel precisely the opposite.'

I was completely correct in those initial judgements though I tried hard to work with him for a while at least to find out if there was any more depth.

From a team that had played fast, flowing, inventive football, Holly and Walley wanted little more than lumping the ball aimlessly goalwards every time we got it, from wherever we were on the field. Wimbledon had been successful with this style, but we didn't have the right kind of players to do it well and I personally was the antithesis of that style. Kerry and, more so, Speedo loved it, because it focused on getting the ball hoofed up towards them constantly. They would clearly be involved all the time, indeed they would be the total focus of the team's play, but I thought it would be counterproductive. When I tried to explain they were getting fewer chances from poorer deliveries in easy-to-defend areas, I was shouted down immediately. Of course in their eyes, it simply looked like a selfish trope from me.

Have a look at how many current successful teams play anything other than the opposite of that style; I rest my case. It was a simplistic and one-dimensional outlook, horrible to watch and awful to play in. If I am jealous about modern footballers at all, it is not because of their money, possessions, houses, flat pitches and fame, it would only be for the fact that this dismal style is no longer de rigueur in the top division and something that is closer to how I tried to play is the current approach.

We still had a good side and to some degree we did well despite this 'Position of Maximum Opportunity' (POMO) zealotry. While the fans were right behind us and still incredibly generous to me, I believed from day one that Ernie was desperate to get me out of the team. Having said that, he seemed to despise Micky Hazard even more, but then he was a superb technical player, far too complex for Ernie's unsophisticated methods.

After coming back from Iraq, the entire thing imploded. The mood was awful, many of us hated the 'tactics', we had a raft of injuries and the poor preparation that led to the squad being too small came home to roost. Nigel Spackman and a few others spoke to Ernie as if he was an imbecile barely capable of understanding English. The lack of respect was palpable, and it was clearly not going to end well.

In January 1986 I scored our only goal in a 1-1 League Cup draw against QPR and it was studiously ignored by the military-minded coach after the game. In February we drew 2-2 with Leicester, and I was blamed for us not winning. Apparently, I wasn't getting enough crosses in, even though I had one assist and created three other gilt-edged chances on a pitch like a paddy field that had recently hosted a Chieftain tank convention.

Speedo who was out injured came down from the stands into the dressing room to make it clear he also thought I was the problem in that game. It felt like it was planned and even though I knew I hadn't played that well, there was no lack of effort under difficult conditions. We were still riding high in the league and serious contenders, or so people thought, but the joy of Chelsea's play from the season before had been ripped out in less than six months.

Our keeper Eddie Niedzwiecki was out injured, and there were a massive number of games to be fitted in after a whole raft of matches had been abandoned during an incredibly hard winter. The final straw was two games in two days, and they were both wins!

The first, a 1-0 away win at Southampton in March put us in fourth position in the league, four points behind the leaders Everton and with two games in hand. There was no doubt that we could have been serious challengers to win the league right at that moment. There was enough talent in the squad, but there wasn't a coherent plan and there weren't enough players.

I almost didn't get to play at the Dell as I had left my boots on the team bus outside Southampton's ground. I went back out to get them but the pristinely dressed, moustachioed, ex-army sergeant major steward who was on the door refused to believe I was a player and wouldn't let me back in. The Chelsea fans around me were laughing at the situation, but he wasn't for budging and obviously I didn't have a ticket to get in. Having said that, the rest of the team were wearing Day-Glo tracksuits and I looked more like a proto-goth, so I could see his point to some degree. I'm not convinced my look would have gone down well in his barracks, but he eventually relented when John Hollins came out looking for me.

The next day we won the Full Members' Cup final at Wembley, beating Manchester City 5-4. Chelsea back at Wembley for the first time in over a decade felt like a big deal and our fans celebrated as if we had won the Champions League.*

We were actually 5-1 up with six minutes to go when they scored two quick goals and then the referee gave them a super-soft penalty with just seconds to go which took it to 5-4. I found myself ranting at the official for awarding it. He said, 'Don't worry, it's just a bit of fun, I'm going to blow the final whistle as soon as you restart.' I liked his style and he was true to his word.

At that moment it really felt like we were on the cusp of something special and that Wembley finals might become a regular thing for us if we could just overcome the tactical battles within the dressing room. Unfortunately the club didn't get there again for another decade, long after I had gone and that afternoon might have been the high point. I loved that day from start to finish and naively thought that our good football in

---

* Yes, it really was the next day. Two games in two days is something the modern footballer wouldn't accept, but it happened on a number of occasions back then. It never seemed to bother me too much. These days on the radio when I am asked about the stress of too many games close together for the current players, I try very hard not to go all Monty Python, with a Yorkshire accent: 'Luxury. We played two games in two days, usually on mud heaps or potato fields. At that time I played seven games in fifteen days. GBH wasn't even a yellow card, I played nearly 850 games in my career when the average for a modern player is well under half that and they get paid not far short of Bill Gates's wages, while I had to sofa-surf at the end of every season. And you try telling that to the kids today and they won't believe you.'

the sunshine at the national stadium might change the direction of travel for Chelsea's style. Maybe Ernie would see the error of his ways?

Sadly, there was no chance of that. He was the high priest of the high ball and he wasn't for changing.

From the outside it probably looked fantastic for me at this point, but at the club the next week I was being told, 'If you take more than two touches at a time before hoofing it into the penalty box, you will be subbed.'

Everything about my game that made me a bit different, a little bit special and successful was no longer required. Vision, beating people, drawing defenders and sliding intelligent balls through to runners, working intricate plays to get me, or overlapping or underlapping players, to the byline – I was to dump them all. Intelligent or complex plays were considered nothing more than selfish indulgences, I was to lump it forward and that was it. 'Just get it in the mixer' was the repeated shout from Ernie on the bench and just as often from the strikers on the pitch.

Even though I had made two of Speedie's goals in his Wembley hat-trick it didn't change a thing.

On the Wednesday I was given my debut for Scotland against Romania, who had the inimitable Gheorghe Hagi in their side. It was joyous, we won 3-0 and it was great to have friends, family and many people I had known throughout my life turning up to the game and waiting outside to chat. It was an incredible highlight that I had been hoping would happen for about a year.* Before that, I wouldn't have

---

* I had a wonderful moment after coming on as sub for Gordon Strachan in that game against Romania. Afterwards, outside the main entrance at Hampden Park, my dad was waiting. He didn't need to say it but this was the moment more than any other that underlined all his hard work had paid off. It also clarified that as a teenager I knew the square root of nothing, and he had been right all along that I would play for my country. Giving him my shirt after the game was a very poignant moment, but both of us being Glaswegian it was done without ceremony. I handed him a plastic bag with my first Scotland shirt in it and said, 'Probably best you keep that.'

dreamt of ever being good enough to be a Scottish international. That said, I wouldn't have dreamt of being intimidated when I got there either.

On our first trip together with the full national team, Brian McClair and I arrived at dinner on the Sunday night to find only two seats left, on a table beside Alan Hansen and Kenny Dalglish. We were staying at the ultra-plush Gleneagles Hotel to prepare for a home match at Hampden Park. We had our own private dining room but there were still liveried waiters providing silver service in a huge high-ceilinged room, impressively decorated in very tasteful classical Georgian style. The world-renowned and respected stars on our table seemed at home there and for entertainment decided to 'rip into' the two new kids who they thought would be shy, defensive, overawed and not capable or brave enough to give any cheek back. The Liverpool dressing room was famous for its biting humour and we were to be the latest victims, in what was considered a rite of passage.

Unfortunately, for everyone involved, they underestimated the attitudes of the two former degree students.

Brian and I had a strong belief that any type of psychological bullying should be met with the same level of fire straight back. Why should we just sit there and take it? And anyway, as a couple of outsiders we never felt the need to play by their rules; they may be the top dogs but we felt perfectly happy to bark back. We instinctively knew about the fine line between boys' banter and bullying and that one can quickly lead to the other in football if you do not stand up for yourself.

Brian's disposition is as inscrutable as anyone you will ever meet, so the Liverpool duo would have been surprised at the reaction when his waspish tongue was let loose. When pushed Brian is far more truculent than me and I couldn't imagine him being cowed by anyone, however eminent they were. He is naturally disposed to kindness, fun and seeing the ridiculousness of any situation but his outward demeanour doesn't suggest that, quite the opposite. Like me, he feels injustice is simply not to be borne, whether in a dressing room, on a football field, in public life or indeed in one of the poshest dining rooms in the United Kingdom.

Kenny Dalglish himself was then known in media circles as a classic dour Scotsman, with a bone-dry sense of humour, although he wasn't like that with teammates most of the time, but Brian could make Kenny look like Billy Connolly in comparison. An initial discussion with the icons about the use of football-based colloquialisms instead of the correct use of English, would you believe, escalated into a full-blown and bad-tempered argument.

Underneath it all it was really about us 'arrogant kids' not rolling over and taking the stick quietly like we were supposed to. It was getting a little bit out of hand, so the manager came over and moved us to another table, away from the legends. The new kids were definitely being stared at throughout the rest of the meal by the rest of the squad. But I did feel that a few of the half-hidden smirks from some of the Scottish-based players suggested they were impressed by our chutzpah – or maybe it was just the general entertainment we provided.

After dinner and a team meeting we headed back to our room. The moment the door was closed Brian and I looked at each other for a moment in silence before he said, 'Did we really just do that?'

'Yeah, I think we just had a blazing row with two of Scotland's biggest superstar celebrities,' I replied. 'And when I was a kid I used to go to see Kenny play at Celtic and sing his name.'

Brian said, 'Me too.'

We couldn't say another word for twenty minutes because of the laughter. Good job, guys! We laughed mostly because they seemed so angry and because of the stupidity of it all.

Luckily Kenny in particular was great with us very quickly afterwards and seemed to respect our cojones, but there wasn't always a perfect atmosphere in those early days. What didn't help was that there was sometimes an unspoken tension between the Anglos (those playing in the top league down south), and those based in Scotland. It took a few years but eventually Andy Roxburgh managed to root that problem out. For some reason Brian and I, and the younger Anglos coming through, seemed to escape that feeling of otherness from the home-based players. I am sure the Scottish based players felt it was arrogance from some of the Anglos in the old days but that was never the case from us in the new generation, even when we moved south.*

My sudden introduction to the national squad was only a short relief, however. Life at Chelsea wasn't fun at this point and it was about to get a lot worse.

We fell apart the next weekend over Easter.

A 4-0 loss to West Ham on Good Friday and a 6-0 (!) defeat to QPR at Loftus Road followed on Easter Sunday.† There were three games in five days and then seven games in fifteen days when we were completely gone as a team, totally exhausted, riddled with injuries and bereft of spirit.

Jokes about us being crucified over Easter were obviously rife but it was the start of a horrible and spectacular downward spiral. We won only two of the last eleven games. Among all the other problems, it was clear the squad wasn't deep enough nor had enough quality to withstand the avalanche of injuries and suspensions. Other sides had quickly sussed what our new tactics were, not that that would have been difficult as they weren't complicated and could have been jotted down on the back of a fag packet, with space to spare.

I truly believed those simplistic strategies had destroyed something that had previously been special and could have got much better. A few weeks later we had an injury crisis up front and, as usual, I replaced Speedie, scoring the winner at West Ham and then the equaliser to get a point against Newcastle in the next match.

Alex Ferguson, the new interim Scotland manager, was there at West

---

* Brian and I were committed team players to the core and never refused to turn up for international matches because it didn't suit us, a real problem with some others over the years. Whatever the situation, we would never turn our country down.

† The massed ranks of Chelsea fans sang constantly throughout the entire 90 minutes of that horrible 6-0 defeat to near neighbours QPR. It was incredibly moving to hear that support even as the goals flew in against us. I don't know many other fans of big teams who would react that way.

Ham, so it vastly improved my chances of getting into the World Cup squad for that summer in Mexico. Fergie put me on the bench for the England v Scotland game at Wembley three days later but then I was dropped for the next Chelsea game. It was an extraordinary time when I thought, *I can't understand if I am playing well, scoring goals, making chances, I am totally committed, I am also playing through constant pain with injuries, then why am I always on the edge of being sidelined?* I lurched sickeningly from the highest highs to the lowest lows every couple of days.

That first call-up in the game against Romania, playing with the likes of Graeme Souness, Dalglish, Hansen and Gordon Strachan, was significant for me but the more important match looming was of course the game at Wembley against England the following month. If I played well maybe Alex Ferguson would put me in the squad for the World Cup a couple of months later. It was a long shot, but I came on and played fairly well on what was little more than a thirty-minute cameo. The key moment for me came when I got the ball inside their penalty box with my back to goal, with Terry Butcher marking me. Yes, the big man again, this time in very different circumstances to my trial at Ipswich.

We were 2-1 down but pressing for an equaliser. Terry had scored the opening goal but I had him just where I wanted him. I twisted and rolled him and as I got past, he caught me clumsily on the side of the leg. It was OK, I could keep my balance. I stayed on my feet and cut the ball back to Roy Aitken who sadly thumped his shot just over the crossbar. I didn't think any more of it until after the game. Alex Ferguson as you probably know is a proud Scotsman and not a particularly good loser either. He said a few positive words through very gritted teeth afterwards about the lads' efforts, but he was hurting and seething.

He then came over to me and said, 'Did big Butcher catch you in the box?'

'Yes, but I managed to keep my balance and…thought that…big… Roy…' I tailed off as I realised where he was going with this. He didn't say I should have gone down for the penalty and there was to be no hairdryer treatment. It was worse, much worse.

For a few moments he was totally silent. And then he simply walked away. Unsurprisingly I wasn't picked to go to Mexico. He never suggested I should have dived or even 'made the most of it' as they say in the game, but it certainly felt as if the idea was hanging there, and more to the point he obviously had me down as someone who did not precisely share his view of the game.

Having played hundreds of first-team games by that point, I had never once cheated by diving. It wouldn't even have entered my mind, but was I right? I suspect an episode of *The Moral Maze* would be needed to help me sort that one out.

I don't dive, so that is fine.

But what about my teammates and indeed my manager? Might they look on it differently? They may feel that because there is contact, it is a foul and I should make it look as bad as possible. What about the fact that in the same situation someone in the other team would have gone down and got them a penalty? Am I disadvantaging my team by being too honest, or in their view just being bloody annoying? When was I given the sole guardianship of the keys to the squad's ethical standards?

Forget about my teammates, my entire country might be annoyed and disagree with the fact that my principles might just have led to Scotland losing to England! Is that a reasonable stance? What if I'd known that if I dived, I would be on that plane to Mexico and a World Cup? Would I have done it then on purely selfish grounds?

The answer – you won't be surprised to hear – is an emphatic no! I would rather not take part than use the dark arts to succeed.*

So. I wasn't going to Mexico. I would have to deal with that.

---

* Even that is not actually the entire story if I am to be brutally frank. It is maybe that I just draw the line in a different place. There were many times in my career when I 'won' penalty kicks by beating a player then deliberately cutting across him to manufacture the situation where he would lunge in and foul me. I don't have any problem with that: it isn't a dark art but I concede it is pretty damn murky. So, where has that big clump of moral high ground I was standing on suddenly gone?

Disappointing yes, but a first-world problem. I would get over it quickly enough.

Alex Ferguson was gracious to a fault, however, and phoned me personally to tell me the bad news.

'Pat, I am not going to take you to Mexico, but you are first reserve if any forward pulls out between now and the plane taking off.'

I thanked him for calling and said I had no expectation anyway. I assured him I would be ready and delighted to come at a moment's notice. I wished him and the team the best of luck and underlined I would be supporting them throughout the tournament like any other Tartan Army fan.

I really wasn't as devastated as some players might have been. Gordon Strachan was chosen and played well. I strongly felt if it was a close thing, give it to the other guy; I only wanted the call if I was clearly the better player.

The next morning after Fergie's call I went into training and David Speedie, my fellow Scottish international forward at Chelsea, who had also featured in that England game, came straight over to me. 'Are you going to Mexico?'

'No,' I replied, 'Fergie called me last night and gave me the bad news. What about you?'

David was fuming and after adding an impressive variety of imaginative expletives he relayed what Alex had said to him. 'David, I am not going to take you to Mexico but you are first reserve if any forward pulls out between now and the plane taking off.'

I kept a straight face and decided not to tell him that I had been fed the same line. It was an uncharacteristic error from Fergie to forget that we were teammates and would obviously talk about our phone calls. But he was only trying to be kind and I felt there was nothing wrong with saying it to both of us. I fear David didn't react as magnanimously as me during his call, but even that would have been accepted by Fergie – he knew the passions involved.

A few weeks later one of the forwards decided not to go. Kenny

Dalglish wasn't going to be on that plane after all and there was a free seat. Fergie took Steve Archibald!*

I still played more games for Chelsea than anyone else that season, but it always felt under sufferance. Kerry, David and I had still managed just shy of 60 goals between us, but I felt totally unwanted. I loved the club but the idea of staying in the long term under these circumstances was beginning to feel unthinkable.

Three games after the high of playing against England at Wembley I was dropped again; it was another four games in eleven days for a side that had been hollowed out. I was again relegated to the bench for the last game of the season. It was another total capitulation from a team that had been title contenders a few months earlier, who then finally limped home in sixth place with only one point from the last fifteen. Holly dropped me (and Kerry) for that last game to 'try' something different (nobody said 'rested' in those days). The team lost 5-1 at home against Watford but it was the discussion in the manager's office that perturbed me most.

I asked John Hollins: 'If you are resting my injuries for this one then I guess you will not need me for the post-season friendlies. So, I'm away after the game.'

Holly: 'Are you asking for a transfer?'

Me: 'No, not at all, I am just going home to Scotland to recover.'

As I shut the door, it really felt like he was suggesting I should ask for a transfer. It could have been a misunderstanding, but it was a very bad way to finish the season. The entire summer was filled with painful thoughts.

Does the club want rid of me even though I have played more games than anyone else, even though I was third-top goalscorer and was again in the running for the Player of the Year award by the fans?

What can I do to change the situation, other than grow another six

---

* I was in the squad that May, left out for the World Cup and then back in the squad right after the tournament was finished – not the last time I would suffer that fate.

inches, start hoofing it into the mixer and getting a few more headers at the back post myself?

Will my love of the game and of Chelsea Football Club be destroyed by this?

Is it really worth carrying on playing when the fun is gone? I promised myself I would only play for the love of the game.

Maybe it is time to go back to finish my degree. Could I really do that after all that had happened in my life in the past three years?

I even made some discreet enquiries at my old course and yes, they would allow me back. I was clearly serious enough about it to find out if it was still an option.

In the midst of it all a situation arose which could have changed things. I was in the Scotland squad again and at that time my usual room-mate for the four days would have been either the Manchester United goalkeeper Jim Leighton, Maurice Malpas from Dundee United or my mate Brian McClair. In his wisdom Andy Roxburgh obviously thought, *Hey, Pat and David Speedie are teammates at Chelsea, we'll put them in a room together.* Considering that I was having trouble spending five minutes in David's company, four days in the same room sounded like hell in a hotel. I almost withdrew from the squad on the spot.

After dinner on the night we arrived I decided not to leave with the obligatory feigned back injury that players often use – I had never done that sort of thing anyway – but maybe it would be worth one last go at talking to Speedo. I could try to understand him and help him understand me. In the same bedroom alone together two feet apart, he couldn't very well shout, moan or turn away in disgust, throwing up his hands in front of a crowd after not getting what he wanted. He would have to explain his actions.

Somewhat surprisingly the discussions were enlightening, and I felt I understood him more as a result of that time together. He explained openly that he would do anything to anyone to succeed, for him and for his family, everything and everyone else was totally secondary. From his position there was a morality to his behaviour and an honesty in that he openly couldn't care less about how his actions affected anyone else. For a man from mining stock, it was a starkly Thatcherite outlook on life, not that I thought it wise to say that to him right at that moment in the middle of some of the worst of the miners' problems. My own initial efforts to explain my team-spirit ethics were laughed at as being airy-fairy nonsense. Anyway, he didn't seem at all interested in hearing my side of things; it just wasn't of any importance to him because it didn't help him. If I could make him goals, which I often did, then we would get on fine from his perspective, full stop.

When we got back to the club the next season, it was quickly back to the same old story. At least I understood it now, even if it appeared to me that taking his sort of stance meant actually working against each other, instead of with each other, within what should be and needed to be a team sport. More than anything else, this type of attitude underlined to me that our team was doomed to never maximise its potential. Others were still laughing at Ernie Walley and his simplistic tactics, but he had the power and the influence and could see no wrong in Speedo and his outlook. It also appeared that Ernie had the manager's ear and could get anyone he wanted dropped, isolated or indeed sold.

Here is the surprising thing: I quite liked Ernie as a man. He was honest and hard-working even if he was a man of very simple ideas. He was completely open. There was no side to him, no dishonesty and to this day I think he missed his calling. He would have been far better employed as a drill sergeant in the army – he was made for that.

If finishing the 1984–85 season in sixth position was considered a triumph, ending the next season in the same spot was a disappointment. At the end of March, we were right in the running to win the league. We had beaten the eventual runners-up Everton at home and drawn with them away while also getting a creditable draw at the eventual champions Liverpool. There was a brief glimpse of glory but it quickly faded.

19/
KICKER CONSPIRACY

By the next season we had slipped to become a fairly middling outfit. Fourteenth in the league and things had really changed within the group. It would be impossible to put your finger on exactly when it was obvious that the special moment had begun to wither. Apart from the change in management and playing style, Tony McAndrew, who in my eyes had been the inspiration for the right attitudes, had left and on the field we were no longer the surprise package for the opposition.

One of the replacements in midfield for Tony Mac was a guy called John McNaught from Hamilton Academical. He was coming from Scotland to join the ever-growing band of Scots at the club. There was Speedie, Joe McLaughlin, Steve Clarke, who I had a fantastic understanding with on the right-hand side, Les Fridge, John Millar, Doug Rougvie, Billy Dodds, Gordon Durie and Kevin McAllister, as well as Duncan Shearer who left at the start of the campaign. And me.

So any Scot arriving down at the Bridge had plenty of Caledonians ready to help out a fellow 'Jock', as the Londoners called us. By this time maybe I had become just a tad more refined over the years, my accent had definitely mellowed a bit, allowing me to be understood better, but this mad-looking lad looked as if he had been hauled out of the back of a boozer in Easterhouse late the night before, brought down south in the back of a van and he certainly wasn't going to change his accent for anyone.

I said, 'Hi there, I'm Pat, you must be John. How are you? Have you just arrived?'

The reply in authentic, impenetrable to most, Glaswegian slang: 'Yawrite wee man, fuckin' great tae see ye, s'bin years.'

'I am sorry, have we met before?'

'Smee – John, John McNaught. Fur fucksake. Y'no remembir mae?'

'I can't say I can.'

At this point I'm feeling more like Bertie Wooster than a Scottish footballer from the schemes. But I just cannot place this guy. *Did I play against him once and I have forgotten but he hasn't? If so, is he just about to punch me for something I've done? He looks like he might.*

'Cannae believe you have furgoaten the auld days. It's me, Mad Nugget McNaught.'

Under-12s, Blue Star and suddenly totally unchanged apart from being a bit taller, there he is standing right in front of me. Now toothless, with unwashed, unkempt hair and swaggering like he just came out of the Griers pub in Easterhouse. He wasn't even good enough to get in Blue Star's first team back then and if I had to pick one player who had no chance of making it all the way to Stamford Bridge, then it would have been Nugget.

John is no longer with us, but his first start for Chelsea will be long remembered by anyone who saw it. It was a freezing cold New Year's Day, we were playing QPR and I still didn't think John would be good enough to survive at this rarefied level. As we stood in the home dressing room and formed a queue, waiting for the referee's whistle and all ready to go out, our assistant manager, yet another Scot, Ian McNeill, piped up, 'Does anyone want a wee swig of whisky to warm ye up before ye go oot?'

I did my usual eye-raising at the unprofessionalism of the idea as did most of the others, but John wearing number 8 was standing directly behind me, as I was wearing my usual 7. (How sweet that we used to run out in order.) Mad Nugget took a huge slug from the bottle and as I saw him do it I grabbed it from him and gave it straight back to Ian.

'Come on big man, us Scots have to show these people we are not amateurs, we have to act professionally and for God's sake it's your first start in the top division of English football. Behave yourself!'

'Sorry, wee man,' but as I turned away, he got the bottle back from Ian and took another long slug of whisky before I had the chance to grab it off him. This guy had no chance, he was out of his depth.

The score after 25 minutes of the game was Chelsea 2, QPR 0 (McNaught 12, 24).*

There was a delicious moment at Chelsea the week after John had received a red card. The notification arrived from the FA with the referee's comments on the sending-off, it read:

'Mr McNaught committed another foul in midfield. My stand side assistant drew my attention to the infringement. When I proceeded toward him, he turned to me in an aggressive manner and said, "Ma Fuckin' missus could dae better than that c**t on the line." I took the

---

* After the end of my career and some years after John died, I heard that his wife and children had no filmed evidence of his career at Chelsea. Few of the games were televised and there would have been no record kept, except for the fact that after every game I used to take home the single-camera match video that the manager had made for his own tactical use. I copied it for myself, then edited it down by mating two video machines. None of the other players would have known about or considered doing this themselves. It was the early days of video recorders, so they didn't figure out its uses for quite some time. I thought it was obvious how it should be utilised.

So I scoured the edited videos I still had and was able to put together a highlights package of John, including those two goals against QPR. I found out his family's address and drove up one night uninvited to deliver it personally. The tenement was about 200 yards away from where I was brought up in Easterhouse. It was lovely to see the look on Mrs McNaught's face when I explained what was on the video.

above player's name and sent him from the field of play.' John had no idea what he had done wrong.*

There might have been plenty of Scottish colleagues around but the good feeling under John Neal had just about completely dissipated, the dynamic was much less inclusive and the team clearly didn't have the same positive group ethic at its core. From a personal point of view, I had to adapt my game, almost always having two players marking me when I got the ball, as well as not being encouraged to be creative by the coaching staff. There were injuries to key players and Kerry, who had been scoring thirty plus goals per season, only got 10 in the league this time. Over the summer I had decided to try once more to make it work and by the end of the 1986–87 season, I even won Player of the Year again.

The last game of the season was played against Liverpool at Stamford Bridge. In the previous home game I had done something very out of character indeed. I had tried to hurt someone during the match. I only did this three times in my entire career; they were all during my time at Chelsea and I made a mess of it every single time.

The first came in a game at Goodison Park, after I had been tackled by Pat Van Den Hauwe, one of the most physical players around and rumoured to be quite unstable too. I got to know him when I signed for Everton and he was unusual more than unstable. I was convinced that he had spat on me after a tackle and I lost my rag. I got up, swivelled 270 degrees and lunged at him two-footed, at thigh height, as he drove up the line. The problem was that as I swivelled round, I had lost sight of him briefly and missed the fact that he had passed the ball. In mid-air I realised

---

* The big man was a bit green for this big city in a disarming way. He challenged Kerry Dixon to a race over 100 yards, not a good idea because Kerry was lightning quick, easily the quickest at the club over short distances. John was probably quite fast in Scotland, in a bombing up and down the midfield sort of way. The bet was laid, John looked confident, Kerry ran the last 30 yards backwards he was that far ahead.

I was hurtling towards Trevor Steven, one of the nicest chaps in football, a man so polite he probably wouldn't spit on the pitch or in public generally never mind at me. I can still see the look on his face saying, 'What on earth are you, of all people, doing this for?'

I managed to take some of the force out of the blow as I reached him instead of following through and mangling his thigh. The referee was so shocked at me doing it, he forgot to book me as I apologised profusely to Trev, who would become a good friend when I went to the Toffees.

It must have been something about Merseyside as my second misdemeanour was across Stanley Park at Anfield. I still have the footage on DVD proving my guilt to this day. I played a ball wide to the left from midfield, pinned the old ears back and sprinted for the penalty box. Ronnie Whelan was trying to catch me but I was ahead of him and he clearly thought I was a danger, so he pulled me back not once, not twice but three times. The third time was the snapping point. I deliberately swung my left elbow back and caught him perfectly on the jaw sending him flying. Like Trevor Steven, he didn't seem angry just amazed that 'soft la' Nevin, as they would say in Liverpool, actually had the temerity to do that. The referee didn't see it, but the camera did, and I should have been sent off.*

My one premeditated action had a more damaging outcome for me and it was in the third-last game of the season against Leicester City. They had a midfielder called Ally Mauchlen and he was a classic small, red-haired, Scottish-terrier type with a stereotypically short fuse. The line at the time would have been: he's a well-balanced Scot, he has a deep-fried chip on both shoulders. The game had been won but he had been kicking

---

* When commenting on games now I try to remember when something like this happens, it usually isn't premeditated, it is a moment of madness in the fever of a game that can strike anyone, even the milder-mannered of us. The phrase is usually, 'What was he thinking about?' Well, he wasn't thinking at all, he was reacting instinctively in the moment, under huge pressure and out of character, just like we all do now and again.

me all afternoon and I spotted my chance to get him in the last couple of minutes. As he turned with the ball into my area I knew he wouldn't see me coming, so I sprinted towards him at full speed. I had it all in my mind, as he passed the ball I would be just a little too late to intercept it but my studs would crunch into his unprotected ankle. I knew how to do this because it had been done to me many times and Ally himself had already crocked me earlier that afternoon. It was payback time.

Actually, it wasn't, I didn't even reach him. As I sprinted towards him my ankle went over in a rut in the pitch and I wrenched the entire joint, badly damaging all the ligaments, one of the most painful injuries you can get. I've had quite a few broken bones in my career, but at the moment of impact they are not as bad as 'doing your ankle' for sheer excruciating agony. Ally breezed away, not even noticing my presence while my season ended there and then, which served me right. I also decided while lying there writhing, that would be my last attempt to 'do' anyone – I was useless at it.*

This led to me having to watch the last game of that season from the terraces. It was Liverpool at home and I had a new kind of dilemma for that game: where to watch it? The idea of me sitting in a club suit in the stands was unthinkable – why would I do that? As a fan I watched from the terraces and didn't see any reason why I should be different now, even if I was the club's Player of the Year.

So ten minutes before the game started, I got the big coat on, pulled

---

* At another game against Leicester, Ally and I had squared up after a scuffle between us during the match as the game was progressing elsewhere. As I walked off the field, I had forgotten all about it, but another Scot who I would go on to play with at Everton, Ian Wilson, came up to me as we headed to the dressing rooms at Stamford Bridge and said, 'Wee man, don't go out the front entrance after you get changed. Ally is nuts, he will probably be waiting there for you with a baseball bat.' I never got to find out if he was, because just in case I spent an extra ten minutes talking to my girlfriend in the players' bar until their bus left. I'm sure Ally is a delightful chap; I just didn't get the chance to find out off the field.

the collar up a bit, hunched the old shoulders, walked along in front of the main stand alone, and got the steward to open the gate to the Shed End. I walked into the middle of the crowd and leaned on a banister to watch the game with the Chelsea fans. I had such a good relationship with them, they were so kind and forgiving of me that it was an honour and a pleasure to stand among them. I also wanted to feel part of that passion again from that side of the fence and hadn't realised how much I had missed it until I stood there. It helped that it was a great game that ended 3-3 and had the amazing and bewildering moment of me singing 'There's only one David Speedie' along with everyone else after he scored our third equaliser.

What was even more fun was that not one single person spoke to me or seemed to recognise me. A few did turn around, had a double take then obviously thought, 'No, it couldn't be' and turned away again. To be fair there were a few young Chelsea fans who were mercilessly copying my style at the time, so I could have been one of the doppelgangers. It was one of the truly oddest days in my time at Chelsea – and there were a few of them. When I told the players where I had watched the game and suggested they should do the same if they found themselves out of the team for any reason, they just shook their heads as if I was off my head. I still thought I was being reasonable, but I could see why they thought those actions were strange. Maybe being a little nondescript guy at five foot six helped; it would have been a trifle harder for our tall, blond and striking striker Kerry Dixon to be quite so inconspicuous.

It was an odd end and great fun to stand in The Shed with the fans and be one of them, but much of the rest of the joy in playing for Chelsea had gone and I was struggling to find a way to bring it back. The Player of the Year award, voted for by the fans, was scant consolation, in fact it felt not far from ironic.

20/
NEW DAWN FADES

By November of the 1987–88 season things seemed to have steadied a bit at Chelsea and we were back in the top six. Although our away form wasn't great, things seemed much better after the previous ultra-average campaign. Then disaster struck, our goalkeeper Eddie Niedzwiecki was injured once more with a snapped anterior cruciate ligament and we fell off the edge of the proverbial cliff yet again. Chelsea managed to win only one league game following on from his injury right up until the end of the season. That was one victory in 26 league games. Looking through the team now and the quality of players we had, it is still difficult to understand how that was even possible.

Even the times with the Scotland national team were difficult at that point. We were used to qualifying for every major tournament but in the campaign for the Euros in 1988 we found ourselves in the same group as the Republic of Ireland, Bulgaria, Belgium and Luxembourg. Our downfall came at Hampden Park when playing against the Irish. We were expected to beat them but they were a superb side and hugely underestimated by most, though not by us. With Liam Brady, Paul McGrath, Ronnie Whelan, John Aldridge, Kevin Moran and Mark Lawrenson among other top players in their line-up, we couldn't break them down. Davie Cooper and I sent in a barrage of crosses from the bylines on either side but they stood strong. Lawro scored with an early goal from a free kick taken thirty yards away from where the initial incident happened and our chances of qualification were just about scuppered there and then.

Now, my family came over to Scotland from County Kildare in Ireland just two generations before me and they still feel themselves to be, at the very least, partly Irish. I myself have Irish citizenship alongside my British passport; a few summer holidays in our youth were spent visiting family back in Ireland, so my own feelings go deep even though I am first and foremost Scottish. As I walked out of Hampden Park afterwards, tired and distraught, there was my dad standing waiting for me. He appeared not to be quite as distressed, in fact he didn't seem particularly unhappy at all. My annoyance was aimed at him for once.

'Dad, you weren't supporting Ireland tonight were you, with your own son playing for Scotland?'

He smiled and after a moment said. 'Not... as...such, but if you are going to lose to anyone, then that is who to lose to.' It was a tense journey back to Barlanark that night where scarcely a word was exchanged.

Later in the campaign we had to go to Sofia to play Bulgaria. Although Scotland were out, if we got a result then the old country, Ireland, would be through. Even though they had Hristo Stoichkov in their side, a player who became a Barcelona legend, Scotland won 1-0 with a Gary Mackay goal. It is still remembered by all Irish football supporters to this day, long after it had been forgotten in Scotland, and my dad was even able to celebrate that Irish win openly.

There weren't that many opportunities to visit countries behind the Iron Curtain back then and I was desperate to see and feel what it was really like in this totally alien environment while I was there. We arrived at the hotel in Sofia before the game and I was already planning a walk on my own to have a look at the city. No one knew me here, so I wouldn't be troubled by anyone, or so I thought. I didn't even get into the hotel before being accosted by a man outside.

'Hello, you are Mister Nevin, no?'

'Yes I am, can I help you?' In those pre-internet days, behind the Iron Curtain, actually knowing my name alone was extremely impressive.

'My name is Rumen Yankov. Mr Nevin, is it true you love Bulgarian folk music?'

The answer, maybe surprisingly, was yes. The 4AD record label had brought out a compilation of Bulgarian folk songs sung by local choirs and they were/are beautiful.

But how did he know that I loved 'Des Voix Bulgares'? Apparently, a combination of smuggled copies of the *NME* and John Peel's World Service show at the time was the answer. This guy had been waiting for me and the upshot was that later after training he walked me across the city to his house where, in the front room, he had assembled the all-female choir each in their intricately decorated white folk dresses. It was a beautiful, mesmerising and incredible performance that they provided for me. They were so proud of the music, the heritage and so delighted that someone from the West liked them, it was an unforgettable special personal concert. Years later after the Iron Curtain was lifted, they did eventually perform abroad, touring the world to great acclaim.

As we walked back to the hotel two things happened. First, we walked past a dowdy shop in which everything seemed to be that unique grey-brown colour that communism specialised in. He asked me in his classic Euro-Soviet accent, 'What do you think shop sells?' There was nothing more than an assortment of little pieces of metal, bulbs and valves strewn around. I had no idea.

'This is a TV shop; you buy each piece and when you finally have all the parts you assemble it yourself.' Communism was lagging further behind Western consumerism than I had imagined.

The second thing was even more striking. I asked him what he did for a job.

'Until yesterday I worked in car factory, but I give up job to come and wait for you at hotel.'

I was aghast. 'But you have a wife and two children, are you mad?'

'Oh, do no worry, this is communism, I get another one tomorrow. They are all terrible and pay peanuts, nobody cares about their jobs here.'

I suppose that's why they made Trabants and Ladas instead of Mercedes and Audis.

The trip was a brief respite from the pressures of what was happening at Chelsea. I was obviously still unimpressed with the long-ball, over-simplistic style we used too much, which wasn't getting the best out of the players we had. To be fair that was beginning to change just a little bit at the beginning of the season – or maybe we were just ignoring those tactics and playing our own games. Our keeper Eddie getting injured was probably the biggest problem; games that we would have won or drawn before with the help of Eddie's brilliance, we were now narrowly losing. As a group we knew he was world-class between the sticks, but we hadn't realised quite how pivotal he had been in the past four and a half years. He never played again, having to retire at the age of 27. It was a tragedy because he had eight or nine great years left at the very top.

Other things were happening too, not least that the confidence was beginning to drain from the group, a common problem when teams go through a bad period. The run of bad luck would have been funny had it not been so distressing. There were many games when we hammered the opposition, hit the woodwork countless times, they cleared miraculously off the line and their keeper would have the game of his life – then we lost to a breakaway goal. I am not a fatalist in any way, but if ever anything was written in the stars, it was our ignominious end to that season.

The difference between success and failure at that level can be very small. A single refereeing decision, a ball hitting a post and staying out instead of going in, does end up being the difference between relegation and safety. Those small single incidents happened to us on dozens of occasions; had any single one of them gone in our favour instead, it would have saved us.

Many fans blamed the coach John Hollins and he was sacked midway through the campaign, but by then he was working hard under incredibly difficult circumstances, attempting to adapt after the long-ball fiasco. I still got on very well with him, even when he made me sit out four games to see if that would help change our fortunes. It was the first time I had ever been dropped for any length of time. That was very hard to take when all you want to do is help the team on the field.

I refused to let it affect my professionalism, so I kept as fit as ever. I was running along the Embankment down by Pimlico one night while I was briefly out of the team. I actually did that when I was in the team too if there were no midweek games, just for the love of running. I thought I still needed those ten-mile runs to keep me in peak shape. As I was powering along, suddenly a car screeched to a halt. It was Holly, the manager.

'What on earth are you doing, Pat?'

'Eh, running, gaffer, can't you see?'

'Don't we train you hard enough to keep you fit enough?'

'Well, to be honest, no, not really. Not for me anyway.'

He wasn't angry, he accepted the point but did insist I get in his car to drive me home to keep my legs fresh. I was quickly back in the team after that moment.

I had almost never felt tiredness unless I was ill or carrying an injury. During games I could run for hours with no pain – I just bounced along effortlessly at that age. It is the most joyous and empowering feeling, something I still miss today when I go on my regular runs. Unsurprisingly it didn't last throughout my whole career, but it was helpful at the start and obviously with the ignorance of youth, I thought it would last for ever. However, I was getting ill more often, which years later I discovered to be grumbling appendicitis. That season saw me hospitalised twice, but neither time led to my missing games. Somehow, I always managed to recover from the vomiting just in time!

John Hollins always accepted my attitude was unwavering. Around that time after an away game against Nottingham Forest he talked to me on the way back to London and all but apologised for not sticking by me more during that season. It was impressive of him to say that when he was under extreme pressure himself.*

* I liked John Hollins and he is still a friend to this day, even after all the trials and tribulations and even after inadvertently almost setting me up for an ignominious fall. He once asked if I would go and talk about my football career to the sixth form at his son's school. I was happy to help with that and I blithely set off in the little old MG with a map on the passenger seat. In my school in the east end of Glasgow the sixth form was tiny, maybe a couple of dozen students who were keen to make it to university, unlike the vast majority who had already left looking for real jobs. I had it all planned: I would sit on the edge of a desk at the front of the class and simply chat. These kids wouldn't be that much younger than me anyway. What could possibly go wrong?

As I approached the driveway to the Sevenoaks School, I realised that I had not given this oration serious enough consideration. The driveway seemed to go on for miles and when the school came into view, it looked less like St Andrew's Secondary in Glasgow's east end and more to my eyes like a grander version of Chatsworth House, or how a youngster today probably imagines Hogwarts.

I know Bertie Wooster got into very similar scrapes by the hand of P G Wodehouse, but he had Jeeves to extricate him, I was on my own. Still, I thought to myself, it might be very posh but it's only a few kids. I was met by the bursar (what the hell was that?) and was shown into a very grand library room. Moments later the head entered. I was desperately trying to get a hold of what was happening here, so her introduction was informative but also delivered in an accent posher than the Queen's.

'Good day Mr Nevin, thank you for coming along. The boys seem very excited about the prospect of listening to you talk about your foot-ball.' She appeared not to know it was a single word. 'In fact so much so that it will not only be the sixth form in attendance, the rest of the upper school have also been given leave to attend if they wish. We have moved your talk into Big Hall due to the high level of interest.'

'So how many do you expect to be in there?' I asked rather tentatively.

'Maybe two hundred or so.'

Knowing that I hadn't done a single scrap of preparation or spoken publicly before, I desperately tried to glean a little more information while still trying to look relaxed.

'So how long would you like me to speak for?'

'Oh certainly no more than forty-five minutes to an hour. Mrs Thatcher was here a while back, she kept to the point and was interesting. Mr Ted Heath, however, droned on interminably about yachts and that didn't go down at all well.'

I couldn't be angry with Holly, I liked him too much. He was and is too nice a person, too personable and his heart was always in the right place whatever mistakes were made. Sadly, I couldn't feel the same way with Ernie, whose attitudes about football were still the antithesis of mine. Communication is always important and usually enlightening, so in that final season I decided to try very hard to talk to him, to explain why my game was so different and why I thought the long-ball policy wasn't working, that maybe we should at least consider a middle way.

'Ernie, we have some very good football players here like Micky Hazard, Tony Dorigo and Stevie Clarke,' I began. 'They are international standard, and this one-dimensional thinking is destroying their creativity and effectiveness. This POMO football is taking away everything that is special about us. I will not have anywhere near the positive impact I could have if I can't have at least some freedom to create on my own terms. Is there any way we can work on some sort of solution to the impasse between what most of the squad want and believe and what you are demanding from us?'

As I finished my long, considered and heartfelt soliloquy beside one of the pitches at the Harlington training ground, I realised he was looking away from me, over my shoulder into the middle distance. Had I got through to him? Was he finally ruminating on my ideas? His considered response to my outpourings was:

From breezing along in my car five minutes ago I was now expected to deliver my first ever formal speech with no preparation and no notes in front of an audience I had nothing in common with. I was also expected to upstage at least two prime ministers and doubtless many other world-famous distinguished speakers. My handful of press interviews and the debating society at my secondary school might be of limited help here. I asked for ten minutes just to tidy up a few things in my speech and went to the loo. I furiously wrote down notes on anything I could possibly talk about and reminded myself of the odd story I had. *Thank you, John Hollins, for throwing me in at the deep end.*

In the end it went down very well, particularly when I hammed up how hard it was in my youth in those 'desperately violent' backstreets of Glasgow.

'Look at those two boxer dogs over there playing, aren't they great?'
He then jumped up and bounded off to have a rumble with them.
I'm not sure he had listened to a single word I had said.

A while later in the build-up to a game at Stamford Bridge, Ernie
reiterated his favourite mantra to me, this time with a kindly but
patronising smile and an unwelcome arm around my shoulder.

'Here is what you do, Pat: every time you get the ball just put it into
the penalty box, in two touches or less, no matter where you are or who is
in there. If you take more than two touches, we will substitute you right
away, got that? Now off you go, kid.'

He had said it before but this time it was absolutely crucial to me.
I would rather not play football at all than play it that way. Obviously, I
was going to ignore the advice, but in that moment, even though I don't
like making snap decisions, I knew I had to leave the club. The actual
snapping point was his treating me like a child. As we know already, I
didn't react well to that.

With my contract running out at the end of the season I put the wheels
in motion to see if anyone else wanted me.

I had never had an agent but Athole Still found out about my position
and let me know that a move to Paris Saint-Germain could be organised
at the end of the season. Hanging about in the cultural capital of Europe,
learning French and playing with some classy football folk who didn't
think the word 'skill' was blasphemous – what was not to like? My mind
was made up again almost in an instant.

It didn't hinder my efforts for Chelsea. I still loved the club and I
certainly still felt the same affection for the vast majority of the fans. If
anything, it made me more determined to help the club survive in the top
division. Near the end we got draws against champions-elect Liverpool
and two other sides from the top six, Everton and Arsenal. We clearly had
a decent team, but no luck.

David Speedie had got a lucrative move to Coventry City, so even
though we lost a good player, it made life a lot easier for me and a few

others. During the season Ernie and then eventually John Hollins were sacked, so maybe I could have changed my mind and stayed at Chelsea. By then, however, I had a different problem: the club simply didn't offer me a new contract.

With it being reported that my contract was running out, many fans were asking, indeed begging, me to stay, but I didn't want to stir up emotions by letting them know that the chairman Ken Bates hadn't actually offered me anything. I knew he would offer me a contract at the very last moment; if he didn't, I could leave on a free transfer, which obviously he could never allow as it would be financial madness to let me go without a fee. The minimum he was legally allowed to offer me was precisely the same as I was on, less signing-on fees. I might even have considered taking that at a push, but it was clear they didn't want me to stay. There would be a new manager, Bobby Campbell, taking the club in a new direction and to be fair I think they needed some cash at the time. In their view I was little more than a saleable asset.

There was one final lunch with Ken Bates, where he continually asked me to ask for an annual figure I would sign for. I gauged that this was so he could say to the fans, 'He asked for too much money, he was too greedy, so we had to let him go.' I wasn't going to fall into that trap, but I tried to get it across that I wasn't in the business of sledging him or the club once I had gone anyway, so he needn't worry about me bad-mouthing him in the press. He finally got it, and we left the lunch on good terms, laughing at what was clear – that it was time for me to leave, something neither of us could say openly but both of us knew fine well.

The final part of the season was like a version of that nightmare we have all had, when you are trying to run away from something but your legs will not move. The bottom three would be relegated – fair enough, that is the norm – and we finished a comfortable seven points above those three, so we weren't that bad! We were eighteenth with two other teams on 42 points, both of which had a better goal difference than ours. For two seasons only, in 1987–88 and the one before, the fourth team from bottom would go into a play-off competition along with teams from the league below. It was a completely bizarre situation, never to be repeated, arising from the decision to slim down the top league from twenty-two to twenty teams.

In retrospect the goalkeeping scenario seems the most obvious cause of our slump; we scored more league goals that season than QPR, who came fifth. Only one team in the bottom half of the table outscored us, so we still made and scored enough goals. The problem was that only one side in the entire division shipped more league goals than us and that was the bottom side. Still, we had the play-off games to get ourselves out of this jam.

We hammered Blackburn Rovers 6-1 over two legs in the play-off semi-final. We played well and I was being marked by my old friend John Millar (we last met him going walkabout with me in Baghdad) who was by then the left-back at Ewood Park. At one point in the away leg I scored from twenty yards and John's reaction on camera is pure Basil Fawlty after thrashing his Austin 1100 in *Fawlty Towers*. It is tough ruining the dreams of a close friend but that is how sportspeople must be when competing, totally focused on winning while friendship is completely parked until afterwards. I had no feelings of sympathy at all until we walked off together, shook hands and hugged. As an athlete you learn to compartmentalise things most of the time, not because you want to but because you must.

The play-off final against Middlesbrough was without doubt the most disappointing game of my entire football career. We were 2-0 down from the first leg but our fans turned up en masse for the second leg at the Bridge and we knew we were good enough player for player to claw it back. Not for the first time that season we battered the opposition, we made chances, we hit the woodwork several times, their goalkeeper had a blinder, our pitch was more like the Sahara desert than the lawns of the modern Premier League, so using skill as a weapon was difficult. You name it and it conspired to scupper us. After going into the play-offs due to goal difference and only one goal short of safety, we were relegated by one solitary goal at the end of it all, losing 2-1 on aggregate in our final game. Of the four play-off games, we won three, but still went down. It was a form of torture and a decent number of our fans decided to have a riot on the field for old times' sake, just to add even more pain for the club.

Truthfully, I did not have a single thought that day along the lines of, Well, I'm OK, I'm swanning off to PSG anyway. That was filed away for another time; the compartmentalisation of my feelings was total. I was disconsolate for the fans. Bobby Campbell had taken over as coach and it would have been great had he been able to salvage the season.

But the die was cast and it was clearly the lowest point of my football career thus far. I had a last meeting with Ken Bates a few days later but it was a half-hearted affair on both sides. We were just ticking boxes, I knew that I wasn't required.

Some newspapers were asking me to spill the beans and do a story about my ill-feeling towards the club. I was offered a five-figure sum for the juicy headline, but I wouldn't say anything negative about the club I had such an affinity with, even though I was personally no longer wanted by them. I did not want to add bitterness to the sadness.

I knew how it looked from the terraces, that I was the rat slinking off the sinking ship. I knew that some of those fans would be unfairly angry with me, but I was convinced I was doing the right thing. I thought it was more important they stayed on good terms with the club and thought slightly less of me, rather than me somehow trying to turn them against the club they supported. From my point of view that would have been small-minded and very, very selfish, so I never let them know that I had not jumped off that ship, I had been pushed.

After the last meeting with Ken I walked out of his office into the ground itself, trudged up the steps and sat at the back of the main stand. It was a beautiful, warm, summer evening with one of those atmospheric scarlet sunsets that London does so well at that time of the year.

I sat for an hour or so just watching the planes glide noiselessly into Heathrow in the distance, getting my head around just how much I would miss this place. The club, the players, the fans, Stamford Bridge itself, my friends and London too. I still love the city. I even remember the track playing on my headphones: Simple Minds, 'Somebody Up There Likes You'. By then they were far from my favourite band, but that beautiful track hit the spot.

It was an important, poignant, sad moment and yes, I admit, utterly self-indulgent too. I soon managed to cheer up in the end with the thought process I have since used on such occasions:

Oh, get over yourself, you arse. You were lucky you had the time here and there are adventures to come that might be just as exciting. Most guys would give anything to be in your position. So lighten up!

I had played 245 first-team games in five years for Chelsea; the bald statistics would say I scored 45 goals but I created many more than that. That is usually how you are judged these days, but more than those figures, hopefully I gave some joy and entertainment to the fans who had been so supportive of me. They would always be my club, no matter how it ended. Lots of fans wrote to me with poignant messages over the summer asking me to stay and I was touched by every single one, but it was now impossible. All I had were memories, most of them were very positive and all of them helped me grow into a better person who was more capable of dealing with the ups and downs that life throws at us all.

PART THREE
EVERTON

21/
HIT THE NORTH

My time as a Chelsea player was in the past, a life in Paris was on the horizon, but first Annabel and I went to Corfu for a summer break. We stayed in a scruffy little taverna with a simple room on the first floor, in Vatos, out on the quiet west coast of the island. There was a secluded beach at the bottom of a steep dirt track that was just what we needed. I knew this place, having been before; it was a haunt of Aussie travellers with their VW vans and the more intrepid explorer types of youngsters who weren't interested in the nightlife the island had to offer. It was also a Nevin family hang-out, as my older siblings had also visited regularly over the previous twenty years. It was less being at the discos and more being like the Durrells. I wanted to get away from it all and it would be easy there, or so I thought.

One lazy afternoon Spiro, the taverna's owner, came running all the way down the hill to the beach. 'Mr Patrick, there is a telephone call you must take. The man says it is important.' It was Pete Welsh, my flatmate back in London and one of the original bunch of best friends from my college days. He was cool and measured with the information.

'Pat, Colin Harvey from Everton has been on the phone and says you should talk to him before you sign for anyone. He wants you to sign for Everton right now.'

I paused for about five seconds and said, 'Oh, all right, tell him I'll sign for Everton, I'll be back in a couple of weeks.'

Pete being just as laidback as me said, 'OK, I'll let him know when he calls back tonight.'

I doubt if Colin had ever had such a short discussion, via a third party who wasn't even an agent, to sign a player. In fact, I later found out he thought something was amiss, but Pete reassured him:

'If Pat says he'll sign, then he will, don't worry.'

'But we haven't even talked money yet.'

'It's not that important to Pat, he isn't like that,' Pete replied. 'So just relax, it will be fine.'

Pete knew me well.

There was a follow-up conversation with Annabel that afternoon while lazing side by side on the beach. She asked, 'What was the main reason you wanted to sign for PSG anyway? Was it the football or was it swanning about in Paris for a few years?'

She knew it was more the latter than the former. She gently reminded me that I should do the right thing for my love of the game and that was clearly Everton. In those days the Toffees were considered a significant step up from Chelsea as a football club. No promise had been made by me to PSG, in fact I hadn't talked to anyone there personally. It was all being arranged by Athole Still, so I didn't feel too guilty about my sharp change of mind.

I flew back to London for the evening and then on up to Manchester where Colin and his assistant Terry Darracott were waiting to drive me to Liverpool. Two minutes in Colin's company and I knew I was with a man I liked, respected and trusted implicitly. Some people are just like that, they exude honesty, and Colin is one of them.*

---

* It is worth underlining here for any younger readers, PSG weren't anything like the force they are now, they weren't even the best team in France. I played in a good team at Chelsea, but they have been incredible since the advent of the 'Roman Empire'. Everton at that time was a club that had recently won the

Colin Harvey started his car at Manchester airport and chatted away but in the background the 'radio' was playing some pretty impressive songs. Every band that came on was one of my favourites and this was not common for daytime radio. When Joy Division was followed by The Fall and then Cocteau Twins, I smelt a rat, although a rather pleasant one. He admitted that his daughters, who were into their music too, had made a mix tape to make me feel good on the journey. They nailed it!

We went straight to Colin's house where I met the daughters and his wife. If anything, they were even nicer than Colin if that was possible. This deal was a shoo-in – I loved the idea of working with such good people around. The next day I met up with Athole Still. He wasn't officially my agent, but because he had done so much in the planning for the PSG move, I thought he deserved at least a bit of a payday. I explained to him that I was going into the meeting with the Everton officials first but only to ask one question, 'What is your offer?' They told me what their initial offer was, and I said, 'Thank you, Athole will take it from here.'

I went back out and told Athole what I had been offered and said, 'Whatever you can make for me on top, you can have 20 per cent of that.' After all, hadn't I got that first offer all on my own? I knew it was a first offer and Athole could make his percentage, but I didn't agree with the idea of any agent getting 10 or 15 per cent of all my annual earnings, before tax!

Athole was such a gentleman about it and although understandably he didn't like my thinking, he just laughed it off. He got me some more after haggling and as such did get a very handsome reward for what was in the end, a day's work. We stayed friends; he even came to my wedding – although I went back to doing all my own deals after that.

It soon became clear that Everton were going for it in a big way in

---

league, the FA Cup and a major European trophy. They were the real deal and I couldn't turn them down.

the transfer market. The new signings were all paraded on the same day: Neil McDonald, Stuart McCall, myself and – breaking the British record transfer fee – Tony Cottee from West Ham. I knew the standard of players that were already at the club, so I thought this was going to be extra special. I had landed very lucky indeed. The first real game of the season was against Newcastle and it could only be described as glorious. Goodison Park was bursting at the seams on a warm sunny day, the playing surface was like a carpet – a luxury I didn't have at Chelsea, whose pitch was like a potato field for large parts of the season. The team was brilliant on the day and I had a particularly good game as well, even if I say so myself. We won 4-0 and it should have been many more. Boy, had I made a good decision. Everywhere I looked around me in the team was a very good player in blue. Neville Southall was probably the best keeper in the world, Kevin Ratcliffe was a world-class defender, I knew that from playing against him. New lads McCall and McDonald were looking strong too and every time I watched Ian Snodin, in whichever position he played, he seemed to get better. If Graeme Sharp and Tony Cottee could strike up a partnership it could be unstoppable and with the likes of Kevin Sheedy and the brilliant Trevor Steven along with me around to supply them, it was mind-boggling how good this could be.*

In the meantime I had to look for somewhere to live. The club had put me up short term in a rented apartment in Southport. On the first day there I decided to go down to the main street to do some food shopping. An hour later I got back into my car having bumped into five different Everton and Liverpool players. I went straight to the boot and got a map out. There was Liverpool, Southport was just about due north of

---

* The only tiny downside that day was my dad turned up and said, 'You know you've done it again.' What had I done? 'You've only gone and signed for another team wearing blue and white and as a Celtic man I just can't bring myself to wear a blue scarf.' Poor Dad, my next two teams after Everton wore blue and white as well.

Liverpool, so where was due south? Because that is where I was going to look for a house. I couldn't imagine working at a club and then constantly bumping into the players when I was off duty too.

Due south was Chester, a place I had never visited but it turned out to be a good decision as it is a fabulous little city.

A few weeks after I bought the place an Everton fan came up to me in the players' bar at Goodison.

He said, 'Do you like opera?'

'Absolutely,' I replied.

'I could get my hands on some tickets for the upcoming Pavarotti concert if you like.'

'Excellent, that would be amazing, they are like gold dust. How can you manage that?'

'Oh,' he said, 'I do the big houses of wealthy people up in the north of Scotland.'

'Are you a painter and decorator or something and they will get the tickets for you?'

'No, I mean I "do" the houses, I'm a burglar. I spotted some on the mantelpiece of a place I was in the other day and I could go back and get them for you.'

I managed to quickly say that he shouldn't bother as I might be busy that week after all, but the open 'honesty' of his first conversation stunned me. As he walked away he had an interesting parting shot.

'How are you enjoying 23 Elizabeth Crescent in Chester? I have told all the lads not to "visit" and, by the way, your alarm system is rubbish.'

Welcome to Liverpool!

The next game was a 1-0 win at Coventry, with Tony Cottee stealing the goal. TC and Sharpy had scored all five goals so far and the stars seemed to be aligning in every possible way. I felt very happy, incredibly hopeful and now totally relaxed about the decision to leave Stamford Bridge and come to Goodison Park. There was no doubt in my mind that this would be the biggest, best and most successful part of my career.*

The coming week held a lot of promise too. It was Annabel's birthday on the Sunday and the day before we were playing Nottingham Forest at home. The perfect weekend was planned: I had bought the ring, would take her to a restaurant and propose on Saturday night after the game. I was definitely going the whole way and getting down on bended knee. What could possibly go wrong?

Another sunny day and 35,000 fans came along ready to cheer on another scintillating performance. Once again I was up against the full-back I relished facing most, Stuart Pearce.

As the game started, I felt I could do no wrong. In the first twenty minutes I had skinned him with ease three times and got to the byline to put in dangerous crosses. The fans were as positive towards me as those Chelsea fans had been for the previous five years – there was an incredible buzz every time I got the ball. Everything felt just right until in a moment of thoughtlessness I made one tiny mistake.

The last time I went past Stuart I made a crucial error, and I have no idea to this day why I did it as it really wasn't my style. As I cruised by him and he languished on the ground in my wake, I looked back at him. It wasn't meant to be dismissive or cheeky or arrogant but it sure as hell would have looked that way from his position. I knew exactly what was

---

* Around about then a man was waiting in the players' bar for me and I immediately recognised him with his shock of grey hair. Jimmy Lumsden, one of the two men who had let me go at Celtic as a sixteen-year-old. I went over to say hello, but he spoke first.

'I came down here and waited specially to talk to you, Pat. I just wanted to say, you have done brilliantly in your career and we made a big mistake not signing you back then. Sorry about that.'

It was big of him and unnecessary but very classy. I had always liked him anyway, but was even more impressed with him after that. I said there were no hard feelings and there never were. Years later I was delighted to see him as my old friend Davie Moyes's right-hand man at the Toffees. He always struck me as honourable, honest and one of the good guys.

coming my way the next time I got the ball.

Moments later I picked it up on the halfway line and headed towards him again but this time he wasn't jockeying me down the line. Instead he appeared to be running at pace directly towards me, his eyes fixed not on the ball but somewhere around my sternum. I had pushed it too far and clearly this was not going to end well.

For once in my professional life, discretion seemed the better part of valour. I turned away from him inside the pitch with the ball still at my feet, still looking at the now appropriately named Psycho hurtling towards me. Unusually I didn't look behind me before I turned as I had other things on my mind. Brian Rice, who had the reputation of being about as tough a tackler as me, went for the ball. I was unprepared. His tackle caught my leg as it was 'planted' on the ground and my anterior cruciate ligament was shredded. It was totally my own fault and later, as I lay on the physio's couch, I had plenty of time to ruminate on what happens when you chicken out, even if it is very rare and maybe even understandable in the circumstances.*

I didn't realise how serious it was at first, in fact I played on for a good twenty minutes, but my leg felt like it was about to fall off from the knee down. It is amazing what you can do with adrenaline coursing through your veins. Then a ball landed between Stuart Pearce and me. I knew I couldn't even attempt that 50/50 tackle, my knee was such a mess. It was beside the dugout and instead of tackling I just limped straight off the pitch. Had I made that tackle my career would probably have ended there and then.

---

* Brian Rice had been a colleague and was a good mate. We had been together at Celtic as 'S' Forms when we were kids, and he even played in the Euro U18 Championship final alongside me with Scotland back in 1982! He was a lovely player, but not only was he known for not being a tackler he was also loved for being particularly slow for a pro player. His classy vision and ability were enough to get him by. The slight, wispy midfielder still managed unintentionally to give me my first serious injury, not some massive thuggish defender – how disappointing.

The club physio and the doctor checked me over and sent me straight to the hospital. The consultant had one look and said, 'You're staying right here and I will operate on you first thing tomorrow morning. You have badly damaged your anterior cruciate ligament.' I knew what this meant; I could be out of action for up to a year.

That was obviously very bad news but it had to be dealt with later. I explained the more pressing problem to the surgeon.

'But I was going to propose to my girlfriend in a couple of hours, I've bought the ring, booked the table, I think she might even be expecting it to happen tonight.' Well, she had pointed out a ring she liked in a jeweller's shop on Kensington Church Street a few months before. 'Surely if I'm sensible with the leg and it is in a cast now anyway, I could just come back first thing in the morning and go under the knife then?' He took pity on me and off I went to meet Annabel.

Even that didn't go to plan. The down-on-one-knee stuff wasn't happening now as I was unsteady on the crutches and my left knee was in less than perfect shape. But I put thoughts of the injury to the back of my mind. This was to be a special night, I didn't want to ruin it and didn't dwell on the seriousness of the injury. I was planning on asking the question over dinner but hadn't decided exactly when. If I asked during the starter and she said no, it would have ruined the entire meal! I decided that after the main course would be the right time. The thing is with some of restaurants they aren't exactly completely private and I didn't want anyone listening in to my undying love speech. I am from Glasgow after all, it doesn't come naturally.

The table next to us was uncomfortably close, but fortunately there was no one sitting there. Just as the main course plates were being cleared and I was having a quick swig of the Amarone before popping the question, a couple were shown to the table beside us and would hear every word. I looked round to check them out: it was Alan Hansen and his wife. There was absolutely no chance of me going through with it in front of another footballer – one who played for Liverpool, who was a national team colleague and, as the nation found out later, was not shy with his acerbic opinions. You just know he would comment on it in his trademark way: 'That's a terrible effort, ah can't believe you've asked her like that. What were you thinking about? You played that like an amateur.'

So, I asked her to marry me outside the restaurant after dinner and she said yes – well, I was getting the sympathy vote standing there on the crutches. The next morning, I was under the knife and I had to learn how to deal with my first long-term injury.

22/
DOUBTS EVEN HERE

After stitching the ligament back together again, the surgeon said he felt the procedure had gone well and my first question on coming to was the obligatory one: 'How long before I can play again?' He absolutely refused to give me an answer, which was infuriating. I soon learned that no one on the medical staff at the club would be willing to answer that question either. First of all they didn't know for sure when, or indeed to some degree if, my knee would fully recover. More specifically, with longer-term injuries the feeling was that if you knew about the long months ahead it could get inside your head, leading to depression. If that road seemed too long, there might even be an unwillingness to work as hard in the meantime to keep yourself fit through the countless dull hours of weights, swimming and eventually cycling.

I was frustrated for a variety of reasons. Why didn't they understand I could cope perfectly well with the information? Didn't they understand I would work as hard as anyone to stay fit; I was a fitness fanatic and loved doing the work, and it wasn't a chore! I was also mentally very strong, so I knew I would cope. Of course they couldn't know all that, they hardly knew me at all; I was just in the door.

The biggest frustration was that I couldn't help the team. After the great start they then immediately went on a run of only one win in the next seven league games and I felt guilty because I might have been able to help out had I been fit. There was also the small matter of the club having paid nearly £1 million for me, which was a very substantial sum back then.*

To put it into perspective, my new room-mate Tony Cottee had been bought for £2.2 million and at the time it was the highest fee in history for a player transferred from one British club to another. I like to think that means I would be worth £40 million in today's market; I like to think that anyway, even if it isn't true!

While I was injured, I began to feel at least some of the weight of that transfer fee in a way I hadn't when I was playing. I clearly couldn't show that I was good value for the investment, I couldn't do anything to repay the club or help my new teammates, not while I was stuck in the physio's room. Because of that, I was determined to be in there for the shortest time humanly possible.

Les Helm was the head physio and we got on well. He was a no-nonsense old-school type and not easy to please. He knew the medical side but also recognised the difference between those who wanted to work hard and those who were enjoying a break from the pressure a little too much. I had to be held back rather than pushed on. I wanted to be the quickest player ever to recover from an ACL tear and all the other damage that had been done in my knee. There was medial and lateral collateral ligament damage as well as meniscus damage, so the entire knee was a bit of a mess. My attitude was simple. 'I want the rest of my body to be in perfect shape when I am finally allowed to run again and if that means swimming, running with buoyancy aids in the pool, cycling and doing weights, then you are going to have to physically stop me from doing all of them all day long.'

---

* Today that figure sounds laughably small, when you think of players being sold for north of £100 million. I can't think about it without imagining the *Austin Powers* Dr Evil character saying, 'One million pounds', while lifting his pinky finger to his mouth.

The operation was on 11 September and by late November I was standing on the pitch at our Bellefield training ground ready to play in a bounce game that had been arranged to see if, unbelievably, I was already recovered enough to come back. It surprised the medical staff and maybe even me too. There are usually a series of barriers to overcome even after the physical healing, like your first jog, first sprint and the first time you strike the ball with full force, but they held no fears for me.

The only psychological problem I found was that first block tackle I had to deal with. There was a background fear that the ACL might tear again, even if it was unlikely, so it was a huge relief when I managed it. It was troubling me a little, but as soon as I had that one tackle the concern disappeared immediately and never came back. The brain just seems to kick in and allows you to move on regardless.

A more unusual effect happened during training that first week back and it was the brain working of its own accord again. I went to turn at the same angle that I had when the original injury happened. With no conscious input from me as far as I could gauge, I jumped straight up in the air even though there was no one near me. Quite clearly my brain just took over and removed me from that situation – I wasn't even consciously thinking about it. It only happened once and after that the brain rebooted and I never thought about it again.

There was, however, still something missing: match fitness. I had worked incredibly hard but there is a different type of fitness needed for 90 minutes of football and I needed that to get back in the first team. I went to see the manager Colin Harvey and asked him, 'Can I take a week off so that when I come back, I will be ready, fully match fit?' I instinctively knew exactly what to do. He agreed and seven days later, after seven long-distance, two- to three-hour hill runs, mostly in north Wales, I was ready again.*

---

* I had gone up to Scotland to do some hill running there too, to aid my match fitness. On the way back down one night, driving south along the M74, the road was suddenly closed ahead. I had no idea what was going on and the only

My first game back was against Bradford, less than 14 weeks after the injury had happened, but something had changed at the club while I had been recuperating. Not everyone is going to get on at a football club, there are too many relationships and too many complications from the dynamics within. We often try to put bad feeling down to one reason, think of it in terms of a simple cause and effect as to why the relationship does not work, but it is almost always more complicated than that. Some people just aren't compatible or do not want to be compatible in a certain situation that doesn't suit them.

There were clearly some players who didn't get on with each other at all. When I had first arrived, there was obviously tension in the dressing room, but I had never known a dressing room without at least some tension. It is normal, it might even be desirable to a degree to have a charged, ultra-competitive environment like that. Players not getting on and then not working well together is another matter.

That tension at the start of the season that I put down to a healthy competitiveness was clearly more than that. Without being poisonous yet, the new team certainly hadn't bonded well. An argument during a training game would be picked over afterwards instead of being dealt with and forgotten when the session finished. Something as simple as players from one group raising their eyes to the heavens, then towards each other when one of the 'others' made an error, started becoming more noticeable. It is a small detail, but it is important in what it signifies. In good teams with good attitudes, you have your mate's back and you get him out of a jam instead of looking away shaking your head.

---

other way back to Chester was to go back up to Edinburgh, then south past the Borders on the east coast, a huge detour that would mean I wouldn't get back to Chester until 4am. I was a bit miffed until I turned on the radio to discover that a few miles in front of me a jumbo jet had 'crashed' onto the town of Lockerbie, and some wreckage had landed on the motorway I was travelling on. It was just the perspective needed for any lingering self-pity or annoyance I was feeling at that moment. Those poor innocent people had all my thoughts and suddenly a little sore knee seemed very inconsequential.

It can take a while for new employees to be accepted in any workforce but this is dangerous at a football club and clearly this was taking too long to settle. It didn't help that when I had limped out of the team we were in third place in the league and by the time I came back they were hovering around mid-table.

How deep the problem was became clear at the Christmas party.

The Christmas parties were legendary for the football clubs in Liverpool. A ticket for Liverpool's, Everton's or even Tranmere Rovers' parties were the hottest tickets in town.* The idea was that the price of the tickets for the party at 'The Conti' (Continental Night Club) were extortionate, unless you were a good-looking girl or group of girls – for them entry was free. By the time the party got underway it was roughly ten girls to every guy. I thought it grotesque even in those days; in more modern times it sounds like they might have consulted Caligula for organisational tips. My trick was to bring my brother-in-law along to make sure nothing untoward happened with me or more importantly was said to have happened.

The overriding idea for the party was to bring the players together with a night of drinking and partying. I had been aware of a clique of older players being unhappy with the newcomers. But on this night it really came to the fore. At one point, the old guard started up one of their favourite (admittedly borderline moronic) drinking-party sing-along songs and it was greeted with groans from the others. That was their bonding song and I guess it was important to them. When the newcomers rejected this, mocked it even, the atmosphere went from frosty to icy between the groups. There were no great fall-outs at that point, just a distance and a wariness that the occasion was supposed to resolve.

There were still the initiations though – surely these would help melt the ice wall. As one of the new lads I was expected to stand up and sing in front of the entire audience at the club. I had planned it well, I thought.

---

* I found out later that Tranmere's was by far the maddest and best organised by some distance.

I walked on to the improvised stage wearing my Tom Cruise navy whites from *Top Gun*. Which was meant to be ironic from a committed scruff like me.

I then removed the uniform in the middle of the heaving night club, leaving me with only a loin cloth and red ink on the palms of my hands before donning a straggly long brown wig. They all looked understandably confused and surprised. One amazed player immediately said 'Jesus!' And I answered, 'Yes, my son?'

I had talked Trevor Steven into strumming a few chords behind me but he had legged it, leaving me alone, arms out wide, to start singing 'Always Look on the Bright Side of Life' from Monty Python's *Life of Brian*. It went down well and everyone sang along. Maybe that could become our entire team's drinking song? Sadly not: the night that could have brought us all together, maybe the best chance we had and at the right moment, was missed. From then on, the divisions just got deeper.

It is not unusual for there to be some tension when a group of new players come into a team. I had felt some of that when I initially arrived at Chelsea, but back then the new group became successful right away and some of the players who were being sidelined left in a cull soon afterwards. For those reasons there was no lasting problem. At Everton it was different; the previous group had been extraordinarily successful and weren't ready to move on and it was clear that the new players were brought in to be their long-term replacements.

In some respects it is totally understandable that they would feel unhappy. Whatever your job, imagine if your manager brought in someone to replace you but expected you to work alongside them and help them to integrate, so that they could take your job even more quickly. What about if some of these incomers also got paid more than you even though you were the ones that brought the company success? Be honest, how many wouldn't rail against that? I fully understood where they were coming from although it was never openly articulated from either side.

There was another problem: the older players were very tightly knit and seemed to bond on nights out with plenty of alcohol. The new group weren't habitual drinkers as a rule and were all recently married, so regular nights out during the week or just some weekend 'partying' was not going to happen. Howard Kendall had been the manager during the great days and he believed strongly in the usefulness of drinking as a bonding tool, with him front and centre.

The older players appeared not to rate the incomers; that may have been fear or they may have been right, it all depended on your perspective. But it was hard to be successful in a team that didn't have anywhere near the spirit it should have had. I absolutely didn't take sides. In fact some time later when Colin Harvey was at his wits' end with the effects of the schism, he said to the entire dressing room, 'We have two separate cliques in this dressing room and it doesn't work, we cannot be successful with that going on.' He paused and then said, 'Actually there are three groups, Pat you're in one on your own.' It was intended to be humorous and maybe lighten what was a very difficult moment because the resentment was all unspoken up until then, but I took it as a huge compliment. I wanted to get on with everyone and for the most part did. I could see the problem the rift was causing but I couldn't do anything to mend it. It needed a much bigger, stronger personality than I, or anyone there who was not taking sides, could bring to bear.

Having said that I didn't take sides, when we had the rare family get-togethers at our house in Chester it was generally the new lads and their families who accepted the invitations. It would be Tony Cottee, Stuart McCall and Neil McDonald, with eventually Peter Beagrie and Peter Beardsley and their partners coming around too. Kevin Ratcliffe and his wife were especially friendly and unfailingly supportive to Annabel and me at the time.

In the end the coldness became poisonous and was probably the one thing more than anything else that stopped the team from being as good as it should have been. But why should it have such an effect? Surely you can still play well with people you do not get on with personally off the field?

You can, but you will not maximise your potential as individuals or indeed as a group. Simple things like certain players celebrating more, or indeed only, if one of their mates scored a goal. That is noticeable within the group even if it is not as obvious to the fans. That didn't seem to affect me but there were times when I felt that I could wait forever to get a pass from certain players because they would always look for their mates first. This is the sort of thing that shouldn't happen beyond the age of eleven, but I have seen it with my own eyes from certain players in the Premier League over the past few seasons!

Most of the time things were fine and we managed, but when times got tougher for the team the problems surfaced. It is sad because the biggest losers in all this were the fans. I couldn't accept the fans getting short-changed. I just wanted to bang heads together and say, 'All of you are superb players, you can be really special, you just have to work together, it's not complicated.' But it seemed impossible to get the group to truly bond for any length of time.

The problems it caused Colin Harvey were grossly unfair on him. He was doubtless shocked to see it happen because, measuring things against his own character, he couldn't have conceived of behaving like that himself. It may well have been that a purge was needed and he wasn't quite ruthless or callous enough in those situations. If it is a fault, it is about the best one you can have in my eyes. He cared about the older players and respected what they had done for the club. Maybe he cared too much.

Colin once arranged a trip to Spain for some golf in the desperate hope that the group might finally bond. It rained every day, there was no golf to be had and instead everyone was cooped up together, with plenty of drinking. Surprise, surprise, there was a fist fight after some pointed jibes were exchanged. The 'jolly' backfired spectacularly, but it had been the right thing to try.

In that first season we were still battling to be successful and the cups were a good opportunity. I certainly felt better about things when I scored the winning goal in two semi-finals to get us to two cup finals at Wembley that season. The first was the Simod Cup, the trophy put in place to make up for the fact that English clubs were still banned from Europe following the Heysel Stadium disaster. I scored the only goal against QPR and that led to a final against Nottingham Forest. We were beaten 4-3 after extra time in what to an outsider must have been an entertaining game, but even though it was Wembley and a final it was small beer as far as Evertonians were concerned.

Their eyes were on the FA Cup, and back then in 1989 it was a big deal, much more so than it is now. We still had to get past Norwich City in the semi-final at Villa Park and they were a good team. It was another beautiful sunny day and this time with the real cup final as the prize the team played very well as individuals and as a unit too. I scored the winning goal once again and as we left the pitch I was as elated as I had been after any game in my career. The FA Cup final awaited, I would certainly be starting, that goal had paid off a huge chunk of my transfer fee and Everton felt like a bonded team again just at that precise moment. We finished a hugely disappointing eighth in the league; I had done better than that a couple of times at Chelsea but winning the FA Cup would make it an acceptable season in the fans' eyes.

As I floated off the park Mike Ingham from BBC Radio Sport was waiting to interview me. The gentleman that he was, before going live he gave me a warning.

'I think you should know, Pat, something awful has happened at the other semi-final at Hillsborough between Liverpool and Nottingham Forest, the details are unclear but there are certainly dozens of dead Liverpool fans inside the ground.'

Moments later we were live on air and I think it was clear in the gear shift in my voice during that first answer how happy I had been to how devastated I became in just a few seconds. It did take those moments to compute the full horror but it was the highest high of my time in football to the lowest low in less than twenty seconds. He asked a couple of questions and then I said something like, 'Actually I really don't want to talk about playing football right now, it feels totally wrong.' He agreed and we finished the interview there.

I trudged slowly towards the dressing room just in time to see the celebrations suddenly stop. As soon as the team was told there was total shock. We were left silent with no thought of what had happened to us; our thoughts were with our friends from across Stanley Park.

Afterwards I walked in a daze to the car that was waiting along the road for me. Bill, my father-in-law-to-be, and his wife Ann, along with Annabel and my dad were outside looking incredibly happy. They hadn't yet heard what had happened at Hillsborough. I hated having to tell them and gave it a few minutes as we walked away from the stadium before I let them know. I wanted them to have that moment of joy with me, even if I couldn't have it myself.

The goal, the most important of my career, never was shown on TV. *Match of the Day* was rightly curtailed that night; there was no football other than a report on the disaster. I, like many others, would have been personally offended had they shown our game. The BBC got that one right.

The hours, days and weeks that followed were very difficult for football in general, but for the city of Liverpool and the families of the dead above all, it was horrifying. I had to drive through Liverpool the next day while heading to the training ground for a talk about what might happen next. I came out of the Mersey tunnel from the Wallasey side and drove up past the Royal Liverpool hospital and there were so many people walking around aimlessly on their own, standing on bridges, at the side of the road or randomly on waste ground just staring vacantly, desolately, at nothing. It looked like a scene from a dystopian horror movie, not real life. These people were still in shock and they were everywhere.

They could have been those who had lost family members or friends, maybe they had been to the game and survived, maybe some had made their way down to the hospital to try to get news of those friends and family. I suspect many were also simply citizens of that proud place who were in total shock and hadn't even been able to start the grieving process the entire city still had to go through.

Many people have written more eloquently than I ever could about what the families of the 96 had to go through, but being there at that time I know why their anger was so fierce and why it was certain they would never stop fighting for their justice. They have my undying admiration.

There were so many funerals to attend, with many taking place at the same time, we had to go in separate groups on rotas. As Everton players representing the club we went to as many as we could and it was the most heart-wrenching time imaginable. Every funeral I went to seemed to be that of a young fan. I was completely emotionally broken by the end of the week and I didn't even know any of these kids personally. What made it more poignant was the honourable and respectful way the funerals were attended by all Liverpudlians. I am not sure I could have had anywhere near their dignity. Even as I write this I am thinking of 'You'll Never Walk Alone' being sung at each of those ceremonies and I have tears welling in my eyes.

Not to be moved by the carpet of flowers that covered Anfield was impossible too. There have been other memorials since in British life and maybe the carpet of flowers was 'a thing' previously but I had never witnessed or heard of it before. We went to visit as a team together to show our respect.

My city of Glasgow had gone through it in 1971 with the Ibrox disaster after a Rangers v Celtic game but I was too young to understand the significance and I think my parents shielded it from me anyway. However, eighteen long years later and innocent fans were still being killed in football grounds that weren't fit for purpose or indeed basically safe. It was an outrage and I certainly accepted that whatever the downsides of all-seater stadiums, if they were safer, then they were necessary at that time.

As the weeks rolled on, at no point did I think the Cup final would go ahead and in fact when asked I said that I thought it shouldn't be played. A gap that year would underline that football understood the importance of the tragedy and it would be the most fitting way to memorialise it. I could only think, *Yes, it is the Cup final but it is also only a silly game of football in the end.* It turned out I was wrong.

The families of those who died were the right people to choose and they appeared to agree unanimously that the game should go ahead. They felt that football was so important to their loved ones; they would not want other true fans to miss out on the day. It also helped that it was an all-Merseyside final – it couldn't have been anything else.

It was an emotional build-up to the game but I still had to do a few interviews on TV and if you look at them now I come across as very serious and intense. Out of the context of what had happened it even seems silly, but I couldn't bring myself to crack even the faintest smile when talking about the build-up to that game.

Even so, we were not going to be anything less than Liverpool's toughest opponents. Very few people on the planet wanted us to win that day and a fair percentage of the planet's population was watching but, through respect, we were not going to give anything less than everything.

What did make me happy was getting a decent number of tickets for family and friends, so I was able to invite many of the most important people in my life along. My dad was there of course but my mum also being there was special and rare; she hadn't wanted me to be a footballer but was grudgingly accepting that for now it would be OK, for a while at least. She loved the day.

Among the other friends was John Peel and his wife Sheila. Being a Red I thought he would have toned it down a bit as I could only get them tickets among the Everton fans. My family informed me he was dressed head to toe in his own team's colours. First, he could get away with it because he was Peely but secondly, Liverpool and Everton fans were still mixing at the games, especially this one. That was one of the joys of playing in a Merseyside derby, you could score a goal, look up and see Liverpool fans and Everton fans standing side by side. Sadly, that doesn't happen any longer because of the segregation that understandably followed due to the 'Taylor Report' on Hillsborough.

The game itself was a classic, or so I am told, having never watched a moment of it to this day. Maybe I should finally watch the highlights all these years later because I am writing this? I vaguely remember making a decent cute pass in the build-up to our first goal, but maybe not – we got beat so who cares! It was 3-2 after extra time with Stuart McCall, one of the other new signings, getting both of our goals, though I do hold that Liverpool cheated during extra time. They brought on Ian Rush as a substitute – surely that is unfair? You can't bring someone as brilliant as him on from the bench. He scored two goals and they won the day, much to the relief of just about everyone unless you happened to be a Blue.

There was a moment during extra time when I did have a bit of a wobble. The thought suddenly crossed my mind that *If this game is drawn after extra time, the replay is going to be on the same day as I am due to get married.* I can't imagine how I would have dealt with that one.

The vague fading memory I do have of the game is that because I was playing on the right wing for Everton, when we didn't have the ball, I had to track back and mark in front of their left-winger, John Barnes. On a boiling day, for 120 minutes, in the dying embers of an injury-ravaged season. Part of my problem was that John didn't seem to be charged with doing the same to me. I had almost nothing left by the end. Before the ACL injury it was hard to remember being tired at all, but after that I began to feel less superhuman and more human.

You always hear tales of glory in football but what happens to the losers? First of all I didn't give a damn about the medal, in fact I dumped it at the ground but someone spotted me dropping it in a bin and sent it back to me. I have it somewhere but have never bothered to look at it, or for it, for three decades.

What about the party that was arranged in case we won? Well, there was a dinner and some drinks and an overnight stay in London but it was dreadful. Everyone was pleasant, wives and children were around, but the thought of what the celebrations would have been like had we won hung heavily in the air. I didn't think about it at the time, but had we scored to make it 3-2 for us, it could well have turned our shared history in such a way that the schism within the group might have melted away. We would have partied all night together, the older players would have had to accept the new ones were winners too – a newbie in Stuart McCall had scored our two goals at Wembley after all and I had scored the goal that got us

23/
SHINE ON YOU CRAZY DIAMOND

It does all sound a bit bleak but there were many good times at Everton in those early days, it is just that the expectations were so high and we didn't quite reach them. The individuals were an interesting bunch though and I was newly and very happily married to Annabel.

Neville Southall was not only bizarrely brilliant as a goalkeeper but was also surreally funny, with no discernible filter on what he said. That has not changed to this day as any of his Twitter followers will attest. I loved his crazy craic. He would sit at the back of the coach dealing out abuse to all and sundry and I loved it, especially when he aimed it at me. My clothes, what I was reading, my vocabulary, the music I listened to, everything was fair game, but even though it was done with a biting humour and sarcasm it was never done with spite.

He had his own nicknames for everyone: the brilliant and lovely Trevor Steven, whom no one ever had a bad word for, was Tricky Trev to everyone else but was always Ralphy to Neville. I eventually asked him, why Ralphy?

'*You know, like Ralph Coates.*' It was a typically obscure Neville reference, this time to the former Burnley and Spurs player from the 1970s who had an almost totally bald head by the end of his career, set off by a comedy combover. It was his way of saying Trevor was thinning a bit on top. Trevor would very rarely bite but Neville took great pleasure in getting a rise out of even the most controlled and mild-mannered teammates.

When Trevor left for Rangers, Neville and I acquired a toupee from a joke shop and sent it to him at Ibrox with this message typed on official Everton notepaper: 'Dear Trevor, we found this crying and whimpering beneath the bench where you used to get changed at our Bellefield training ground, does he belong to you?' I had a cheek; I lost my hair much quicker than Trevor did.

Neville was very funny in training too but not always by design. He would often do something so brilliant that everyone would just stop and applaud or laugh at the seeming impossibility of his saves. His physical build looked all wrong for a goalkeeper but his cat-like reflexes and what seemed like an ability to defy physics by changing direction in mid-air were astonishing. It was also the regularity of these 'once in a lifetime' saves that was incredible to witness.

In one training session the coaches set up a shooting drill. The entire team lined up facing the goal thirty yards out. One player knocks the ball up to another who has his back to goal, he lays it off about twenty yards out and the first player tries to score with a shot from there. There were some very good scorers in that team like Tony Cottee, Kevin Sheedy, Graeme Sharp, Mike Newell, by this time also Norman Whiteside, myself and others but after about fifteen minutes still no one had actually managed to score against Neville. That is all very impressive until you understand the big man wasn't using his hands! He was reading the shots and wherever we hit them he was saving with his chest, feet, shoulders or any part of his anatomy other than his hands. Even when we tried to bend it into the top corner, he would read the trajectory and get his head to it before it went into the net. After a while we were laughing so much, we could hardly reach him with the shots.

Another training drill is when you are played through on the goalkeeper for a one v one. Even though all keepers hate this drill, because they are always second favourites, once again Neville was brilliant at reading and saving in these types of situations. He always got the angles precisely right and those reflexes rarely let him down. His innate skill was his ability to read your body shape and know what you were going to do with the ball most of the time. Slip it to his left or right and he was generally down there waiting for it before you knew it. But I had a special ploy of my own that could beat him, one I used throughout my career in these situations: the scoop!

If I was one v one with a goalkeeper and he had covered all the angles, I had just about perfected the skill of scooping (not chipping, it was at a much higher trajectory than that) the ball to about twenty feet in the air over the onrushing keeper. No matter how good Neville was, unless he had a trampoline handy, he couldn't stop it as it glided over his head and bounced gently into the net. It was infallible and there was absolutely nothing that Nev could do to stop it, so he dealt with the problem in his own unique way.

The big man's strategy was unforeseen and did made me think twice about using the scoop against him for a while. In a training game he came running towards me, I scooped him again but instead of stopping to watch the ball go over his head he kept on running and, with his entire fifteen stone, rugby tackled me at full force. He was even more enraged the next time I scooped him; I was ready for the rugby tackle and shimmied past him but he kept chasing me all the way out of the training ground. It is safe to say Neville didn't appreciate the scoop and of course eventually it made me try it more often instead of less! I did quickly learn to sprint in the other direction as soon as the ball left my foot. He was a big lad, but fortunately not as quick as me.

I regularly put the scoop to good use in first-team games. There was a 3-2 win at the start of my second season at Everton against Manchester United when I had a one v one with their keeper Jim Leighton after a superb through ball by Kevin Sheedy. I knew exactly what I was going to do thirty yards before I did it. I had scored with an even better scoop earlier in the year against Charlton at Goodison, but it wasn't shown on national TV, so it wasn't as well received.

Years later Karel Poborský who played for Manchester United would famously use the same technique playing for the Czech Republic v Portugal in Euro 96, and for a while it became known as doing 'a Poborský'. I should have taken a patent out on it! It was inventive and unusual but it wasn't meant as disrespectful in any way, even if it may have felt that way if you were on the receiving end. There was a slight trace, though only at homeopathic levels, of guilt from me in the Manchester United game because Jim Leighton was a good friend and often a room-mate on Scotland trips. My more regular Scotland room-mate Brian McClair was also on the field that day, and oddly I didn't feel the slightest bit of guilt about him losing out.*

---

* I liked having sensible but interesting room-mates such as Brian and Jim. Tony Cottee at Everton was similarly sensible and easy company most of the time. Some managers, however, took it upon themselves to put the untrustworthy ones in with me, hoping I would be a good influence.

The secret drinkers I could cope with, the high-energy, non-sleepers were awful as it affected my rest the night before the game. The inveterate lovers who seemed to need a girl in every town were surprisingly only the second-worst type of room-mate. The worst came later in my career at Tranmere when I was put in with an Irish trialist. He sneaked out drinking at midnight, which is not a great idea when you are on trial, and the next thing I was aware of was a strange noise at 4am. I groggily opened my eyes to find him standing on my bed, blind drunk, relieving himself over my duvet! He didn't last long at the club. I made sure he then slept in my soggy stinking bed and I slept in his dry one, not that he seemed to notice the damp patches.

I always thought that the sharing a room thing was a bit odd in an almost Morecambe and Wise old-fashioned way, though at least you didn't have to share a bed. Lots of ideas were promoted as to why players should room-share, but I think it was originally just to save money by halving the number of rooms the club had to pay for. After that it just kind of stuck even when money was less of a concern.

This picture, from February 1985, appeared in a Scottish tabloid. I had a decent idea of how some rough football fans might have reacted. I think I was channelling a Billy MacKenzie of The Associates meets Green Gartside of Scritti Politti look. No, my teammates didn't understand either.

Chelsea back at Wembley after winning 5-4 against Manchester City in the Full Members' Cup final, 23 March 1986. There might even be photos of this moment where I am actually looking at the camera.

Dribbling in the Merseyside derby, 20 May 1989, against John Barnes, back when every top team still had at least one creative winger.

Playing for Scotland at Hampden Park, 27 May 1989, shadowed by Chris Waddle and Paul Gascoigne – two world-class footballers and part of the reason we lost on the day.

After scoring for Everton with my trademark 'scoop' – not showing a great deal of sympathy for my old friend Jim Leighton in goal for Manchester United, 9 September 1989.

Promotional photo for 'Introducing With Pleasure', a 1987 exhibition organised by the British Arts Council at Hayward Gallery, London, for which I was one of the guest curators.

Out for another curry with John Peel, this time in Glasgow, trying to persuade him that there were more great bands from Glasgow than from Liverpool.

The moment I saw Annabel and decided not only to ask her out, but that I was going to marry her…if she would have me! June 1986.

Scoring the winning goal against Norwich City in the FA Cup semi-final, 15 April 1989. Utter joy that turned to devastation at the end of the game when we heard what was happening at Hillsborough in the other semi.

Newbies Tony Cottee, myself and scorer Stuart McCall celebrate after equalising in the 1989 FA Cup final for Everton v Liverpool. Sadly it was not to be the great new beginning for the team I had hoped.

After scoring for Tranmere Rovers against Bolton in front of another group of
fans I quickly grew to love, April 1995.

DJing at The Victoria in East London, December 2018.

In that second season at Everton I was confident that Colin Harvey could pull things together. After the win against United we beat Arsenal 3-0 at home when I managed to get a couple of the goals against what was a famously mean defence at the time. Things were looking good.

The return game at Highbury wasn't eventful, a narrow 1-0 defeat, but the rest of the night was.

I stayed down in London and went round to my old place in Kensington, where my former flatmate Peter was still living. The poll tax riots in central London had kicked off big-style that day but that was in the centre of the city, so there was nothing to worry about, unless I fancied joining in. I had arranged for a number of my old London friends to meet up at my place as I hadn't seen them all for a while; a nice quiet night in with a few glasses of wine and stories about the 'old days' would take my mind briefly off the day's defeat to the Gunners.

The gang were all together having a nice time but there was one missing – my ballerina friend Fiona Chadwick hadn't turned up. That was strange as she said she would come. I got a phone call in the early evening and it was Fiona at last and she didn't sound comfortable. Having danced in the afternoon with the Royal Ballet, the Opera House was now cut off, with rioters in the streets and mayhem all around. She was trapped. She was trying to sound calm but she clearly wasn't and judging by the news on TV it was already dangerous and likely to get a whole lot worse as darkness fell.

What can a gentleman do? I had no choice but to jump into the MGB GT and drive into town to get her out to safety. It was like a war zone by the time I got up there minutes later, but fortunately I still remembered all the back streets into Soho pretty well. There were cars being torched as I neared Covent Garden, with bricks and bottles being thrown everywhere as the protesters staged running battles with the police. Right at that moment coming in from Kensington in a little green sports car, while the proletariat were considering rebellion to be the only sensible course of action, I will admit to feeling a little bit exposed as well as looking as if I was on the wrong team.

Fifty yards short of my agreed destination to pick up Fiona a guy ran towards the car with furious intent in his eyes, and that brick in his hand was going to play havoc with at the very least the paintwork of the car but more probably the windscreen. I wound down the window and in my gruffest Glasgow accent said, 'Whit are ye daen, big yin?' The Scots were famously all against the poll tax, more than anyone else in the country having been used as the guinea pigs, so it was worth a try.

I got lucky. It was a fellow countryman. 'Awe sorry, wee man, ah didnae know it wiz you.' Off he trotted with a cheery smile and his half-brick was lobbed at the nearest shop window instead. Seconds later I spotted Fiona, she jumped in the passenger seat and we were off at speed through Soho.

That acceleration was just what I thought was finally going to happen for us at Everton now, or was I deluding myself about that too?

Some of the players we had brought in were very good indeed. Norman Whiteside had arrived from Manchester United and he was one of the best and most misunderstood players I have ever come across.

Norm scarcely ever gave the ball away or lost possession from a tackle in games or even in training. His vision was exceptional, his strength on the ball immense and his match intelligence was up there with the best I have ever seen. That season he was well into double figures for league and cup goals scored, which was especially impressive because he was a midfielder and his injuries meant he was playing while limping most of the time.

Many who played with him felt that if he hadn't damaged his knee when he was playing as a teenager, he could have become one of the greatest players of the age and I agree. He was playing at a World Cup at sixteen and looking perfectly comfortable there. He scored a brilliant winning goal for Manchester United in a Cup final beating Neville Southall from twenty yards when he was only twenty. I had watched him play centre-midfield and centre-forward at the top level and he had been equally good at both. Not many can do that.

Most people pointed to the two weaknesses: he wasn't quick and he liked the booze a little, or much, too much. There was a reason why he wasn't quick and it was because of that initial injury. How the circumstances unfolded were unfortunate and very sad.

When the injury happened to the young Belfast boy, United ensured the operation was carried out in a hospital in Manchester by their own specialist. The entire cartilage on his knee was removed when he was only fifteen! That would be an unthinkable decision for most surgeons today, because that meant his career length would be severely shortened, bone would eventually hit bone and that would be it, time to hang up the boots. An operation that left as much of the cartilage intact as possible would have been more sensible. The pace he previously had disappeared. Norman told me himself how speedy he was in his youthful days – 'I was Giggsy quick as a kid' – so it wasn't in any way his fault he was slow for a footballer, it was purely down to the injury.*

Of course, there was the famous Norman Whiteside, Bryan Robson and Paul McGrath drinking club at Manchester United and although each one was a world-class football player, they were also allegedly world-class drinkers. Norman could sup with the best/worst of them. The time we flew to Japan non-stop, Norman had started drinking before we got on the plane. I think Dave Watson (Waggy), our utterly dependable centre-half, stuck with him pint for pint but fell by the wayside somewhere over northern Finland. Graeme Sharp took up the baton and nearly made it to Ulan Bator before conking out, by which time Waggy was back on the juice to keep Norman company until we reached Tokyo. It was an epic bender by Norm.

---

* Had he stayed in Belfast for them to do the work on his knee instead, it would certainly have been a much better outcome, as he explained to me.

'Belfast surgeons were the world leaders in knee surgeries for the obvious reasons.'

The obvious reasons?

'The kneecappings that were routinely dealt out as punishments by the paramilitaries during the Troubles. They had more practice than anyone else with knee reconstructions.'

I was one of the three people who had to carry him onto the bullet train afterwards, much to the shock of the ultra-polite Japanese commuters. As we poured him on, he might have delayed the train by about twenty seconds. At the time I had no idea how big a deal that was in Japan, they were seriously put out.

Why did he drink? Only he will know for sure but I am convinced part of it was that he knew how fabulous a footballer he was, how good he was going to be and how much was taken away by the injury and that operation. You cannot be that talented and not know it. How do you then deal with having all that taken away? It would be difficult for anyone to cope with.*

The day when Norm finally had to accept the inevitable and retire, aged just 26, was a painful one. I regularly brought my brother-in-law Liam, who was a student in Liverpool at the time, into the training ground at Bellefield. I was still struggling to get others to do extra training with me! When all the players had gone home, usually by 2pm, Liam and I would play football in an area behind the gym. It was grassed, about forty yards wide and perfect for playing long shots. We would get the full-size portable goals positioned, I would shoot at him and he would try to save, then he would shoot at me, always from around twenty-five or thirty yards. It was the same game I played constantly with my older brother

---

* Norman doesn't even watch much football nowadays. Deep down that pain must still be there, but you wouldn't know it when you talk to him, he is unfailingly delightful.

In the time I knew Norman I never heard him swear and found him to be one of the most intelligent footballers I ever came across. He became a podiatrist after his career prematurely ended and I suspect he might even have become a doctor had the exams been available to him. He is also someone who consistently downplays his intelligence and talent, a rare quality in modern life that I have always admired. His popularity within the team was universal. Each time he walked through the door he was greeted with a chorus of 'Norm' by everyone, exactly like the character in the hugely popular sitcom at the time, *Cheers*.

Michael over a decade earlier, except we now had real goals, nets, a pair of Neville Southall's old goalie gloves and perfect turf to dive around on.

I loved playing in goal and we would leap around like lunatics until eventually after an hour or so we would be exhausted, the score something like 21-19, to me obviously. It did help improve my shooting skills but it was more about the pure childlike high of playing football just for the love of it – that was the real reason we did it. I had no idea why more players didn't do the same; we got to be carefree kids again, delighting in our fabulous youth, fitness and health. What's not to love about that?

One warm and rainy day – the best kind, because diving to make a full-length save in the mud was great fun – I suddenly stopped. With the score at 20-20 there was a movement below a sodden tree forty yards away. It was Norman standing there in his big grey overcoat watching Liam and me joyously throwing ourselves about. Norman wasn't laughing, he was staring stoically through the rain. He would have given anything to be able to do what we were doing, but the injuries had finished him. Our joy dissipated immediately into silence. The moment didn't need words.

We also went to Beijing on that tour. It was not that long after the Tiananmen Square massacre and it was a very delicate time politically. The Chinese government were keen to put on a show, so after the game against their national team, they laid on a huge banquet for hundreds of party officials and us. The food was fabulous and I was keener than anyone else to try the unrecognisable oriental delicacies, whatever they were! Much of it looked like what the contestants are forced to eat on *I'm A Celebrity* these days.

The head chef was impressed with my enthusiasm for his food and so at the end presented me with the ultimate delicacy of a huge fish head with eyes, brains and everything else still intact. He stood beside me waiting for me to tuck in. I couldn't offend him or indeed the hosts – I didn't fancy causing an international diplomatic incident – so I made a decent effort at it, even the eyes. The lads thought it was hilarious and served me right for being so open to another culture.

The game against the Chinese national team was played in front of a full house, who back then had no idea what on earth was going on. Goals were scored to silence but a huge hoof up the park by Neville Southall got a massive, ear-bursting roar. I believe they have come on a bit since then in their knowledge of the technical side of the game.

As usual I wanted to see the sights, with two specific places high on my list. The Great Wall was one, but I could not get one single player to make the journey with me, even though free VIP transport was laid on. I also wanted to go to Tiananmen Square, and once more I had no takers, which by then didn't surprise me too much.

I wasn't alone when I did go down to Tiananmen, however, because ignoring the cars waiting to ferry me, I decided to walk from the hotel to the square to get a feel for the history, ancient and modern. The Chinese secret police made no attempt at subtlety when they followed me; they made it clear by walking in a decent-sized posse right behind me. How dare they call themselves 'secret' police! It took away some of the poignancy of the moment, though it was interesting to walk with that sort of tail, particularly when I deliberately veered in unexpected directions. Each time I veered off I turned around and smiled or laughed, to see if they understood that I was having fun with them. Every face was set like stone.

Ian Snodin was another fabulous player at Everton then and would certainly have been England's right full-back had he not badly damaged a hamstring at just the wrong time. I felt bad about that personally: his hamstring 'pinged' as he chased a ball, one I had threaded through to him on the overlap. It was maybe just a tad too far in front of him, hence his injury while over-stretching.

Martin Keown had also been brought into the squad. Martin was lightning quick as a player and was as good a man-marker as there was in the game. It always made me laugh when he said before games, 'Whatever you do, don't pass the ball to me.' The creative side of the game seemed to hold no interest for him – the antithesis of my outlook, but each to his own, I guess. As a pure out-and-out defender, marker and destroyer, however, he was superb.

Martin was lumped in with the newbies in a way that Norman Whiteside wasn't, and it was clear that the schism was still festering within the team. Martin was getting wound up regularly and it was clear to me that rattling his cage would eventually have consequences. I don't think he took kindly to being christened BOB, which stood for Brain of Britain. This was meant as sarcasm, suggesting that he wasn't the brightest banana in the bunch. That is a particularly harsh criticism I suppose, when, from the outside, footballers are not considered as the cleverest cohort in the community anyway.*

When Martin snapped and eventually took his frustration out on Kevin Sheedy, it was not a pretty sight. Even if I did see it coming from a long way off, there was no way I could stop it. It failed to lance the boil and in fact seemed to entrench the antagonistic attitudes even further.

Martin was such a good defender, that he was another that I always wanted to play directly against, this time in the Friday seven-a-side game. I loved to beat him because it was an achievement. There were many players I could get past with no real effort at all and where is the joy in that? But he never ever let his guard down in training or a game. He was always full-on, loath to give anything away.

That season we finished sixth, with Chelsea already back in the top division finishing one place above us. I was perfectly happy that my old team were back where I thought they belonged. There was no bitterness or jealousy on my part, just relief that they didn't plummet the way they had done a decade before.

---

* I actually disagree with that idea. Footballers are a perfectly normal cross-section of young men in terms of intellect, in fact they are probably well above average in terms of 'street smarts'. The fact is that for many, regular education took a back seat because they had been studying obsessively for another very tough career. That's not their fault.

Chelsea might have felt that was success but the attitude at Everton was different. Sixth place in the top division from their perspective was considered an abject failure and I was perfectly happy with that outlook. At home we had as good a record as any team in the league, but away from home our points return was awful. That might well have been down to the lack of cohesion within the group. It is often said that you need a great team spirit to be winners on the road and we didn't have that. While 45 out of a possible 57 points at home is a magnificent return worthy of winning the league, a paltry 14 from 57 away from home said it all, even if nine of the thirteen away defeats were by a single goal only. The margin between success and mediocrity again was smaller than many would think.

I suppose that is why I still thought we were very close to being successful and even realistic challengers, by the end of the season we were still only four points from third place. I still genuinely believed at that point Colin Harvey could turn it around without too much trouble, it was well within our grasp and maybe his quiet revolution would bear fruit next season.

The penultimate game of the season was the visit to Stamford Bridge to play Chelsea, the game I had been dreading since leaving there. I didn't really know how the Chelsea fans would react – after all, it looked like I had left them in the lurch two seasons before. I needn't have worried as they gave me a wonderful welcome 'home'. But there was a nagging thought.

What if I find myself through on goal, one on one with their keeper at the Shed End? Can I really score against them? Can I really do that to the fans who were so incredibly kind to me for those five years, who always supported me even when I was having less than great times?

I decided that I shouldn't worry too much, the likelihood of getting a one v one was remote.

In the second half I got on the end of a Kevin Sheedy through ball at the Shed End with only Dave Beasant the Chelsea keeper to beat, one v one. I had enough time to think, *Should I deliberately mess this up?* It did cross my mind, but only briefly. Call it professionalism, respect for my own teammates and indeed the Everton fans, who had also been kind to me, or just say it like it is: I was a soulless swine and rounded Beasant before sliding it into the empty net. It was horrible and I couldn't bear to look at the Shed End as I turned away with no hint of a celebration. They were fantastic and many Chelsea fans even applauded their own team losing a goal to me! Then again, they did win the game 2-1 with Kerry Dixon scoring twice, so they could afford to be magnanimous.

It nailed it for me, there was no doubt that at the end of my career Chelsea would be 'my team', even though I would still have great affection for the others I played for.

Unfortunately, the end of that season had the further disappointment of yet again being overlooked for the Scottish national team's squad, this time for the summer's Italia 90 World Cup. As usual I was back in the Scotland team by September, but I had missed the global gathering. There wasn't a specialist attacking wide player/winger in the entire squad; so clearly the 3-5-2 system Scotland were playing wouldn't have left a place for me to muscle into it anyway. I would be lying to say I was crushed; the idea of spending a month to six weeks away from home with very little likelihood of getting on the field was a decent counter to any longing I had to be at the tournament.

I will be honest, though, and say that this time, on balance, I felt I should have been in the squad. That's about as bullish as I get, but it didn't have a devastating effect, so I moved on, keeping little more than a vague eye on the competition. If Scotland were playing, I was interested, I still loved the country and wanted them to win, there was no residual bitterness, but other than that I scarcely watched it. At the time I just wanted to be alone and on holiday with my wife, it was still that glorious honeymoon period of our marriage and that certainly trumped watching football any day.

24/
THIS CHARMING MAN

There have been a number of times in my life when I have been privy to moments that would have made others who shared my tastes exceedingly jealous. Sitting with Robin Guthrie from Cocteau Twins in his studio one evening as they made the *Heaven or Las Vegas* album was one such moment. As Robin showed me the heartachingly beautiful noises he could make with his guitar – it is bordering on impossible to describe what he could make that technology do – I honestly thought, *Why don't you just release an album of those noises? No rhythm, no drum or voice needed.*

By the time I was at Everton, I'd also become a close friend of Vini Reilly from The Durutti Column. There were quite a few afternoons spent over at his house just sitting listening to him play guitar, working on his new compositions, which was close to heaven for me.

One afternoon Vini ventured, 'Shall we go and visit my friend Steven in a couple of days?'

'Steven who?'

'Morrissey,' he said a little sheepishly.

Vini had co-written Morrissey's first solo album. I had really liked The Smiths and Morrissey would be a very intriguing person to meet anyway. His fame was enormous in the music world and indeed wider society.

His personality was the bigger draw, though: he had a very different outlook to, well, just about anyone around. He was not only an outsider, but he appeared to be the champion of all outsiders in society. He still is a significant figure but just then he could only be described as an icon for many people as well as a ridiculous figure of fun to just as many others.

So yes I would love to pop round to his place!

On the morning of the proposed visit, I was at training as usual, which on this occasion was a lot of fun. It is hard to explain why some days are like that, but everyone seemed to be in a good mood. Most of the time it is very simple, we had won at the weekend, so everyone was chipper. Usually the training, even the hard running, is fun at these times.

One of the most painful training tasks was 'doggies' the length of the entire pitch. It is disguised running that doesn't look as hard as it really is. So you run from the goal line to the six-yard line then back. Next it is to the eighteen-yard line and back to the goal line, then the halfway line and back, all this without stopping and at a high pace. You are not finished yet. You next go to the far eighteen and back, then the far six-yard line and back, then the opposite goal line and back. If the coach was in a really sour mood, you then came 'back down', hitting all the lines again on the way back. It is close to 1,400 yards, just below a sprint, but the real killer is that you are turning all the time at the lines, which kills your momentum.

Even that didn't stop the buzz around the training ground that day and the seven-a-side at the end was one of those games nobody wanted to stop, we were all having such a good time. There were a good few days like that. I just wished that there had been more, particularly at Everton.

Getting changed in the dressing room after showering, I remembered the visit to Morrissey's house and because I was in such a good mood I carelessly asked the lads:

'Does anyone know the best way to a place called Bowden? I'm going to visit someone over there with a friend tonight.'

Norman Whiteside pipes up, 'I do, I know it well, that's where I live.' I mentioned the road name.

'That's my road,' yelped the big man. 'That's where I live! Why don't

I come along with you, you could introduce me to your mates and then we can all go out on the lash?'

Norman's suggestion wasn't really working for me. I hadn't told him it was Morrissey I was visiting. The famous teetotaller was also a famously pained artiste, not piss artist. I made a mental note then and there to swerve Norm's house as it could get very messy indeed.

Nevertheless, I fancied I might bring Norm along next time, when Morrissey invited me back as a firm friend! I do like putting very different people together, and then listening to and observing the interesting exchanges. But maybe that was a bit too ambitious for our first meeting.

Driving along the M56 from Chester I wondered if I should stop off and get a present for Morrissey, but I just couldn't imagine what to take. A bottle of wine was out of the question and anyway that whole idea of a gift seemed a bit middle-class and conventional for the current king of the indie scene. It didn't cross my mind to think of topics to discuss or even particular questions to ask. I always just turn up and chat to people, listen to what they have to say and allow the discussion to flow, no matter who it is.

When Vini and I arrived at Moz's pile, it underlined my belief that it definitely wasn't the right night to take Norman along. Sitting in the poet/singer's kitchen in those slightly awkward opening few moments my mind jumped back just a few hours to how starkly different my other life was to this one. Twenty-odd grown men grunting and sweating through a punishing run, heavy with laddish banter and tales of heavy drinking peppered with industrial language. Here it was quiet, incredibly reserved, with sparkling use of English about our favourite artists and the offer of some raspberry tea in china cups, with a saucer!

That initial awkwardness was lasting a little too long for my liking. I knew we shared a special liking for Jayne Casey and for the music she made with her band Pink Industry, so that chat helped things along a little. There were plenty of things we had in common that we could converse politely on. Morrissey had made his second album with the talented songwriter Mark E Nevin from Fairground Attraction. I had met my namesake introducing him, Eddi Reader and the rest of the band onstage for their recent Liverpool gig. Morrissey also seemed intrigued by the radio show I had been doing in Liverpool on a radio station set up with the DJ Janice Long and Pete Wylie from the band Wah!, who were among my favourite bands from Liverpool. People always seemed to be surprised to find that I DJed and that has never changed. Morrissey seemed satisfied when I confirmed that, 'Yes, I do regularly play The Smiths when I DJ at a club or on radio.' There followed a discussion about the various merits of Wah! v Echo and The Bunnymen v The Teardrop Explodes and of course Pink Industry, who we both insisted should be part of the debate.

Another effort on my part went down less well. More than once I had been mistaken for Johnny Marr at gigs in London. At an Aztec Camera concert a guy had come up to me insisting I was Johnny Marr and would not believe me when I said I wasn't. That was until Annabel said to him, 'I can prove he isn't Johnny.' 'How can you do that?' he replied. 'Well, if you turn round and look ten yards to your right, you will see that Johnny Marr is actually standing over there.' Unfortunately, there was still an iciness between the two former partners and Morrissey moved the topic away from the genius songwriter and guitarist very quickly.

He was still being a bit guarded, clearly trying to get more from me than he was willing to give of himself and I totally respected that. He was one of those people in the public eye who was loathed as much as he was loved. When your personality, as well as your art, gets that much abuse in the media, it doesn't matter how much bravado is shown on screen, you would be naive and stupid to trust everyone you meet right away. I understood that but I had already got a bit exasperated by what was coming across as a defensive preciousness. I had to put him more at his ease, so I asked him a question which I really wanted to know the honest answer to.

'Tell me, Steven, do you like football? I cannot imagine you do, but was there ever any point in your life when you had some interest or even just went along to see what all the fuss was about?'

I knew enough about him then to know that he loved giving unexpected answers, to blindside the questioner, no doubt sometimes just to be contrary. The correct 'Morrissey the personality' answer would be to say he had never had the faintest interest in the game, but was the contrarian willing to go out on a limb and suggest the opposite?

He mused over it for a little while, probably too long to make me believe I was getting a straight answer – it was a thin line to tread – then he said carefully, 'I can't say I have ever really thought about it. My mind and my thoughts have never ventured towards that area, my soul was otherwise engaged.'

Good answer and one that wouldn't give offence to a footballer asking him. Even though I wouldn't have been slightly put out had he said, as I thought he might, that he hated the game. I decided to try a final little teaser on the subject.

'I only ask because another player from our team was going to pop round with me tonight, his name is Norman and he lives not far from here.'

He answered quickly, probably too quickly this time:

'You mean Norman Whiteside who used to play for United and moved to Everton last year?'

'Not bad knowledge from a guy whose soul is engaged elsewhere!'

He smiled broadly at his own contradiction and that moment seemed to break the ice – from then on Moz was fantastic company, I think he enjoyed the verbal and intellectual challenge as a game and the tight-lipped uncertainty was replaced by a more trusting smile. He quickly dropped the more melodramatic side of his act and the evening became a memorable one. He shot a glance at Vini, our mutual friend that seemed to say, yes he is OK.*

---

* Maybe I was looking for too much in what he said about football. He knew who Norman was, he said 'United' not 'Manchester United', and there was a tone in his voice that wasn't antagonistic. Did that mean there was maybe some slight preference for the red over the sky-blue side of his city? It seemed to suggest it, but I couldn't be sure and I couldn't get more from him on the subject.

With any uneasiness now left behind I decided to push it a little further.

'Steven, why don't you show us around your house, give us the guided tour?'

It was a huge, imposing, turreted Victorian affair that his success with The Smiths had earned him. He came from a fairly humble background like me, I thought, so wanting the chance to show off such an impressive abode surely must have been hidden deep down in there somewhere. Of course he was also famously introspective and incredibly private about his own personal life, I knew that. I was convinced few people would have come round for the first time and been bold enough to ask to be 'shown round' right off the bat, so this impudence just might work and I was very curious to see more. He demurred for a while but from where I come from, a guided tour of someone's house, however big or small, would be quite a normal thing to suggest and be granted. Eventually he gave up, after a surprisingly meek struggle, and showed us around.

Each room was fabulously and tastefully decorated. I particularly liked the one that was an homage to Oscar Wilde. It had some impressive first-edition Wilde works in the library area and was furnished opulently with heavy, deep-coloured curtains and a lush sofa with sumptuous, classic-period armchairs. The only thing it seemed to lack for the perfect Georgian gentleman's room was a well-stocked bar filled with sherry, port and decent malt whiskies.

Another room was swiftly bypassed on the stairs with a flick of the wrist and a 'You wouldn't be interested in that one' comment. Like hell I wouldn't be interested, that was the one I wanted to see most, now that he had dismissed it with just a little too much disdain! I was already envisaging a picture of Dorian Gray, but with an ageing Morrissey in the frame. He changed his mind and then relented again after some gentle persuasion. He turned the key in the lock so sluggishly and opened the door to the room so slowly that it was even more obvious that he was embarrassed about its contents. I just wanted to push past him at this point, it was such a painstaking palaver.

The door finally opened to reveal the very last thing I expected to see: a fully kitted-out multigym with all the most modern equipment.

The final upper lounge room was the most interesting of all. In a sparsely decorated space, there was a brand new and rather beautiful baby grand piano. Vini, a classically trained pianist as well as an astonishing guitarist was visibly impressed and said, 'Steven, I didn't know you played.'

I am pretty sure his reply would have impressed Oscar Wilde himself.

'Oh, I don't, I just bought it for you to play for us this evening. I thought it would be rather lovely.' Vini did and it was.

At one point later we played a bit of football in the garden. It is one of the few times I look back and wish we'd camera phones.

I liked Morrissey a good deal, although nowadays I suspect we might not see eye to eye politically. He was a gracious host and invigorating company that night. I drove home at about midnight in the knowledge I'd had a special day. The night hadn't ended for Morrissey however. An hour later a strange drunken man appeared to be trying to climb over his garden fence and set the burglar alarms off. A blue light was soon flashing outside the property, but fortunately our Norman had legged it by then.

The next day at training I apologised to Norm for not being able to 'find' his house and I agreed to go out with him that afternoon for 'a couple'. I was called to the manager's office on union business at the end of the training session and by the time I got downstairs Norm had gone, dragging John Ebbrell, our young, up-and-coming midfielder out instead. That night Norman lost his driving licence, allegedly doing around 20mph in the outside lane of the M56. I have always felt slightly guilty about that; I should have been there to save him from himself. Big-hearted as ever, he offered to give me his big Mercedes for buttons now that he wouldn't be needing it for a while. My guilt wouldn't let me accept, but he insisted I borrowed it for a while to visit my mum who had started to become ill back home in Glasgow.

I never saw Morrissey again. He sent me a postcard – 'From one dribbler to another' as he so perfectly put it – that could have been a perfect Smiths single. I am not great at keeping things like that, but like all my cards from Peely, I still have that one. He phoned the house a short while later, but with our busy lives, him making albums and touring, me playing football and being a devoted husband and father, we never got round to having that second raspberry tea.

25/
HERE COMES THE
SUMMER

That summer, as usual, I kept working on my fitness while everyone else concentrated on the World Cup; I wanted to come back in really great shape. By this time the family holidays included a visit to the Isle of Arran, famously known as 'Scotland in miniature' and an utterly beautiful place. Along with Annabel's brothers and sisters and their families, and her parents too, a great gang of us would retreat to this beautiful place. Unspoilt, fantastic vistas, mountain walks, lovely people, fabulous food, great golf courses and it is scarcely affected by modern life – just the place to get away from it all.*

My real joy was and still is mountain running on the island. This is also the perfect way to prepare for pre-season training. My daily mountain

---

* Wait a minute – on second thoughts, I don't want to spoil the quiet solitude. So, it is awful, bordering on medieval. There is nothing to do except take shelter from the rain and the vicious midges that cover the entire island in biblical swarms. You would hate it.

runs gave me a great start in the competition for a place in the team, the other benefit being that with my *pre*-pre-season work along with the club's own programme I usually started the campaign as if I was in mid-season form. In competitive industries you have to look for every advantage you can find – I always thought this was basic logic.

The run up to Coire Fhionn Lochan is stunning, especially if you can dive into the crystal-clear water when you get to the top in the middle of the run. I decided to run up to Loch Tanna instead, also on the west side of the island. After supper I casually called out a goodbye to Annabel and her mum and dad, saying I was going for a run, before jumping in the car to drive the ten miles to my starting point.*

The run from Catacol to Loch Tanna and back is 8½ miles with a testing, rough-terrain, uphill slog to get to the top of the hill where the loch is. It may be only 342 metres high but it is a hard run, in places often jumping from boulder to boulder without a path. It's just the sort of thing I love doing on a warm summer evening. By the time I had driven there, warmed up and then run to the top it was well after 9.30pm. That is no problem: on a clear night such as this, it can stay light until well after 11pm and anyway it was downhill all the way from here. I'd be back at the car long before darkness fell.

The temptation to take in the view for longer than I should have was too much to resist. As the sun sets over the Mull of Kintyre with its dying rays reflecting on the Atlantic Ocean beyond it, there is almost always a stunning red, purple and yellow glow across the entire sky. It is different

---

* Annabel's dad was maybe the finest man I ever met, a GP very much of the old school, on call 24/7 for the local community where he was deeply loved and respected. In his speech on our wedding day he warned me about Annabel: 'This is no bed-warming, housekeeping attachment you've got here. This is the family volcano, a smouldering beauty that you ignore at your peril.' It was noticeable he didn't tell me this until a few hours *after* we were married. I hadn't seen the eruptions up to this point. They are rare but fierce and, like a volcano, they are impressive in their own way, but generally only to be seen when she is defending others.

every night depending on the cloud formation and if I am not running I will just get in the car and drive to the beach or a headland and sit there watching the spectacle unfold. Beneath the sky, the peaks of the hills along the Kintyre peninsula stretch all the way from Tarbert to Campbeltown. As night falls the beautiful greens on the mountains slowly turn to grey, then blue and then only black in silhouette as the sun dips, still blazing its red glow in the sky above those hills. All the while, in front of you the still waters of the Mull of Kintyre reflect everything to double the effect. Even I can take photographs here that could make their way onto a Scottish Tourist Board calendar.

Like music these panoramas can lift the soul, and when you add that dose of adrenaline you get from running, I guess it's like the high from many other drugs. The world seemed so perfect that night and it felt like nothing could dampen my near euphoric mood, which is possibly what affected my judgement.

After a short stop at the top to take in the view and then walk up to my waist in the loch's refreshing cool waters after that tough run up, I took my first step on the way down. I immediately turned my ankle on a stone that moved unexpectedly. It is easy to say 'turn your ankle', but as we all know going over on your ankle and damaging ligaments is incredibly painful. Like many players, especially the creative ones in those days, my ankles had been savaged many times by overly aggressive defenders. I usually played with protective supports called stirrups made from bandages and tape, cut in a very intricate and imaginative way to safeguard what had become an inherent weakness in the joints and tendons.

Once the pain had subsided and I realised I couldn't walk, never mind run, the reality dawned on me very quickly: *I am in a bit of bother here! It is now well after 10pm, I am over four miles up on a hill in the middle of nowhere in Scotland. I told absolutely no one where I was going, I am only wearing a T-shirt and shorts, it is a bright, clear, moonlit night, which on the positive side will help me a little in finding my way down, even in the parts that have no path. On the negative side it also means it is going to get cold very quickly. Even walking well, it will take about two hours, never mind crawling along with no usable left foot. Shit!*

I knew no one else would find me for many hours and even that might mean sending for the mountain rescue team. As a Scot who knows the dangers of the hills I first felt stupid for getting myself into this situation but quickly decided that any self-indulgent feelings such as embarrassment or anger at myself would have to be shelved until I found a way out of this dilemma. It goes almost without saying this was before mobile phones were ubiquitous, but even that would have been useless back then, with the lack of coverage in the area.

There were questions to ask myself and indeed to answer.

Is the ankle broken? I didn't think so, but I couldn't be sure. *So, that's kind of positive.*

Did I see anyone on the way up to or at the loch? No. *Not good.*

Did I pass any buildings or possible shelters on the way? No. *Also not good.*

Is there any chance someone will come up the hill at night and spot me? Not a hope.

Can I make a fire, to keep myself warm, and what about trees to shelter under? Nope. *And you're clutching at straws now Patrick, get a grip.*

I had to sort this myself and somehow, no matter how painful it was going to be, I had to get myself back down to civilisation under my own steam. It is amazing how quickly your mind sets to work when you realise things are suddenly serious. I did have some time to think, because it took about half an hour for the very worst of the pain to recede.

My close observation of the various physiotherapists strapping my ankles over the years was my first big help, followed by the previous injury therapies that I, like all sports people, had learned to rely on. I didn't have a handy ice pack, but I did have a nearby stream that ran down the hill. I froze the ankle, submerging it in the stream – water in the hills in Scotland is always freezing whatever time of the year it is! I then took off my socks, which were fortunately long football socks, and fashioned a stirrup of sorts tightly round the ankle to stabilise it.

I tried to make some progress down but it was too far, too slow and too painful. At that pace I wasn't going to get to my car before midday the next day. I needed more help and after a couple of hundred yards finally found what I was looking for. I had picked up a few sticks already, but they were either too small or too brittle. Finally I came across one just about the right size that could also take my weight. It wasn't quite a crutch, but it made for a decent-sized walking stick and it meant I could disperse my weight better and take some of the pressure off my ankle. I set off again, this time in higher spirits, letting my mind wander to the long trek taken in Scotland by Davie Balfour in *Kidnapped* by Robert Louis Stevenson. That thought and that story saw me through the next few hours as I imagined myself to be Davie and considered the tougher struggles he had than mine. He didn't have a car waiting at the bottom of the road each night even if he did have Alan Breck Stewart to help him.

I hobbled on, sometimes tripping in the increasing darkness and I will admit to the odd expletive when my ankle was shot through with pain as I fell in the heather and bracken. I didn't care about the extra cuts and bruises, or the tears to my skin made by well-camouflaged thorn bushes jumping up from nowhere; I just had to get to my car.

Eventually I made it back to safety. I must have looked ridiculous, not that there was the slightest chance of anyone seeing me in the gathering gloom other than the odd old deer.

Through a little ingenuity and a lot of pain, by 2am I was back in the car at last and driving back to the warmth and safety of the house we had taken back in Blackwaterfoot. Thank God I had an automatic car – a clutch pedal would have been impossible with the pain. I expected to see the various members of the family at their wits' end as I reached the house, having faced death – well, a pretty nippy night on mountainside anyway and maybe a touch of hypothermia. Not one of them had noticed I was gone; they were still playing cards, chatting merrily and drinking wine. Thanks for the concern, guys. I said nothing other than 'I think I'll have a wee whisky and pop off to bed.'

The injury wouldn't clear up right away but fortunately that summer we had a couple more weeks left before returning back to training after our jaunt to Arran. We were lucky enough to be able to just about afford a trip to the sun as well and that is what we did next, allowing my ankle time to heal.

In that late summer of 1990, there was a scenario which is not only peculiar in retrospect but seemed utterly bizarre at the time. I got a call from someone who I only vaguely knew. When I had originally moved to Chelsea many of my student friends also came down to London to do six months' work experience. A bunch of them went to work with a small travel agent called Sunfare. This 'bucket shop' was run from premises in Notting Hill Gate by a guy called John Boyle. I had heard of him through my friends and the link was that he had done the same degree course as us in Glasgow, just a few years earlier.

Through my good friend John Campbell, Boyle asked if I wouldn't mind helping him out. I was living nearby anyway, so it wouldn't be any bother. He was buying another travel company but wanted them to know he was a cool employer. He arranged a football match between the two companies to announce the takeover and the plan was to then take everyone down the pub afterwards to celebrate and get to know each other, which he did every Friday night with his own workforce anyway. My part was to come and play in the game to add a little bit of pizzazz. Because we weren't flashy about it and everyone else was similarly laid-back, it was a very successful day and, in the end, a very successful merger.

I didn't hear from John Boyle again until five years later in that summer of 1990. He called to ask if Annabel and I would like to join him on a yacht, sailing from the Greek island of Rhodes, then taking in a few other stunning islands on the way. By coincidence we were going to be on Rhodes anyway, so we agreed to go even if the idea of a flashy yacht trip wasn't really our thing. It turned out to be what I would call a stunning big F*** Off boat rather than a yacht. There were some other friends on board, such as my old mate Campbell, so we literally sailed off into the sunset.

I spent the time swimming ashore (I am a fanatical open-water swimmer wherever I am in the world) to various islands and then going for runs up their hills in the stifling heat to make sure I was fit for the upcoming pre-season. In among the water-skiing and an apology one night for only having Grand Cru Chablis instead of champagne available, it was an eye-opening, once-in-a-lifetime experience for me. Modern players could do that sort of thing every week if they liked, with their own yachts to boot, but for us it was a special treat.

On the last evening John Boyle asked me to join him at the front of the boat. A bit the worse for wear from the free-flowing champers, he told me there was an ulterior motive for asking me on the cruise.

'I've done well in the holiday business over the years and I am considering buying a football club in Scotland,' he explained. 'I've had all the due diligence done already on a club, I can afford to buy it and I think I can make it work financially.'

That's all very nice, I thought, *but what has this got to do with me?*

'Well, you know football and I don't know it at all. You are fairly smart so maybe you could run the football side of the business for me while I do the business side of the business?'

Now this was a bit of a push considering my circumstances. 'John, I'm only 25, in the middle of my career and still playing for my country. That is a lot to give up to run some little Scottish club.'

'Well, you could run it and play for the team as well. What's the problem?' John replied, offering what seemed like something approaching a rational concept, but only because it was that late at night after a considerable amount of wine!

'Oh right, I suppose in theory it is possible. So, which team is it?'

'It's Celtic.'

'What? Are you mental? They are massive!'

I thought it was the wildest and probably daftest idea I had ever heard and wouldn't have considered it for a second, but how extraordinary it could have been in some respects. In the end he wasn't able to acquire the club anyway and eventually a few years later Fergus McCann bought it instead. Fergus ran it very well and left Celtic in great shape after his promised seven years in control. Every Celtic fan to a man, woman and child can with my blessing say, 'We dodged a bullet there!'*

In the build-up to the coming season Everton decided that a nice little friendly game in Istanbul might be just the ticket. Galatasaray fans are quite excitable generally, but they surprised even me on this occasion because in a pre-season friendly to honour their long-serving goalkeeper Zoran Simović it all got a bit out of hand. Things had been going well for them in the first half, they were 1-0 up on home territory and creating chances while our side seemed content on making sure there were no injuries so close to the start of the new season. I didn't want to aggravate the lingering ankle injury I still had from Arran. At half-time Colin Harvey was fuming and made it clear to the team that there was a level of pride to be played for.

He rarely shouted, but that night the power and the passion came from his love for the club. 'Does that blue jersey mean anything to you lot?' he fumed. 'Have you come all this way to be embarrassed? You are embarrassing me and the entire club out there. At least show a little bit of respect for our fans who have come all this way. Make a few tackles and then show them you are a top side with some character and some fight.'

Not for the first time, or indeed the last, Martin Keown took his instructions rather literally. When the first ball in the second half came up to their much-loved striker Tanju Çolak, Martin went straight through him, wiping him out completely. Martin infamously calls this a 'reducer', though it is nothing more than a euphemism for plain old thuggery. He didn't do that sort of thing much – he was such a good marker he didn't need to – but in extremis or under orders, he turned into an asset, in a very Jason Bourne sense of the word.

We managed to up our game, I moved into the central area and scored a couple as we won 3-1 with a much better and more physical second-half performance to impress the gaffer. The Gala fans also seemed to notice our changed attitude but were less impressed. The atmosphere turned

---

* I spoke to John only a couple of times over the next decade before I got another call. 'I'm buying another club, fancy it this time?' I took him up on that offer and it led to the most bizarre adventures of my life.

toxic and with five minutes to go it was clear that when the final whistle was blown, within seconds there would be thousands of unhappy Turkish football fanatics on the pitch heading towards us.

The referee sensibly went round the players and explained that the next time the ball was kicked long from our keeper Neville Southall, we shouldn't chase it, but instead leg it straight for the tunnel to get out of the danger zone before the fans noticed what was happening. Unfortunately, I didn't get the memo! So, when Nev launched it miles up towards the right wing I chased it, not knowing that every other player and all the officials were sprinting in the opposite direction towards the safety of the dressing rooms.

By the time I noticed the thousands swarming over the barriers and running towards me, I realised that maybe scoring those two goals hadn't been such a great idea after all. I turned and made my way at pace towards the dugout, dodging and jinking as best I could, but it became impossible to run through the throng. There was only one thing for it in such an extreme situation: become very British indeed. I channelled my inner Denholm Elliott and walked purposefully but in a friendly manner with a polite but firm smile, saying, 'I say, excuse me, could I just get past? Thank you very much. I say, old chap, would you mind? That's awfully kind of you. If I could just squeeze through here, thank you so much, jolly decent of you. That's frightfully helpful…'

Amazingly it worked and somehow I managed to nod and chat my way to the tunnel after what seemed like an age with scarcely a hand laid on me. The lads thought I had been caught and probably battered within an inch of my life, but when I walked into the dressing room unflustered, they were impressed.

'You know guys, they're not a bad lot out there.' Warming to my narrative, I carried on: 'When you come from the rough end of Glasgow you get a sixth sense of when there is real danger and those guys outside are perfectly fine, in fact they were really nice.' I chose not to mention the very English Denholm Elliott act at this point, but in their eyes the little guy was the only one brave enough not to run for his life.

It dawned on me a little while later as I got changed that it might have been something to do with the cameras being there. If I was attacked, they would have been caught on camera and you don't need to have seen the movie *Midnight Express* to know that a Turkish jail isn't the same as an open prison in the Cotswolds.

When we boarded the coach after showering I was still telling the lads that 'There was never anything to worry about, they were just excitable fans the same as you would find anywhere.'

I carried on in this vein as we turned onto the road. Seconds later a hail of bricks, rocks and bottles rained down on the coach. Every single window was smashed, there were scores of fans with handkerchiefs covering faces smashing the side of the bus with six-foot metal poles. I was under one of the tables taking cover alongside Neville Southall and Kevin Ratcliffe who between nervous laughs were saying, 'So tell us again Paddy boy, about how nice these fans are, why they aren't dangerous and especially about that sixth sense of yours…You Arse!'

I was gleefully ignorant, not for the first time that night obviously, of something else that happened during the game. Galatasaray's owner went over to Vince Cooper, one of the people who helped organise the game, who was also working as a sports journalist in Istanbul and who was, incidentally, a big Chelsea fan. Grabbing Vince he pointed towards me as I beat a few more defenders who were clumsily lunging at me. 'Who is he and how much does he cost? Find out right away, I want him here.' Vince said he would do just that.*

---

* In verifying the facts for this book, I met up with some old friends and checked their recollections to make sure my memory wasn't playing too many tricks on me. Memory isn't infallible, in fact it is very untrustworthy, especially in stressful times. I am acutely aware that our brains process things in a way that suits us and our own inner storyline. Vince told me that because this game was a testimonial of sorts, I might have been right after all about the fans being friendly when they ran on. It doesn't, however, totally explain the destruction of the team bus.

26/
I'LL BE HONEST

I started off well in almost every season in my career. I suspect it was because I entered the fray in at least as good condition as anyone else because of my summer fitness regime. It also helped that the pitches were suited to the more skilful players in the first few months. This time I flew out of the blocks and was probably in the best form of my entire time at Everton. Newly promoted Leeds United arrived at an immaculate Goodison Park for the opener. Disastrously we were 3-0 down by half-time and even though we had a second-half comeback, where I made one goal and scored the other, we lost 3-2. That match, however, is only ever remembered for the fact that at half-time Neville Southall, instead of coming in for the team talk, just sat on the pitch with his back against his goalpost.

I don't think anyone in the team or on the management side even noticed Neville wasn't in the dressing room. If anyone did, they would have thought, *That's Nev, he is a bit odd and he does his own thing to get his head sorted out, no problem.* Understandably it didn't play that way in the media. Most thought he was undermining the manager, but I was sure that wasn't the case. Nev concurs to this day: he was just clearing his head in the best way he could. The narrative, however, was decided then and it stuck even if it wasn't true.

I find myself talking in the media quite a bit these days and I am asked about things that seem of great consequence to the public watching them unfold. Usually it is nothing more than a little misunderstanding of a situation blown out of all proportion. You are pushed to sell the story on air a bit, but I find it tiresome. I prefer the truth and try to explain what is really happening, not focusing on developing the story and the hype around it.*

By November I had already scored six goals (I count one against Sheffield United that was wrongly given as an own goal in the press) as well as weighing in with a few assists. The problem was that made me top scorer and we weren't winning enough games or scoring enough goals throughout the team. I still thought we weren't far off getting it right and that Colin Harvey only needed a bit of time after a shaky start to the campaign, but you don't get that time in football. The final straw for Colin was a League Cup defeat away to Sheffield United. It was clear the knives were out for him beforehand.

Colin called me to his room on the afternoon of that game. I knew it hurt him to say it:

'Paddy lad,' he began, 'I'm dropping you for this game. I've tried everything and it is just a roll of the dice. You haven't done anything wrong and I know you are scoring for us as well as creating and—'

I stopped him there. 'Gaffer, you have enough on your plate to be spending your time worrying about me and my feelings. I think you are a fantastic manager and I will do anything for you. I totally respect you calling me in, but it isn't important, I am here for you and if you need

---

* A similar thing happened years later with the Chelsea keeper Kepa Arrizabalaga refusing to leave the field in the Carabao Cup final against Manchester City. I knew it would blow over but it didn't stop the press and even some ex-players saying he should and would be sacked that week. Nonsense at every level, but I suppose it sold the product, be it a newspaper, TV station, radio station, pundit, podcast or whatever.

me from the bench I will be there willing and able to give you everything I have, if and when you put me on. If you don't need me on the bench, I will be our biggest supporter in the stands. I want the best for you and for Everton Football Club first and foremost. That is what it means to be in a team.'

Now some players who are dropped go in a huff and immediately go sniping to the press behind the manager's back or whining to their agents, or more likely to their mates in the team. They deliberately become disruptive in the hope that if things do not go well for the team, they will then get back in. Those characters destroy any chance you have of developing a good spirit. You cannot hide this behaviour; those bottom lips can be seen from the other side of the room. In fact, they often make it their point to be seen as disruptive.*

By this point the atmosphere was toxic, with the remnants of the schism still smouldering away and the run of defeats adding to the discontent. I honestly think some of our players were secretly happy we were losing in the short term and for that reason I understood why the club felt they might need to wield the axe. I was saddened, frustrated and angry that the wrong guy was being sacrificed. In my eyes, the man who cared most was paying the price for others' unprofessionalism.

Colin's team talk before that game was interesting as he knew it could be his last chance. He read out the team and named me on the bench. He then explained what had happened in his room, that I had told him I would do anything that was needed for him and the club, that my own position was secondary. He then said, 'If all of you had the same attitude as that little guy, not only would we not be in the position we are in, we would be right at the top.' He then walked out and awaited the reaction

---

* I have known a world-class player who, in a decisive international qualifier, in order to get the manager back for dropping him, pretended to be injured when asked to go on as a sub, even when the manager had every right to have him as a sub. His injured pride at being on the bench was more important to him than his country's qualification for a major championship.

on the field. We were 2-0 down by the time he brought me on as sub, I managed to get a goal back, even if it was credited in the press as an own goal, but it was too late.

Colin Harvey was as much the reason I came to Everton as the great standing of the club. I was upset for him when he was sacked and called him a few days later to let him know, but he said not to worry, in what seemed like an uncharacteristic, dismissive way. I thought that casual, uninterested reply was uncalled for but soon found out the reason why he didn't want to speak.

Before the new manager was to be announced we played one game against QPR under the stewardship of Jimmy Gabriel, which we won 3-0, and I scored again. Before the next game Howard Kendall was back as manager and he brought in his favourite coach to be his number two, none other than Colin Harvey! It was almost unheard of for a sacked manager to come straight back in as the assistant. Wasn't he too proud to fulfil that less senior role? Would the fans accept him? And how would the players react? Fortunately, Colin was and is one of the least egocentric people you will ever meet in your life. The fans loved him because they knew what type of person he was, how much he loved the club and that he only wanted the best for it. Howard and he had been the partnership during those great days in the early to mid-eighties so from the inside it was a complete no-brainer, even if it looked counterintuitive from the outside.

The last time I was at a club when they changed the manager, it spoiled everything for me, so there was the thought in my mind that this might happen again. On the positive side, Colin was still around to ensure fair play; on the negative side I had felt that John Hollins would be much more on my side back at Chelsea and that didn't work out. Howard quickly brought in Polish international Robert Warzycha as my replacement so that wasn't a great sign for me, but I felt I could show him I was a better player, if certainly not quicker. He was lightning, and at that time pure pace and power were becoming ever more dominant in the English game.

Robert Warzycha, however, was mild-mannered and thoughtful, and we got on well even if we were vying for the same position. The one moment when he lost his composure was when our Dutch full-back Ray Atteveld rocked up in a very hip CCCP T-shirt. It was a style thing and not meant as a big pro-Russian political statement but for a Pole at the time it was hugely offensive. Robert was in a fury and wanted to attack the T-shirt with a large pair of scissors, with its wearer the next target, much to the astonishment of Ray. We never did see that T-shirt again.

Apart from being quicker than me, Robert had one other major advantage. Having been bought for a lot of money, there was pressure to play him. I was by now the union rep and on the PFA management committee so I was aware that if Robert, or any other import, didn't play a set percentage of games then his work permit would be revoked and he would be sent back. As such, if it was a close call between the two of us, he would certainly get the nod.

Howard clearly liked the players who were still around from when he was manager before, so the players who had arrived in the interim had to be very special to impress him. I was willing to work as hard as anyone to show him how good I could be.

The FA Cup that year threw up something of a fifth-round saga in February 1991 against our great rivals Liverpool. The first game at Anfield finished 0-0. It all hinged on a penalty claim involving the late Gary Ablett and me. He later came to play with us at Everton and he was a lovely man, but on this occasion he basically cleaned me out inside the penalty box. It was a clear foul, an obvious and certain penalty. If you wanted to look up the rules of what is and isn't a penalty kick, then a video of that incident would be a perfect example of a 'stone-waller'. Except that it was at Anfield. The referee waved play on.

I could not believe how ridiculous this decision was at such a crucial moment and I let the referee know my feelings forcefully – forcefully enough to deserve at least a yellow card. I was incensed. By the end of the game I had calmed down slightly and in a post-match TV interview I was asked if I thought the penalty should have been awarded. I said, 'You have the pictures, I think they are crystal clear, but sometimes referees get it wrong and he did this time. We are all human we all make mistakes.' I thought it was very measured considering how I really felt and years later referee Neil Midgley did admit he blew it, but that didn't help us or me then.

When they played my interview later on the TV it was followed by an interview with Kenny Dalglish, who was by then the Liverpool manager, and his take differed dramatically. 'Nevin dived, so it wasn't a penalty.' What?! I was amazed at the brazen daftness of it, especially with the footage there for all to see, but I was much more offended at being called a cheat. I managed to play an entire career and I hadn't dived once, so it felt like a personal attack on all I stood for. I was livid all over again.

I wasn't as angry as my wife Annabel – she didn't take well to anyone questioning my integrity, no matter who it was.

'You have got to stand up to him,' she insisted. And as the phone started ringing with journos wanting a reaction, she was now getting annoyed with me for not laying into Kenny. An intelligent, mild-mannered girl most of the time, this was pushing her too far. The volcano was rumbling menacingly.

'But Annabel, you have to understand it's the living legend that is Kenny Dalglish, a Scottish national hero, arguably our greatest ever player. There is no need for a slanging match, the video evidence is clear for anyone to see. Anyone with any sense can see I didn't cheat. What is there to be gained from calling him names and ending up with the red tops having a field day?'

I had never given the media that sort of fuel and wasn't ready to start then. If anyone couldn't see it, they were wearing deeply red-tinted spectacles.*

---

* Some months later at the end of the season, Annabel and I were at the Gleneagles Hotel celebrating our wedding anniversary. During dinner in the plush restaurant I brought up the subject of Kenny's comments and she was still adamant that I should have reacted more vociferously. 'Yeah, but would you

That the game finished 0-0 turned out to be a good thing in a football sense even if it wasn't great for Kenny in the end. The replay at Goodison Park was a classic, under the floodlights in front of a packed, hyper-excited crowd and shown live on TV, which still wasn't that common in the pre-Premier League days. Liverpool were at their best on the night but they couldn't shake us off. The game ended 4-4 after extra time with us constantly coming back from behind. It was a spirited performance that underlined what we as a team could do against the very best when we were altogether. With this sort of display the hope was still alive that we could get back to the very top.

Most people involved in sports events have their own perspectives on momentous occasions that differ from the fans' viewpoint. If you are one of the actors, then what impacts you personally will colour your memory. So yes, I do recall the brilliance and the excitement of the game but in personal terms it was another impact that affected my performance. David Burrows caught me with a thigh-high tackle early in the game and left me with a dead leg. In modern football he would have been in danger of getting a straight red card; back then it was no more than a stern warning, again. Every step after that was painful for me and got worse as the game wore on and the haematoma hardened. So, much of the fun was taken from me as well as the ability to be at my very best.

In the second half we had a high press on the Liverpool back line – yes kids, that wasn't invented over the last few seasons whatever some modern coaches might suggest, they just use fancier jargon – and after a Stuart McCall tackle the ball landed at my feet twenty yards out. I

---

have said to Kenny Dalglish himself that he was talking nonsense?'

'Absolutely!' came the reply.

Excellent. I leaned over and caught the attention of the couple sitting directly behind Annabel; it was Kenny and his wife. He came over and I said, 'Kenny, I think Annabel has something to say to you.'

To be fair she did say exactly what she thought but in a very polite way. I was impressed and so was Kenny. He was very generous in return: he laughed and said, 'Obviously it was a penalty, but I had to back my player.'

was being closed down quickly by defenders while the Liverpool goalkeeper Bruce Grobbelaar was haring out towards me as was his style. No problem, I only had a second to think but this was perfect scooping territory. I nonchalantly lifted it high over the charging Zimbabwean who was beaten. But I gave it just a little too much and instead of landing beautifully in the goal, it hit the crossbar and bounced over. It would have been a goal worthy of the game and might well have helped us win it.

The entire 120 minutes was played at an incredible pace; there were eight goals scored and many missed chances. It was fabulous entertainment and our fans were celebrating loudly with us as we came off. We were exhausted but elated because we had been the team coming back from the brink throughout. We made our way through the tunnel and up to the dressing room with a positive vibe and plenty of, as the Americans would say, a-whoopin' and a-hollerin'.

It quickly turned to silence when we started hearing what was coming from the other dressing room: they were arguing and shouting at each other in a most un-Liverpool-like way. We couldn't catch the gist, but their famous team spirit certainly wasn't matching ours at that moment. The next day Kenny Dalglish resigned as manager, which was a huge shock. A legendary figure at the club, it wasn't as if the team were doing badly. A 4-4 draw in a Merseyside derby at our stadium and another rematch to follow at Anfield surely couldn't be the entire reason?

What were they arguing about? Certainly, I heard many rumours, and in that city it was an historic moment that had to be discussed and dissected constantly. In later years Kenny has stuck by the fact that after Hillsborough and all the trauma he had been through with that, he simply could no longer cope with the stress he was under.

We won the replay 1-0. I couldn't play because of the injury sustained in the first replay, but the important thing was that we were through to the sixth round to face West Ham. There were eight teams left but, having beaten Liverpool, we should have been among the favourites, if not now the outright favourites, to win the trophy. That night at the old Upton Park ground was, in retrospect, a turning point for me at the club – and certainly in my relationship with the manager, Howard Kendall.

A couple of things had changed and certainly the drinking culture was being, to put it kindly, tolerated more again. It was very noticeable that, the night before away games, in the hotel at dinner there were far too many bottles of wine on the lads' tables. The manager seemed perfectly happy with that. I do like a glass of wine with a meal, but a bottle the night before a match isn't a great idea for most players. I was uncomfortable with the way certain standards were slipping but of course that made me and one or two others just sound like prissy spoilsports. At Upton Park, Howard was not absolutely on the ball for this vital game, there had been a few drinks taken beforehand and when he read out the team, he actually named the same player, Stuart McCall, at least twice in two different positions.

Apart from being far too defensive with the line-up against a team we were well capable of beating, there was a tactical mistake too and an obvious one. West Ham had one real danger for us, their left-winger was incredibly quick and we felt that we should be ready for that. Yet the tactics didn't allow for it, in fact they positively encouraged him to run unmarked into space.

By half-time their flying winger had torn us apart and we were all but out of the competition. It was such a blatant tactical error that I even tried to change it on the field myself. One of the 'Stuart McCall twins' and I started giving much more cover in front of our full-back/wing-back area, but the horse had already bolted.

At half-time with feelings running high, the boss asked who had changed the system during the latter part of the first half. I jumped in before Stuart and said indignantly, 'It was me. I didn't think you were capable of doing it, because your judgement is impaired.' The insinuation was clear, even if it was unspoken by me and the others: he had had a few too many.

Try as we might we could only get one goal back and a raft of things infuriated me even more as we headed up the motorway towards home. I felt our chances of success had been taken away and it was not totally our own fault. I also felt for the fans, as I always did: they had travelled all that way and spent their time and hard-earned cash to be there, only to be let down by rank unprofessionalism. Yes, being principled in those situations was my downfall, but it felt like a moral duty to speak out at that moment. I was rarely the outspoken one but there were certain situations when I just could not keep quiet. I wasn't Howard's favourite before that night but he never trusted me again after it.

Andy Hinchcliffe had arrived early in the season from Manchester City where Howard had been his manager. Andy, perhaps for similar reasons to me, couldn't see eye to eye with the boss. So, when he arrived at Everton, he made it very clear in the press what he thought of Howard and he didn't hold back. Just a few weeks later Howard walked through the door of the dressing room at Goodison as the new manager and his first words were, 'Hello Andy, lovely to see you again.' He said it with a smile, and it was very funny, which Howard could often be, but I know Andy felt gutted that his big move could be scuppered after only a few weeks.

Andy and I were soon the outsiders, untrusted and, as the gag went, we were considered dangerous intellectuals because we had both read a book. Quite a few of us didn't fancy the return to the old ways of 'camaraderie through alcohol'; from the perspective of some others, however, that method had served that group incredibly well in the past, so in their eyes it was worth a go again.

For my part I felt the game had moved on, it had become more professional; they simply could no longer get away with not being in peak condition and still be successful. Modern attitudes in the sport have proved that to be correct. I never bought into the heavy drinking culture at any point in my career anyway. Some people could get away with it in their early twenties and manage but it is much harder, bordering on impossible, to keep boozing into your late twenties and then thirties. There are always opponents who will be younger and fitter who are not abusing their bodies. Simply put, an average player who is very athletic can often overcome a very talented player in poorer condition.

From the others' perspective I might have appeared to be aloof and apart on a night out, that I felt that sort of loutish behaviour was beneath me. But it wasn't that at all. Though I have never had a beer in my life, I love wine and good malt whisky and, yes, now and again I have had too much, but I didn't overindulge regularly. I felt it was incumbent on every player to be in the best condition he could be in, to provide the best performances for people who had paid good money and invested so much time, effort and emotion. Surely if you are a professional sportsperson you should be able to hold back from abusing alcohol, at least during the week?

Maybe there was something simpler going on too: maybe Howard just didn't rate me. Well, that's fair enough. It has happened to nearly everyone in football at some point when the manager changes. The new one wants to get credit for his methodology, and he feels that is more likely to happen if he produces a new group of his players and gets rid of some of the former manager's men. It happens in many other businesses too. I have always thought that is a bit of an over-simplistic outlook to have. A manager should actually get *more* credit for taking the previous incumbent's group and getting more out of them than his predecessor did. The problem is that some fans and media will always say, 'It was the former guy's team who won it,' so a cull is almost inevitable.

In training hard work was replaced with head tennis and fun games, which is fine but it led to some players limiting their work rate and as such fitness levels suffered. There was one pre-season when it was made clear by the boss that those at the front of the very limited number of runs were, wait for it, going too fast! Going above half-pace in any pre-season run at Bellefield was then banned.

I was struggling in this alternative universe. Within a week of this crazy diktat I decided to do my own runs after training to make sure I kept in shape. Within a few days other players who felt Howard's new method was just unprofessional rather than there to 'save our legs', had come to join me. Neil McDonald and I were hammering along when I said to him, 'I hope the manager doesn't find out we are doing this.' We had to stop running due to our laughing at the stupidity of this, the incredible fact that, like naughty schoolchildren, we felt we had to hide our willingness to work hard and stay fit.

It wasn't all awful; training did have a lot of laughs at that point. It was even quite funny when I was 'fined' for not being drunk with the rest of the lads on that pre-season tour. Obviously, I didn't pay, being the union rep, which was another thing calculated to make me unpopular with the management. I could just imagine them trying to get that one past me, the union's legal team and eventually Gordon Taylor himself. I think not.

When I write about the rest of the lads drinking, that never included Neville Southall. The big man never drank. I asked him once why this was the case and the picture he painted was not far off the Marvel character Hulk when he is in a particularly foul mood. Knowing Nev's power and his strength of conviction when he believes in something, abstinence is definitely a sensible ploy. Funny that nobody argued with him or fined him for not drinking. They wouldn't have dared.

27 /
LET'S STICK TOGETHER

At the PFA, Gordon Taylor was as ever on top of everything that could and would happen. I'd been scammed into being the union rep at Everton. Adrian Heath (Inchy) couldn't dump the job on me quickly enough. When he asked if I would consider taking over as union rep from him, I said yes, I would think about it. The next thing I knew all the paperwork was being sent directly to me! Cheers, Inchy.

Within a year I was co-opted onto the PFA's management committee in what turned out to be an incredible time for the organisation. The first rumblings about the new structure that would become the Premier League were beginning to surface. The game was evolving, and the top clubs in particular wanted to maximise the value of their product at home and abroad.

Everything was up for debate from the union's point of view. The players had historically waived their rights to personal appearance money on TV transmissions as long as the union would get a percentage, usually 5 per cent, of the TV deal to spend on good causes and the welfare of its members, past and present. That cold hard cash was the crux of the matter as ever but there were a number of other concerns voiced.

The new contracts for the players would have to be reconsidered too. That might sound like dull, dry, legal work, but that is only because it absolutely is dull, dry, legal work. It had to be dealt with and if you are having a contractual dispute in football with money involved then Gordon Taylor is definitely the man you want in your corner – and we had him.

In November 1991 a strike ballot was held which added some excitement though the voting wasn't exactly nail-bitingly close: there was 99 per cent backing for the union's position by its members. Who, I wanted to know, was the turkey that voted for Christmas? The real shock was that professional footballers turned out to be the most radical group, in terms of pro-union strike voting, that the Electoral Reform Services had ever seen in its history! I will admit I am not proud of all footballers' behaviour all the time, but I was impressed with them the day those figures were announced.

Five per cent of TV revenue wasn't a lot in the past, but as we have witnessed over the years since those original TV deals worth hundreds of thousands, they eventually became worth billions of pounds. Gordon had rightly guessed that was the direction of travel and understood the importance of winning that battle.

Part of the reason Gordon became so famously well remunerated was because he could show how positive the effect his negotiating tactics had on the union's finances. In time it became the stick to beat him with, as well as the thing we personally disagreed about most when I eventually became chairman in 1993. However, the power the union gained from his stewardship and the good that it did for so many members, ex-members and their families as well as the wider community in football, is incalculable.

There were regular management committee meetings lasting eight to ten hours – I told you it was tedious – covering a multitude of complex issues, from those actuarial valuations to educational grants for young players, to money given straight from the hardship fund to help older former players who had fallen on hard times. That could be anything from paying some outstanding household bills to sorting out a new hip. I cannot reveal the identities of those we helped but some were the most legendary names in the history of our sport.

You rarely hear about it because it is either confidential and personal or worthy and not very exciting, but the union did some fantastic work through its efforts in re-education, benevolent funding, medical help, retraining, the pension schemes, anti-racism campaigns – I could go on.

Mistakes were made along the way. But they were made when trying to do the best for the members. Those mistakes were massively outweighed by the positive work, I have absolutely no doubt about that. I know, I watched it, experienced it and have nothing to gain financially or otherwise from taking sides. I understand those who question the work Gordon Taylor has done for the members over the years, but on balance the positives have been incalculably large compared to the negatives.

I was happy to make the effort for the benefit of my colleagues. It was unpaid, time-consuming, necessitated lots of studying and, when I became chairman, it was even more arduous and tiresome but still voluntary. I really believed in the positive services a good and powerful union could provide, and of course it appealed to my tiresomely worthy side, but the downside is that it ate into my family time. It also makes you less employable because many companies do not want a leftie troublemaker or someone they see as a union firebrand on their books. It is unspoken and unprovable, but it certainly is the case in football as well as other industries.

The other counter-intuitive thing was that some fellow players seemed to resent the role I played with the union. If I listed the union's benefits and good works, it would get a Python-esque response: 'Yeah, but apart from the benevolent works, pensions, legal help, accident insurance, education, social campaigning and a lifetime of back-up when we retire, what has the union ever done for us?'

It seems unfathomable that you could dedicate your time for their benefit but could still be seen as, to use their phrase, 'busy'. Busy in this context meant meddling, being too clever, only being interested in your own ends or being involved only to gain some sort of power or status. I have never quite understood the allure of gaining power in any part of life, other than having it to aid the benefit of the greater good for society or colleagues, particularly those in need. Power for power's sake is an alien concept to me. Just like Douglas Adams used to say about Zaphod Beeblebrox, I reckon anyone capable of getting themselves into a position of power should be automatically banned from it. That said, every player who found themselves needing help was suddenly a big fan of the union and the work we were doing. Bloody typical.

So was I walking about with a dark cloud over my head at this point? Not at all. Back in the real world I had a happy marriage, I was still in the team much of the time, was earning a decent wage and I had other entertaining interests. There were still great gigs to go to in the north-west such as Danny Wilson, The Blue Nile, The The, Radiohead, A Certain Ratio, New Order, Cocteau Twins and lots of other smaller bands. There were also great art shows and theatre in Manchester and Liverpool. So, life was still good even if I knew I had a battle on to keep my place in the Everton side.

So, while I was beginning to fall foul of the manager Howard Kendall more regularly, I still didn't consider asking for a transfer. Even when it got more difficult for me to get a start, I refused to yield. I had agreed a contract and honouring that really meant something on my part. Asking to leave (or God forbid acting up in order to manufacture a departure) was not on my radar. What was on my mind was showing everyone, from the manager, to my teammates, to the fans and to myself that I was good enough to be playing every week. In retrospect it was naive and almost certainly a mistake in terms of my career, but just about any move from Everton at that time would have been a step down and more importantly in my mind an acceptance of defeat.

I had been told that a couple of clubs were interested at this point, including West Ham and Celtic, as usual. While visiting family in Glasgow I was contacted by an official at Celtic and agreed to meet him. Somewhat surprisingly it was done out in the open, in a hotel foyer in the centre of Glasgow with no subterfuge attempted. They wanted to know if I was interested.

'Of course I am, being a Celtic fan and Everton looking like they are going in a different direction then I will at least consider it. It must be done correctly though, there will be no pushing from my side. If there is to be a deal agreed it isn't to be done through the media or by meddling agents. You should simply contact Everton and use all the correct channels.' The Celtic representative seemed perfectly happy with that position.

Rangers were dominant back then, winning nine titles in a row from 1989 to 1997, and it would have been a tough ask to challenge their dominance, but Celtic had a decent side too with the likes of Paul McStay, John Collins and Tom Boyd, who were all Scottish international teammates of mine. The next contact was when the same guy called the next day and asked the classic question that Celtic fans at the time would have understood only too well: 'You're not a greedy boy are you?'

With Rangers spending untold millions there was a running joke at the time that Celtic had a 'biscuit tin' mentality. Instead of high-flying, sophisticated financial ideas to try to take the club to the next level, they just looked in the biscuit tin to see if there were a few crumbs left. Years later after what happened to Rangers with their financial meltdown and subsequent liquidation, that biscuit-tin mentality didn't look quite as ridiculous!

I did play a friendly game for Everton against Celtic at Parkhead in the pre-season of 1990. It was a very unusual day for me. I had played for Scotland against the Scottish Football League at Hampden the day before but I still wanted to finally play at Celtic Park where I had grown up watching and loving football. Before the game I felt a bit unwell and had a word with the doctor. After a bit of prodding around he still couldn't figure out what was wrong with my stomach. Colin Harvey came in and asked me what was wrong. I explained the symptoms and he just started laughing.

'What are you laughing at, Boss?'

'I know exactly what is wrong with you because I have it as well today.' Colin was Celtic-minded like me and explained. 'It's just that you have clearly never suffered from this ailment before: you're nervous!'

So aged 26, having played in an FA Cup final, dozens of top-level derby games in England and even played for Scotland v England at Wembley, I finally get nervous before a pre-season friendly game! In some ways it makes sense; these were my people, this is where I came from, I wanted to impress them more than any other crowd I had played in front of in my life and my entire family was there, though they were probably supporting Celtic right enough. But I wanted to show them all.

Finally, I got myself together and walked out of the tunnel to warm up pre-match, signing the odd autograph but generally trying to be as small and inconspicuous as possible. Suddenly a large roar went up and I turned around to look for their new star, Charlie Nicholas, who had just re-signed for the Hoops. But he wasn't there. After about ten seconds, it dawned on me that it was me they were cheering. I had spent so much time telling the world that I was a Celtic fan, it had not gone unnoticed and those next few moments were among the most cherished of my entire career.*

For whatever reason though, the expected bid from Celtic never materialised after our meeting or at least it wasn't relayed to me. That is not unusual, and neither is it in any way incorrect. A contract is a contract and I was still honouring mine; it would take a lot more for me to change that outlook, but the seed arrived in more ways than one, just before the end of that season.

---

* To think that now for complex reasons Celtic are no longer my favoured side in Scotland, you can imagine how heartbroken I was when that happened. On top of that, on social media I get more abuse from a certain group of Celtic fans than I do from all other fans of all other teams added together. It is a long story that deserves and may well get a couple of chapters in itself one day, but in short when I went back to Scotland I was shocked that the sectarianism in Glasgow and its surrounds was almost as bad as it ever was.

At 4am on Saturday 13 April our son Simon arrived after a protracted twenty-six-hour labour for Annabel. I stayed throughout that entire time at the hospital, apart from two hours of training early on, for the most life-changing thing that can happen to anyone. I was quite calm, but Annabel was incredibly focused and brave through the pain and various traumas. The labour was not straightforward and with Annabel exhausted at the end of it all, suddenly as he emerged there was panic in the room – something was wrong with him. The medics stayed calm and worked efficiently but they were deeply concerned. It was difficult to know how much Annabel was aware of the alarm. She had given so much she was semi-conscious.

Simon was whisked off to a corner of the room the second he saw the light and was worked on by a consultant and a bunch of other medics. There was a problem with his breathing and it was obvious he was struggling. There was a dreadful moment when I had no idea what to do. Should I stay with Annabel by her side, as she needed support, or go to my newborn son? Maybe this would be the only chance to see him for… well, I don't even want to think about it now.

I stayed with Annabel as the experts needed the space and I knew I couldn't be of much use to them anyway. I reassured her and tried to shield her to some degree from what was happening ten feet away, but I was always straining to see what was going on. I don't know how long it was until they came back with Simon but it felt like an eternity. He still didn't look a great colour but he was breathing normally on his own and that is all I cared about. It was the most stressful and tiring night of my life and I had it easy compared to Annabel.

By 6am on that Saturday morning I was driving out of the Countess of Chester Hospital car park heading home to get some sleep, wife and baby safe and settled at last. I am not a crier, but as I drove home the tears came with the knowledge that life and my outlook would never be the same again. It isn't easy to be as devil-may-care in your attitudes, and pure of heart in your business, when you have a baby to look after and provide for.

I probably slept for two hours, but then I had to get up because at 3pm we were playing against Chelsea at Goodison Park. It didn't occur to me to mention to the manager that I had just become a father a few hours earlier, that we had feared we might lose the baby and that altogether I'd only had about two hours' sleep in the previous two days. Somehow with the adrenaline and the excitement I got through those 90 minutes. I even got an assist as Kerry Dixon attempted a back pass and I intercepted it to make our equalising goal for John Ebbrell.

There were some good moments that season – scoring in the derby game at Liverpool, ending the season with a couple more strikes in London against Spurs and then QPR – but it was all a bit average compared to the hopes we had had at the start. Mid-table mediocrity in ninth place wasn't and shouldn't have been good enough for Everton.

When the season finally ended I was ready to get back to Scotland for a break with my new family, although in my memory those first days back in Chester getting to know my son always feel like they were long, warm, sunny and enchanting. Day after day was spent sitting in the back garden being ecstatically happy together. Simon was a lovely baby who slept well but to some degree his arrival did finally influence my mentality. For the first time in my life, like most parents, I realised that the job and the career were now actually quite important if I was going to provide for my child. Could I really hold on to that stance of playing purely for the love of the game and making decisions based solely on that, when reality was biting – well, sucking on a Farley's rusk anyway? I still believed that it was the best outlook to have and that I would play my best, most creative football if I managed to keep that philosophy, but it was sorely tested by the new 9lb 4oz extra weight of responsibility.

Having never particularly wanted to go pro in the first place, I'd always had a nonchalance about my accidental job. I had never seriously considered the career as precarious up until then. But in the back of my mind I knew that it was. Now with two other people who would be affected by that fragility it crept closer to the front of my consciousness. Fortunately, Annabel never put any pressure on me and just let me do the job, which was a huge help. I was determined to continue to be ultra-professional and dedicated at Everton but it wasn't always easy – in fact it was frowned on more and more as time went by.

We were in Switzerland for a set of pre-season games organised against the local amateur sides. It was bordering on useless as an aid to preparation for the top division in England. We could have won all those games by double figures but there were plenty of 'social' nights to be enjoyed if you liked that sort of thing, which in those circumstances I didn't. The social side appeared to be at least as important as the actual football.

On one night out I tagged along with everyone else to the only hotspot in the tiny alpine town. It turned out to be a nightclub, casino and poorly disguised 'house of ill repute'. The lads were all drinking away merrily. I made the reasonable excuse that I was on antibiotics for a foot infection that didn't allow me to join in the bevvying. Howard came in with one of the directors and sat down before ordering a bottle of the best champagne they had in the house. If there was any atmosphere, him showing up killed it stone dead. The lads wanted to be on their own this time.

Eventually a striking, scantily clad young Filipina 'lady' parked herself next to the boss, doubtless impressed by his big spending. He seemed to enjoy the attention though I am sure nothing untoward would have happened. He smiled and raised his glass to the rest of the team over the other side of the small room. Like me they were all less than impressed by him and his new companion. About an hour later the madam came over to me, one of the only sober ones left, and in halting English said, 'That is your boss over there?'

'Sadly, it is,' I replied.

'He does know that it is a man he is with, dressed as a woman?'

Maybe it was beneath me, but I said, 'Eh, actually yes he does, he is into that sort of thing, just leave him alone.' It was probably also beneath me to then tell all the lads exactly what was happening. My excuse was that it was a bit of banter and I wanted to inject some fun into the evening.

I don't know how he realised but he found out I was the culprit for his being the butt of the joke and I paid the price. The next morning at breakfast, unsurprisingly, Andy and I were the only two down there until Howard showed up. He couldn't really sit anywhere else, so he sat with us but it was intensely uncomfortable for him. We said nothing but were clearly stifling giggles. He was furious with us.

Later there was a rant in front of the team about me and Andy Hinchcliffe being a disgrace because we were too sober and would prefer to read a book than go out drinking with the gang. It was a fair cop.

After Switzerland, there was yet another training camp set up in a north-western county in Ireland, known then as bandit country due to the IRA goings-on. When we arrived at the hotel there were no facilities for training, not even a football pitch! Clearly there were opportunities for social events, but even for the lads this was too much. There was a meeting and then a full-blown mutiny. Most of the lads just left and went to Dublin and a few of the others headed home. I and a handful of others stayed and spent our time running up and down hills, which was still frowned upon. The lack of professionalism was killing me.

That season I started 41 games, came on as sub in 11 more, and, to my reckoning, scored 10 goals (second-top scorer at the club after my room-mate Tony Cottee), with the usual larger number of assists to boot. The figures are decent for a winger at the top level, but now I had to admit that it didn't feel right. The manager clearly didn't rate me or maybe he just didn't like me or want me around. Sometimes no words have to be said between two people, they just don't hit it off. I knew I was one of those that never would with Howard. Just like in my time at Chelsea, I could sense I would be frozen out at the first opportunity by the new regime.

I wasn't wrong.

28/
LEAVING BLUES

Football clubs never stand still; if they stand still they will quickly fail. At the start of most seasons at the top clubs there will be a raft of new players and you either embrace the increase in quality alongside the increase in competition for your place or you see it negatively as nothing more than a threat. Feeling threatened is a normal, understandable human reaction, because in the end every single player is right to be concerned – they all get replaced by a newer, younger or better model eventually. I relished the challenge of the new blood and wanted to work with an ever-improving set of players, but I understood the alternate attitude. It was clear that in this new season, I would have an even greater fight to keep my place. Robert Warzycha was still there, Mark Ward, Maurice Johnston (remember him?) signed in the November from Rangers and we also got Peter Beardsley from Liverpool.

It would be tough competition, but I really wanted to play with some of those guys. Maurice and I were no longer the eleven-year-olds scrapping for the centre-forward position, as well as scrapping on a stage behind a curtain. We had played together with Scotland and even though you couldn't imagine more opposite personalities I thought he was a fantastic player and now got on perfectly well with him. I didn't fully understand how he managed to be so fabulously fit because he certainly wasn't averse to the high life whenever the opportunity arose.

I really admired him because he had been brave/stupid enough to be the first 'Catholic' player to sign for Rangers, though the idea of him attending Mass every week or kneeling in a confessional booth was as likely as finding me at a local Young Conservatives meeting. It was an incredible thing for 'Mojo' to do and Graeme Souness deserves great credit for pushing it through. I didn't think that immediately when he was on the brink of going back to Celtic, but it was an astonishing story at the time in Scottish football. It was a landmark, ground-breaking event and that is no exaggeration. Maybe he did it for the money or, as Souness said later, for the devilment, but it was a mighty blow in the fight to break down one of the biggest sectarian barriers in the country. That sectarian divide that lives on in some communities is still the thing I dislike most about the country I love.*

I once sat beside Mo on a team bus journey with the Scotland squad a while after he had signed for the Gers. He was never my first-choice mate to sit beside as we had so little in common, but I went right over and parked myself there. It was part support as he was sitting alone and part

---

* I know exactly where I was when the news about Mojo signing for Rangers broke. I was driving a van down to Chester from my wife's parents' house in the Scottish Borders with my brother-in-law Liam, a Rangers fan. (A Gers fan with a name like that? He was christened William but in the Borders the connotations aren't so widely known, so Liam it is.) As we passed beyond Hawick, BBC Radio reported that Maurice had signed for Rangers. How we both laughed at the stupidity of the Beeb in London, what an embarrassing mistake to make.

He had obviously just finalised his well-publicised move to Celtic and we chatted about how the BBC would get, as they say in Scotland, 'pelters' (dog's abuse) for that gaffe. Fifteen minutes later when they reported it again, this time with details from a Scottish reporter underlining the fact that it was Rangers he had signed for, I almost drove the van off the road. I have never been so close to wrapping myself round a tree.

interest to see what it was like to be so hated, at that time by most of the fans on both sides of the Rangers and Celtic divide. The abuse aimed at him as we went towards Hampden Park was incredible; there had even been suggestions of paramilitary death threats, from Republicans and Unionists. The oddest thing is that, judging by his demeanour, he didn't seem to notice or care too much. He could have been one hell of a poker player because no human on this earth would be able to totally blank that level of abuse and threat.*

Knowing Mo's history I was very confident that he would also significantly add to my workload as the union rep at Everton. He didn't disappoint. Soon after he had signed, he turned up late for training looking bleary-eyed. That wasn't the problem, the real problem was that he turned up *very* late – it was after training had finished just as we were showering and getting ready to leave. He asked me what he should do. I said I wasn't exactly sure as no one had actually missed an entire day's training here before.

In full union rep mode, I said, 'First go up to see Howard in his office and when you come down fill me in on his reaction. I'll get in touch with the union and we will take it from there. It will probably be a hefty fine, maybe even two weeks' wages which is the legal maximum, but we will try to argue it down a bit. I'll go in and see the boss afterwards.'

Off he went and I waited and waited and waited. I was getting more and more concerned – this was obviously going to get very serious. An hour later Mo came downstairs. 'So what happened then?'

Mo had walked in and Howard had said, 'Happy birthday, let's have

---

* At Everton, it was mooted at one point that we should go on another trip to Northern Ireland to play some local teams and the lads were even asked to have a meeting about what they thought about it. I obviously wasn't concentrating fully as various players made their points. It was agreed we would go, only for a lone Scottish voice to pipe up with a laugh, 'You must be f**king joking!' I spluttered and spat out the tea I was drinking at the thought of Mojo in Belfast and then in bandit country. I'm not sure they had thought that one through too well. Mo didn't go on that trip!

some champagne.' They finished the bottle and that was it. There was no mention whatsoever of the missed training session and they parted on amicable terms. Mo had only four words for me as he staggered out of the door at Bellefield to get in a cab home: 'I love this club!' I was speechless but as the players' rep, it was a great result. Clearly, I didn't appreciate what I thought was more unprofessionalism but on the other hand Mo was well onside with the manager after that. He gave everything he had in every game and in every training session, when he actually got there. So maybe there was some method in the madness after all, sometimes!

Even more than with Mo's arrival, I was hugely impressed that the club had enticed Peter Beardsley to join us from Liverpool. I felt then and still do that he was one of the finest if not the finest English player of his generation. I had played against him at Newcastle and Liverpool, and even then I knew I would love to play in the same team as him. Put him in the modern game at Liverpool or Manchester City and he would be better now than he was then because he would be alongside players who were on his wavelength.

Peter coming was definitely part of the reason I stuck it out for the 1991–92 season at Everton, when, in truth, I should have been preparing to go. I also had my admiration for Colin Harvey who was still there. The fans had been brilliant to me and there was still a connection between us. There was the history of the club which I admired. I always wanted to honour my contracts unless a club wanted to sell me and I still wanted to prove to myself that we could win a trophy or two. Maybe above all that I wanted to play alongside a player I felt a total connection with on the field. Over the years there were very few whose skills I admired to that level, and who I felt I could have a total understanding with on the field. Each in retrospect were ahead of their time. John Collins with Scotland was another one, but there were very few. The English game didn't seem to value these types of players, certainly nowhere near as much as it does today.

The problem was that I had very few opportunities to play alongside Peter that season. I was regularly on the bench and often only given a few minutes at the end of games. Sometimes it even felt like being given those few paltry minutes was a punishment, an attempt to annoy me and provoke a reaction, specifically to put in a transfer request. I was, however, still trying to prove myself in every training session, and even in those few matchday minutes, that I was worthy of a starting place. For me personally it was frustrating and I particularly hated the fact that my dad would travel all the way from Scotland and was hardly seeing me play at all. This was a totally new experience and I was conflicted.

What made it worse is that I felt I was at the peak of my ability, better than I had ever been before because of what I had learned over the years. From being a consistent starter for my entire career suddenly I was in a season where I made only 7 league starts. I did play 23 times altogether with cup games and substitute appearances, but it was nowhere near enough and the joy was being sucked out of it for me – again.

There was one game away from home at Watford when I got a rare start. I thought I played well and laid on the only goal for Beardsley with a through ball he slipped under David James. Afterwards he said to me, 'I would have been proud of that pass.' I took that as the highest compliment! It was the understanding of movement that only two players thinking in a lateral way would have got.*

The final straw came in a league game away at Oldham. Even with Maurice Johnston and Peter Beardsley playing we were behind. I was sent on to help save the day. I made a few chances for both of them but in the end it was me who scored the vital goal. I had chased an errant back pass in the last minute after I gambled that the defender might leave it slightly short. A toe poke just before the keeper got there and we had a precious point.

Going back into the tiny, ancient, wooden dressing room at Boundary Park afterwards I was obviously delighted and thought, *Surely the manager*

---

* Watch De Bruyne and David Silva any time they play and you will get the point. David Silva plays football exactly the way I tried to, and wanted to, play. I would like to underline three times in red, that I am not saying I was in his class as a player, his is simply the style I tried to play.

must give me more of a chance now? His only words to me after winning us a point were, 'Hey, you just got lucky there that the defender made that daft mistake.' Thanks a lot, Gaffer!

I was thankful for that comment because driving home that night I made the decision in my head that my heart had known for a while: *This will never work, I am never going to win Howard over no matter what I do. There is no point carrying on with any hope, it is time to go.*

It was underlined when I was left out again at the weekend away to Arsenal with only a crumb of comfort, getting on as sub for the last seven minutes when we already 4-2 down. I gave everything in those seven short minutes. My attitude was still all about doing the very best I could at every moment, but it was pointless in the long run and I knew it. Even someone as thick as me eventually figures out when he is not wanted, it just took longer than it should have. That delay in getting out certainly damaged my chances of a higher profile next move, something many people warned me about, but I chose to ignore them. A year out of the limelight is a lifetime in top-level football.

29/
WITH A LITTLE HELP FROM MY FRIENDS

There was another problem on the horizon. Euro 92 in Sweden was approaching and this time I really wanted to be part of the Scotland squad. Playing in the tournament and representing my country was of prime importance now and it might not be the worst idea to be in that sort of shop window, in that I was going to need a new club soon.

There had been suggestions in the press that some clubs were interested in buying me but that was in the hands of the club, I still had a year left on my Everton contract. I had no agent, so there was no one out there looking for me and pushing for me. I still felt that my ability should be enough to tempt a decent club. Then a surprising offer arrived out of the blue: Tranmere Rovers wanted to take me on loan for a couple of months beginning in early March 1992. I needed some help, but maybe I could help them too. The Rovers were in the second tier and I have to admit there was a slight problem of status to consider, not in my eyes but, I thought, in the eyes of others: *If I go to this team considered 'unglamorous' by most people, might they think that this is now my level? Will another Premier League outfit come in at the end of the season if they think that is the level that even I rate myself at? If I do well in the second tier, would that even be enough to impress the Scotland manager?*

Lots of friends asked me why I was considering going there, insinuating it was beneath me. I knew I could still play at the top level, but I needed match fitness quickly before the European Championships squad was chosen. I needed to be playing and Scotland manager Andy Roxburgh had made it clear that he couldn't take someone who was only getting a few minutes here and there, even if it was for Everton in the top tier.

It wasn't an easy call to make, so I decided to go over to Birkenhead and talk to the Tranmere manager Johnny King. I would make my mind up using my usual gut instinct. Five minutes with Kingy was enough; he was funny, driven, trustworthy, eccentric, loved football and said the things that I wanted to hear.

'I want you as an attacker, someone who can excite our fans,' he told me. 'We play entertaining, attacking, skilful football here with two wingers and I want you to come and be as creative as you possibly can. Get on the ball as often as you can and just do your thing. When we have the ball, I want you to go where you think you can do damage – you will have that freedom.'

Had he been reading my mind? After the prescriptive play at Everton this was music, sweet music. I totally accepted that Everton had a more regimented style, even if it didn't exactly suit my strengths; it is after all a team sport and you have to sacrifice yourself for the group sometimes. My team ethic always trumped my individual wants during a game if that was what was demanded, as long as the tactics weren't arrant nonsense! This, however, was a golden opportunity to simply go and enjoy it all again on my terms.

Everton often played pre-season friendlies at Prenton Park, so I knew and loved Tranmere's classic old-school stadium. It also helped that it was even closer to our home in Chester than Everton had been, so there was no need to travel or live away from the family. The fact that John Aldridge was there was also a draw. I knew he was an exceptional goalscorer and I thought he was someone I would enjoy creating chances for.*

So the only thing stopping me going to Prenton Park then was snobbery and that wasn't happening from my end! That sealed it. I decided to go for a couple of months and give myself a chance of reaching the Euros, a chance to enjoy playing football again and a chance to let people know that I hadn't lost anything.

As I pulled on my boots for the first training session I thought it might be tricky adjusting to a different, lower standard at Tranmere. I had been used to the international stage and the top of the English game, with decent technical players all around me. After all, it was only little old Tranmere Rovers, so surely I would have to cut them some slack for their limitations?

Before the week was out, I had gone home exclaiming to my wife, and anyone else who would listen, 'Some of the players at Tranmere Rovers are fantastic!' The former top-level players who had dropped down maybe weren't a surprise to me but the youngsters coming through were superb, this was one very good side. In fact, they did not seem any weaker than a lot of the sides I played against in the top flight. Certainly, for levels of pure skill, they weren't of a lower standard at all. There also appeared to be an excellent team spirit – what a joy!

The top level had gone very much towards the power-play style. Back then Crystal Palace, Wimbledon and the likes of Sheffield Wednesday were all having success with physicality and more direct football. They had good players as well, but the emphasis had become very much the old British style. The POMO ideology hadn't died, it had just evolved ever so slightly. Playing the ball long and getting it 'in the mixer' quickly was still a central part of the game; pace and power had become king for many clubs. I personally wouldn't have wasted an afternoon watching

---

* After working with him for just a short while, I realised he wasn't an exceptional goalscorer, he was far better than that, he was a world-class finisher – and I do not use that phrase lightly.

that type of football, even though I accepted it could be successful. Thank goodness there were one or two teams that didn't play that way in the nascent Premier League.

The hype surrounding the new league model was extraordinary, and the public bought into it, so well done building the sport into the international business it became. With my background in economics I openly admired that business model even if I wasn't mad on the product itself.*

The long-ball game wasn't a likelihood at Tranmere although figuring out what the manager wanted wasn't always easy either during the eight games I had signed up for. The team talks seemed to be more like riddles than conventional 'up and at 'em' speeches. Tactics were barely discussed compared to Everton but it was the mass of mixed metaphors that left everyone in the room baffled. Having read a bit of everything from George Orwell to James Joyce, I was happy to search for sense in the similes but in the end, I drew a blank with Kingy. He was the master of the mixed metaphor.

'We are on a rocket trip to the moon, lads, but there are dangers on the way. It is a long journey, we are rocket-propelled but anything could go wrong at any minute. We have the navigational skills to find our way

---

* The more simplistic, long-ball, power-play game is a perfectly understandable method if you haven't got enough skilful players to compete. Maybe you just do not have the money, the time, or inclination to buy technical players. The patience to deal with some of them and their foibles or indeed an ability to develop them isn't easy either. Using physique first is an easier, quicker method and it makes business sense too. It is just that I do not find it a particularly interesting style to watch and never have. It doesn't make it wrong. The phrase 'playing football the right way', when you have a talented, skilful team out there, is nonsensical – it is just a preference. If the team I supported won trophies using long-ball football alone, however, I would be happy for them, but I wouldn't be tempted to go along and watch them. Some fans are committed to their teams, whatever the style; the feeling of belonging is just as valid as any other consideration. I need to be entertained to go along with it fully.

through it all. There could be bad weather on this voyage and on those high seas we might even hit some rocks on the road to success, but if we crash on the road we have plenty of fuel in the tank…'

Wait a minute, I thought we were on a rocket to the moon? Did he mean we might hit the rocks on the Sea of Tranquillity? And where does the road come in?

Nobody piped up but we were all thinking the same thing. Even though I didn't know what he was talking about, I personally loved these stream of consciousness rambles. Johnny King may have loved an unfathomable team talk but he also had that core ability to put a good, balanced team out on the field with committed, talented players, which was far, far more important.

I enjoyed those eight games of my loan spell enormously. Aldo had scored 40 goals that season which was not an unusual haul for him at Tranmere. They had knocked Chelsea and Newcastle United (after a 6-6 draw!) out of the cups and it was clear this was a very good group. With John Morrissey, a very skilful winger and huge character, on the right wing and myself on the left there were a lot of chances created for Aldo and his hard-working, selfless striking partner Chris Malkin. Ian Muir was a player I hadn't heard of before I went there; I soon realised I should have been paying more attention. He was a super striker who would have played every week and scored plenty had Aldo not been breaking records all over the place.

Of the youngsters I thought were very good, the vast majority eventually went on to be sold for large sums to clubs who were in the Premier League at the time, so my hunch was correct. Ged Brannan (sold to Manchester City), Steve Vickers (Middlesbrough), Tony Thomas (Everton), John McGreal (Ipswich Town), Ian Nolan (Sheffield Wednesday) and Alan Rodgers (Nottingham Forest) each made the step up. Others were to follow through what was a superb youth development and scouting system at the time run brilliantly by Warwick Rimmer.

The plan worked a treat. There were games against good-sized clubs such as Newcastle and Leicester. I had great fun, I made a few goals for

Aldo and others, Andy Roxburgh took note and I was back in the Scottish international fold, though still far from certain of getting in the final squad of twenty-three for Sweden. There were a few more hurdles to cross before that happened but it had been the right decision to go to Tranmere in the short term.

The two months were a great release for me, and by the time I headed back to Goodison I had only a few weeks left of my Everton season. To my total amazement I walked straight back into the first team. They had been struggling and were now languishing below mid-table. I managed to score against Manchester City and made a few more goals, but I knew that nothing was likely to change in the long term. The mood music from the manager wasn't good. In fact, the question I asked myself was, *Am I getting a chance here, or are they just getting me fit and in the limelight, so I am more sellable?*

My final game for Everton was at Goodison Park and fittingly it was against Chelsea in the last match of the season. We won 2-1 but the enduring moment happened late on when I beat Erland Johnsen with an outrageous dummy at pace, swivelled past another defender and then tricked the keeper before calmly stroking it past him, only for it to scrape past after hitting the post. It would have been one of the best goals of my professional career, instead it was a perfect metaphor for my entire period at Everton – so close but not quite the success I had wanted. I had a year left on my contract, but Howard made it clear he was not going to use me often if at all next season. It was a sad day walking off the field knowing in my heart it would be for the last time in an Everton shirt.

30/
TAKE A CHANCE ON ME

The season was finished for Everton but not for me. Scotland had to decide which twenty-three players to take to Sweden for the European Championships. It had been a year since I last played for my country and that was in an away game at little San Marino. To everyone's shock, half-time came and went with the scoreline still 0-0. One of Scotland's great sports journalists Ian Archer famously said, 'I looked at my watch and suddenly realised that after an hour of play we were still drawing 0-0 against the top of a mountain.'

I knew I could fix it; Andy Roxburgh often used me as the key to unpick those kinds of intricate locks. There were always at least nine defenders between us and the goal, even when they were allegedly attacking, so it needed imagination. I came on, managed to wriggle through their defence and as I was just about to score I was tackled agriculturally to win a penalty.*

Against those types of defenders, I had a major advantage: I knew

---

* I was brought down for penalties for Scotland against San Marino, Luxembourg, Estonia and the CIS. And should have got a few more – where was VAR when I needed it? I claim those penalties as assists!

they didn't have the 'quick feet' I had. The idea was to run at pace with the ball close to me and use my skill to tempt their clumsy (though this time quite violent) tackles. There was always a decent likelihood of a penalty in the circumstances, whether they meant it or not. It worked, Gordon Strachan scored from the spot, we won 2-0. Even so, I hadn't had another chance for twelve long months. So it was a pleasant surprise when the door to Sweden was opened ever so slightly.

There were a couple of games arranged in North America as a warm-up and an opportunity to help Andy Roxburgh make his final decisions on the last couple of available squad positions. The first was in Denver against the US and the second v Canada in Toronto. The deal was obvious, if I played well over there, then I was certain to get in the squad.

I wasn't the only one trying for the last few available places; another was twenty-year-old Duncan Ferguson, then playing for Dundee United. I had come across Big Dunc already on a previous Scotland get-together a couple of years before. Back then I was part of the squad but this very young kid was brought along to acquaint himself with the national set-up. Playing down south I knew nothing about his progress; I found out quickly enough.

In the first training session Dunc and I were on the same side. I got the ball and beat a few players but was tackled and it went out of play. From thirty yards away Big Dunc called to me while beckoning with his forefinger, the way a particularly arrogant billionaire would call over a waiter: 'Wee man, cm'ere.'

I walked over slowly, curious as to what the young newcomer to the group had to say.

'See when you get the ball, wee man, look up and give to someone who can play, someone like me.'

The phrase 'You couldn't give him a brass neck with a blow torch' immediately sprang to mind. It is one of the more offensive things to say to any pro, even those with limited ability. I would hope I was one of the more skilful players in the group, so to hear that could have annoyed, offended or even angered me. It wasn't meant to be funny; he was clearly serious. Like with Gazza many years before, I thought, *I think I might enjoy hanging around someone like this, someone who clearly has absolutely no filter. I like to be entertained by odd characters and even if there is some danger involved, he is a very promising study.*

By the time we were in America in May 1992, the big man's notoriety had grown considerably and I found him even more intriguing. During a training session at a college football park before the big game against the USA in Denver, Colorado, Duncan was playing up front. As ever the defenders were lumping the ball in his general direction, expecting to see the usual all-action battling style that he was already famous for.

Instead of fighting, battling and chasing, the big man was just watching the ball sail over his head with little or no reaction other than a shrug of the shoulders. He would have shown more interest if a pigeon glided by, but then he was a pigeon fancier in those days. Andy Roxburgh and his then assistant Craig Brown were sticklers for everything being just so, spick and span and all in order. From players training hard to making sure your socks were smartly pulled up, things had to be done right. This negligent approach from the big man just would not do at all – his shirt wasn't even tucked in! The problem was that this attitude had never been encountered by either coach at international level, so there was a dilemma for a few moments while they considered what to say.

Before they could figure it out, Duncan just sauntered off to the side and sat in the small stand talking to a couple of very bonny-looking local student girls. Roxy and Broon, as they were affectionately known, were aghast. From about fifty yards away they shouted to him, 'What's going on, Duncan?'

Big Dunc didn't even deign to stop his conversation, in fact he seemed surprised and slightly annoyed by the intrusion. Instead he held out a hand in their general direction and without turning away from the girls he shouted, 'Ach, sair tae.' And carried on with the chat to his 'lassies'.

The correct thing to do when you have a 'sair tae' (or indeed a sore toe) during training, is ask the manager if you may leave the field of play and go to see the physio or the doctor. Duncan would have to be managed differently from everyone else, but he had enough ability to be worth the effort, for some managers anyway.

I was given a start on the right wing against the USA and with the likes of Brian McClair, Paul McStay, Gary McAllister and Ally McCoist also playing, it would be a great chance to impress. If I could make a goal or two for them, things would look rosy.

On the positive side we won 1-0, I scored the only goal, it was a good one in the top corner from twenty yards and I was also presented with the MVP (Most Valuable Player) award after the game. Typically understated, the Americans had inscribed on the trophy, 'The World Series of Soccer MVP'.*

On the downside, with about half an hour to go I got the ball out wide and had a problem. I could see the USA midfielder Dominic Kinnear (a fellow Scot by birth) coming in from an angle as I beat their full-back. I had talked to Dominic before the game; I was at school with his cousin Maureen back in Scotland and she was a good friend. He seemed a good chap and as such I expected him to slow down and jockey. Instead he flew in at full speed two-footed and went straight over the ball.

I knew I was quite badly injured because there was a lot of pain and I couldn't put weight on the leg, but I wasn't aware at that point he had broken my fibula just above the ankle – it was a stress fracture if we are going to be pedantic. I hobbled off, thinking it was just a bad knock and that it would recover in time for Sweden. I was a quick healer after all, as my previous return after the ACL injury showed.

---

* A year later I went to see a film by Mike Myers (he of *Wayne's World* and *Austin Powers* fame) called *So I Married an Axe Murderer*. Annabel and I sat in the cinema in Chester laughing at a great movie when I suddenly realised, 'Hey wait a minute, that goal they are celebrating and watching on TV was the winner I scored against the US.' My one and only claim to fame that I am really proud of, is being just the tiniest part of a Hollywood movie, and a good one too. It is arguably the funniest scene in the film with 'Heed' in front of the telly! I will not send Mike Myers the bill but if he sends a bottle of Opus One, I'll be sure to toast him.

I was replaced by Duncan Ferguson, coming on for his Scottish international debut. What a huge moment for the youngster. It was a chance to show his quality and maybe even get a seat on the plane to Gothenburg. However, he didn't appear to have the usual reaction of a player pulling on that blue shirt for the first time. Once again there was a distinct lack of the Braveheart spirit from our warrior striker. To all of us on the bench, his look was bordering on disinterested.

At the end I hobbled to the 'locker room', as they say in the States, and sat there with everyone else waiting for the debrief. I was pleased because I knew I had probably done enough to ensure a ticket to Gothenburg and was relaxed as Roxy went around the group liberally using the matey nicknames:

'Marsh [Gordon Marshall]] – well done on the clean sheet…Slim [Davie McPherson] – top defending…Hat [Paul McStay] – great control of the game…'and I was given the positive nod too.

By the time he was saying well done to Choccy (Brian McClair) we had all realised that he was going to have to say something to Big Dunc, who really hadn't made much of an effort. This would be interesting and enlightening.

Andy started on an affable note: 'Duncan, erm, is everything OK? Are you injured, what was wrong out there?'

'Ach nothin' wrang Gaffer, ah just cannae get massel up fur these f***in' park gemms.'

Yes, it was a friendly but this 'park game' was an international fixture, his debut for his country and his chance to make the Euros. Amazingly, Duncan still made it into the squad for Sweden. The raw talent was in there somewhere and maybe the European Championships were sufficient incentive to pique his interest.

There was another game against Canada four days later, which I clearly wouldn't be fit for, but there was also a bit of R&R time to be enjoyed. Big Dunc creased me up time and again without ever being aware of his unintentional inner comedian. We were in a classy joint in Chicago and there was a beautiful, sophisticated-looking woman sitting at the bar.

She was probably the CEO of a multinational FTSE 100 company, totally unapproachable to most mere mortals, I suspect even George Clooney would have flinched at making a pass. Not Duncan, however; he walked over to the bar – a pint of heavy was to be his refined refreshment. He then casually turned to the goddess and delivered his urbane opening gambit: 'Hey hen, whaur d'ye bide?'

A rough translation would be: 'Excuse me madam, where do you live/come from?' She was baffled and had no idea he was speaking English, which I suppose he wasn't really. The barman was similarly confused and even quite upset: he thought he had heard of every sophisticated drink in the business, but this was new to him.

Some would laugh at this inability to see how ridiculous his delivery was, but I truly admired his unwillingness to be anything other than himself. He stayed that way through his entire career.

I knew that feeling well, of the importance of being true to yourself, even if it was manifest in a different way. I continued to watch and listen to Duncan over the years to track his astounding and unpredictable progress through football and life. Maybe the biggest surprise, after unacceptably assaulting another player and ending up in jail, was the sensible assistant coach he eventually became. When I meet him now the question in my head is always the same: *Who are you and what have you done with Big Dunc?*

There was another night out, but this time it was an official function for Scotland's kit sponsors, Umbro. Partway through the evening Andy Roxburgh called me over to his table where he was sitting with the head of Umbro USA. The confident CEO immediately took control of the conversation with his American drawl.

'Well done scoring the winner against us, young man, but I was looking forward to meeting you anyway. We had some videos sent over from Scotland showing your fantastic ball-juggling skills.'*

---

* I had made some videos for the Scottish Football Association aimed at helping anyone from the coaches to young pros to disabled footballers. I did this for free as it was a good cause.

Mr Executive Umbro US continued: 'We took some of those clips and used them in our nationwide TV campaign with you sitting down keeping the ball up, then we spliced it to show the ball going from you to Pelé and then on to Mia Hamm, the top women's player in the US. It looked great and was a very popular ad.'

Andy could see in my eyes exactly what I was thinking. I am no bread-head, but if they are using my image and ball skills in a US-wide TV advertising campaign, first they probably should have had the decency to ask me and secondly, do you reckon Pelé and Mia gave their images for free?

The manager spotted my furrowed brow and slits for eyes but gave me a look as if to say, 'Just leave it this time Pat, please?' I wasn't in a strong bargaining position, still hoping to be picked for the squad, so I walked off and left it at that. Back at my table, I explained to my mate Brian McClair what had just happened. He contemplated for a moment.

'Tricky position,' he said. 'Do you know who is paying for dinner tonight?'

I replied, 'You know fine well it's Umbro, why do you ask?'

With his usual monotone deadpan voice Brian said, 'It was rhetorical.' Just then he slid the wine list towards me and opened it at the back page. This was where all the most expensive wines were listed. We ordered a couple of bottles of Opus One, which now would cost about £1,000 each in a decent restaurant, as payment for my work for Umbro. It was as delicious as it should have been.

There were now only three weeks until the start of the Euros and I had a very sore leg. At first, I couldn't run on it, a week later I could just about jog but the idea of kicking the ball, with what was my stronger right foot, was unthinkable due to the pain. I had an X-ray but no fracture showed up, so it surely was only severe bruising.

Andy was happy to pick me for the squad expecting it to clear up at any moment. The crack eventually showed up later in another X-ray after the tournament, so I didn't know it was 'broken' at the time, but it wasn't going to stop me anyway. For a kick-off we had been drawn in an incredible group with Germany who had Jürgen Klinsmann, Matthias Sammer, Karl-Heinz Riedle, Andreas Brehme and Stefan Effenberg; and the Netherlands who could boast world-class players such as Ruud Gullit, Marco van Basten, Frank Rijkaard, Dennis Bergkamp, Ronald Koeman and a whole bunch of other stars too. Even the CIS (who briefly went under that transitional banner between being the Soviet Union and then Russia) had Alexei Mikhailichenko, Dmitri Kuznetsov, Andrei Kanchelskis and Dmitri Kharine in goal. I was desperate to have a go at them all. Considering that my career and the careers of many others in England had been blighted by the European club ban, this was a chance to play against these great players and judge myself. It would help if I was actually able to kick a football though.

By the time the first game against the Netherlands arrived I knew that kicking the ball more than twenty yards was going to be impossible, but really, did I need to kick it that far? Running wasn't a problem, I could dribble pain-free, play little tiki-taka passes, even if the term hadn't been invented yet. I could manage and in training nobody seemed to notice my discomfort! The biggest problem was that I generally took the corner kicks in most teams I played for, but I managed to surreptitiously relieve myself of those duties – I couldn't get close to kicking it that far. If we got a corner, I suddenly found that my bootlaces needed urgent attention, so someone else had to go over to take it. I also told my mate Brian McClair of my dilemma so he agreed to come over and offer himself for a short corner if I was marooned by the flag.

The first game against the Netherlands in Gothenburg was obviously going to be a fairly defensive affair on Scotland's behalf, so I didn't expect to be in the starting line-up. The Dutch were most people's favourites for the tournament and the thinking from Andy Roxburgh was mostly about holding out and maybe sneaking a draw. Goram, Gough, McKimmie and co. fought valiantly, but after seventy-five minutes Dennis Bergkamp broke through our defences. I was on the bench and it was common for me to be brought on as a wild card late on either to salvage the game or just as a last throw of the dice. This time I wasn't called on and for once

I didn't mind; the injury meant I was well short of 100 per cent. There was no shame in losing 1-0 to the Dutch and most aficionados felt the tactics had been sensible. But it did make the next one against Germany a 'must win' game if we were going to have a chance of getting through to the semi-finals.

The Dutch fans had been loud and noisy as they always are, but the Tartan Army of Scotland fans were incredible. They were a new generation who unlike the old days in 1978 didn't expect to win the World Cup or those in 1975 who would tear up stadiums like Wembley and leave a trail of destruction, while always smiling as they did so. This group were fun-loving fans who just wanted to see a decent performance, witness a good level of effort and have a good time on their travels into the bargain. The new realism was mostly due to the wise words spoken by Jock Stein when he had taken over after the 1978 Argentinian debacle. On top of that, if their good-natured behaviour made the England fans, who weren't anywhere near us, look bad in comparison, then all the better!

The German fans in Norrköping were easily out-sung by our noisy tartan wall. Again, we were to start off cautiously in a tactical sense, but there were discussions within the group, if not quite grumblings, that maybe we should have a bit more of a go at Germany right from the off. Although playing quite well we paid the price for our negativity by conceding goals to Riedle in the first half and then Effenberg just after half-time. We were all a bit miffed on that bench. We played for domestic teams who weren't fearful of anyone and couldn't care less if West Germany had won the World Cup two years earlier, we wanted to get 'intae' them and have a go.

With nothing then to lose, the team was finally let loose and we hammered the Germans in that second half. Sadly, we just couldn't get that first goal back, one which might have spooked them. I got on for the last forty minutes of the game and even though I couldn't kick the ball far, getting past players and creating chances turned out not to be a problem.

Ultimately it was hugely disappointing and, because of the other results, we were already out of the competition before the last game against the CIS. Once again Scotland had failed to get through the group stage and we felt we had let those brilliant fans down. They were having none of it, because they could see the effort and they understood that it was as tough a group draw as you could get; against the current world champions and the European champions. Certainly there was no embarrassment.

It wasn't cheap surviving in Sweden and some of those fans had spent a huge amount of money just getting there. Fortunately, Andy Roxburgh had his finger on the pulse and knew what to do. After the Germany game he got us all together and asked if we wouldn't mind going down to mingle with and say hi to the fans who were camping in a local park in what were pretty basic conditions. I have a clear memory of our huge coach arriving in the gloaming (early evening sunset) and us walking into a camp with small fires all around that many of the fans were cooking on. The atmosphere was warm and quiet, with a soft red haze covering the entire area. It was not unlike a scene after a battle in the movie *Braveheart*, except with actual Scottish people involved. Slowly the thousands there spotted us and came walking towards the team. It was a lovely moment, there was no screaming and shouting or overexcitement. The feeling was more like bumping into a bunch of old mates that you hadn't seen for a while. We chatted, laughed and I think a real bond was put in place on that day. It certainly was from the players' side; we had all agreed to go down to that gathering that evening and every one of us seemed moved.

The last game against the CIS was played back in Norrköping and with no pressure on us we cruised to a 3-0 win. That wasn't bad considering they had drawn with Germany and the mighty star-studded Dutch side beforehand. There is a moment that slightly gives away my predicament at the time, however. On at last as sub I picked up the ball on the left wing well inside my own half. I dribbled all the way to their eighteen-yard box where I was brought down for a penalty kick. It was considered a rather fine run at the time but in fact there were no Scotland players within twenty yards of me at any point, so I couldn't pass it even if I'd wanted to – it would have been too painful. Gary McAllister scored from the spot. It was only twenty-five years later when I gave a speech at the Royal College of Physicians in Edinburgh about coping with injuries, that Stewart Hillis (the team doctor) and Craig Brown found out that I had been playing with a 'broken' leg; they had no idea.

There was a final confusing moment as we were about to trudge off. Roxy said we should go and celebrate with our fans behind the goal following our win. Gary McAllister turned round indignantly, saying, 'Are you joking? We are out, we lost the tournament. What is there to celebrate?' In that moment I felt the same; we had failed even if we had just won 3-0. But we did relent and walked down to applaud and thank those fans who had made the journey, which in retrospect was exactly the right thing to do.

Something exceptional had been happening between the Scotland squad and our fans. Previously there had been the normal 'distance' that there usually is between any set of players and their followers. Some players unsurprisingly find it hard to be too close to a group of people who give them dog's abuse when things go wrong, but this moment seemed to cement a new special relationship which was much closer and changed attitudes. The squad and the fans seemed more like a single united team after that. Andy Roxburgh had engineered an understanding that we were just like those fans and they were just like us. Bringing the players closer to the fans by encouraging more and closer interaction, was a stroke of genius that had a huge and lasting positive effect. The Tartan Army had our backs from then on as long as the effort was there and the squad didn't appear distant or aloof.

The sad reality in the short term, however, was that we were going home and I had no idea where I would be playing or indeed living the next season. I was sure I wouldn't be at Everton, but other than that I couldn't tell. I had heard rumours on the grapevine that clubs such as West Ham were interested, but with a year left on my contract and still refusing to have an agent, all I could do was sit tight and wait and see. After a while it boiled down to a simple choice. Well, not simple, it was anything but simple, however, it was a straight either/or.

31/
NEVER UNDERSTAND

Tranmere Rovers wanted to sign me on a three-year deal and there were plenty of positives there: a good team, youngsters who were improving, a style I enjoyed playing and a coaching staff I liked. The fans had also clearly taken to me while I was on loan and there was a lovely family feel to the entire club. Annabel, Simon and I would not need to move from Chester, as Birkenhead was only a thirty-five-minute drive from our home there. It didn't sound glamorous from the outside, but I had never cared for glamour – the entire celebrity 'thing' had always made me feel queasy.

I have never understood that entire weird celebrity concept and the effect it has on people. The reason why some 'stars' behave in an egotistical way and have a detached-from-reality outlook is because the media and the public treat them differently. Just be normal with people and if they are put out by that, then they aren't worthy of your consideration anyway. Simple? Well, that is how I have got by when meeting famous or prominent people in all walks of life.

With my distrust of fame and what I considered the less important effect 'status' should play in my life, signing for Tranmere didn't pose any problems. The money was fine – not great, not terrible but it was comfortable. I would be leaving the top level in the year the new Premier

League was starting. I didn't know then that the financial impact would be so considerable as the wages in that league were about to go stratospheric, but it wouldn't have changed anything for me. The other option had to be checked out in person and it had to be done as a family.

Remember the game against Galatasaray for Everton with the rampaging fans? Well they remembered and they got back in touch through my old mate and Chelsea nut, Vince Cooper. The club asked if we could pop over to Istanbul for a discreet chat and to have a nice little low-key look around. Istanbul is a great city, so I said we would love to. A couple of days later we flew into Atatürk airport. I was rocking my usual travel-worn unkempt look, that is to say I was a scruff. Annabel was a little stressed caring for one-year-old Simon who was showing none of his future fascination for aeroplanes. As we waited to disembark there appeared to be a commotion outside. I thought, *there must be someone famous on board as there are TV cameras and dozens of press men standing outside, right there on the tarmac. This is a nightmare – we are never going to get Simon's buggy through that scrum. Bleedin' celebrities!*

It was a bit of a shock then, when it became clear that the celebrity they were waiting for was me! This was madness but it was only the beginning. There was a totally unexpected press conference hurriedly set up on the concourse and a difficult moment when I was presented with a Galatasaray shirt and asked to put it on for the photos. I couldn't do that as I was still officially an Everton player, but my reticence still offended some of the people there. An equally unexpected moment came when a limo arrived to whisk us off with no consideration of passport control or customs. To add to the general chaos, hundreds of Gala fans had turned up to welcome their new 'star' player. It was pandemonium with flags, banners and the obligatory rent-a-crowd shouting in front of the cameras. This was not what we originally agreed, or what Annabel and I expected or wanted.

We finally got out of the airport and sped across town, still a little alarmed, before being deposited in a plush hotel suite. We were then taken to the stadium for a quick look, over to the training ground to check out the facilities there and then on to the Galatasaray players' island. We were happy enough with a players' 'bar' back in the UK; giving them their own island was a classy touch. The next day was set aside for negotiations even though I explained from the start that 'this is only supposed to be a look around for us'. The sales pitch started immediately, the hard sell was continuous and unforgiving to a degree that would make a used car salesman sound like a Cistercian monk.

The club president had summoned me to his huge office to make his first offer. It was far more lavish than Tranmere's obviously, though there were some smoke and mirrors being suggested with the taxes. Apparently, this was not uncommon! I didn't like the sound of that one little bit, but I listened on. There would be a beautiful flat overlooking the Bosphorus and a BMW of my own to get me to and from training. I listened politely and thanked him.

'I will have to talk to my wife about it back at the hotel,' I added. 'Remember I am here just to have a look around, to consider everything but not to sign a contract right away. You have to get that into your head.'

'You must sign now!' he insisted.

'I can't do that because it is a family decision. I'll just leave now and talk to my wife.'

'You cannot leave!' he barked with more than a hint of menace. As he said that the two burly henchmen who had been trying, and spectacularly failing, to look inconspicuous in the corner, stood between me and the door, bulging forearms folded.

'Am I being kidnapped or just held against my will?' I tried to make that sound chirpy but was by now getting a bit irritated. In a not untypical way in that part of the world the president changed tack in a heartbeat.

'We are friends,' he said, his arm around me. 'Come and sit down, have some tea and cake, we are just doing the business, this is how it works. You haven't even come back with what you would like yet after my first offer.'

It initially threw him when I said I wouldn't be coming back with any counter-suggestions.

I said frankly, 'Look, just make me your best offer and if it is good enough and we are happy to come, we will.'

I was trying my best to explain that my methods were different from most, Colin Harvey had got it a few years before...But this approach was completely alien to him. He couldn't understand my position and was racking his brains for the catch. After a few moments' total confusion, he gave up trying to figure it out and regained his sales pitch momentum.

'You know we want you to be the provider for our new star striker Hakan Şükür.'

I had to admit that was quite a good pitch, Şükür was a top player in the making and I really thought we could work well together. What's more they wanted me as a number 10, none of this standing out on the wing stuff that I was obliged to do in England. Suddenly he had my attention – and then he took it too far again.

'What we really want is for you to come here and win us the UEFA Cup.'

That was quite a big ask coming right off the bat and I was back in the mad reality of the moment. There is a line to be drawn between healthy self-belief and dangerous self-delusion. I hope I know roughly where the line should sensibly be drawn.

'Actually, I really ought to go now, I need a word with my wife.'

'You are not going anywhere!' The muscle at the door suddenly regained their poses, delighted to be back in service but trying hard not to show it.

'What?'

After what seemed like hours of to-ing and fro-ing, out of the blue he suddenly said, 'You can go now.'

'So why the change all of a sudden?' It seemed strange.

'Well, it is after 5pm and the European deadline has passed for the first round of the UEFA Cup. You had to sign for us before then to play in it.'

'So, I take it the deal is off now?'

'Not at all, when you sign tomorrow you can play in the next round.'

'How can you know you will be in the next round?'

'Trust me, I know.'

The next day there was yet more pressure which although from their position may have felt like showing a real desire to sign me, was just irking me. I made no demands, but their 'final' offer was improved twice even though I asked for nothing more. My *Life of Brian*-like refusal to haggle was clearly bewildering them, but I just wanted time at home to think and talk about it. Just before I left, they asked what my biggest concern was about signing. I put my cards on the table, explaining that leaving home would not be easy for my wife who was close to her family. For my part I loved the prospect of adventure and the idea of living in different exotic cities around the world.

They immediately had the answer.

'She doesn't need to live in Istanbul – why don't you just commute from London? You could fly out each week three days before the game, train with the team and as soon as the weekend game is over, you could fly back again, a fast car will be waiting to get you to the airport or a motorbike if you like, we have close ties with the airlines, it is no problem.'

It seemed a wild and exotic idea, though plenty of people live in London and commute to New York these days. Just now I live in Scotland but work in London, but back then it did seem a very jet-setty and impossibly glamorous lifestyle.

There was another and bigger consideration: my mother had been diagnosed with cancer and the prognosis wasn't good. If I was in Turkey it would limit my time with her and just as importantly limit the time she would be able to spend with her new grandson Simon. This may even have been the biggest factor when the decision was finally made a couple of days later.

When Galatasaray called, I said, 'I have been sorely tempted but I am afraid I have decided to sign for Tranmere Rovers.'

'Who?!'

It really seemed to upset them that I chose a team they had never even heard of, instead of the mighty Galatasaray. The president sounded confused and tried to understand.

'What about our history, the trophies we win, the 30,000 fans packed into our magnificent stadium every week? What about European football, the derbies against Beşiktaş and Fenerbahçe? Is it the car? We can make it a convertible Mercedes. Is it the flat? We can make it a house overlooking the Bosphorus. Is it the money? We will double the last offer and make it all tax free.'

It was time for straight talking. 'I am afraid it is none of that and thank you so much for your generosity, but it really is about the love of the game and the beauty of my life here and my family.'

A moment's silence and then, 'You come back to Turkey tonight and take one look over the Bosphorus and you will see beauty.'

'As it happens, I had a look over the Mersey recently', I replied, 'and I prefer that.'

Clearly this was the ultimate insult. He hung up without saying goodbye.

32/
FERRY 'CROSS THE MERSEY

With a year still left on my Everton contract and the decision made that I would like to make the short journey across the Mersey and sign for Tranmere Rovers, the only way to ensure I could leave was to put in a transfer request.*

I hated the idea of leaving a year early and not seeing my contract through. A contract was more than an agreement as I have said; it was to my mind a bond of honour on both sides. I had never done this before, but it was a huge moral dilemma for me. Before painting myself as the perfect principled peacock, if you ask for a transfer, the other not inconsiderable downside is that you forgo your right to any remaining signing-on fees and, if appropriate, loyalty bonuses.

It was a wrench, but I felt this is what Everton were waiting for

---

* Everyone apparently slaps in a transfer request. I decided it would make a nice change to hand it in politely in person to the Everton manager after the first day back at training.

me to do. I was finally willing to hand over that short letter, to ensure I got a quick and smooth move. I expected Everton to play that game to maximise their position financially and I understood that was a perfectly reasonable position to take. I wouldn't be asking for a single penny from them when I left.

I went into Howard Kendall's office and handed him the transfer request; his position amazed me.

'I am pretty sure I can't see that envelope and it might be a good idea if you put that back in your pocket. The deal with Tranmere will go through anyway so there is no need to hand that in…whatever it is.'

He knew exactly what it was and instead of playing hard ball, he was allowing me to keep that lump sum of signing-on fees as a parting gift. It was an unexpected and welcome kindness. There was absolutely no benefit to Howard in doing that and considering we had little in common and rarely saw eye to eye on just about anything, it was handsome of him.

I believe I had behaved like a perfect pro throughout, always working hard, always being available and most importantly showing him that I wanted to be useful to the club whenever I was needed whatever the circumstances. I put up with being sat on the bench, given a couple of minutes here and there, but even if it meant warming up throughout the entire second half to show my willingness and readiness then not getting on at all, I would do the right thing however miffed I was inside or however cheated I felt. This generosity might well have been Howard's recognition that I had always done the right thing, even if he didn't think I was right for the team.

He also recognised that I hadn't gone moaning to the press or created any bad feeling within the camp, so maybe he was impressed by that even if he wasn't impressed with my playing style. I will never know as Howard has now sadly passed away and is rightly missed by all Everton fans for what he did as a player and as a manager, especially in his first spell.

I was unhappy to leave Everton for a variety of reasons. I liked the club as an idea; it felt like the people's club. I admired the fans for their football knowledge and was thankful for their kindness to me. I can never really remember a complaint directed towards me personally, though I am sure there were a few in the crowd at times, but they were an understanding group in general. What's a shame is that I also felt that I hadn't maximised my potential at the club, but it certainly wasn't through lack of effort on my part and I hope it was circumstances more than anything else that led to that.

I played in 150 games but only had 113 starts scoring 21 goals. If I bend those stats in my favour, then 21 from 113 is a strike rate of around one goal in every five games, a level I felt comfortable with. Some of the sub appearances were only for a few minutes anyway…But am I trying a little too hard to justify myself here? Probably – it is a natural thing for people to do and I accept that others might have looked at it differently. So long as I was creating goals at a better rate than one in five, then I was OK with the numbers.

Leaving the club was the right thing to do but it was still sad. So what would I miss most? The staff at the training ground and at Goodison were unstintingly helpful and friendly. I now get on well with just about every player from that time, whether they were oldies or newbies, whether they rated me as useless and self-indulgent or I thought they were past their best, lazy and living on former glories. It seems a simple thing but playing at that beautiful stadium on that immaculately maintained, almost manicured, pitch was an immense pleasure and I was going to miss it.

Over and above that, the importance of the happiness that the ever-friendly Everton fans gave my father on his weekly trips to the games is incalculable to me. I always wanted to make my father happy and he loved the people, the place, the banter and the wit of the Toffees. They might not always know this is the case and the Scousers get enough rubbish thrown at them, but the way they welcome outsiders is second to none. They made me and my family feel at home and for that I cannot thank them enough.

When I did walk away it dawned on me that for all the twists and turns, when I stripped it back it had been incredibly similar to my five years at Chelsea. A really good initial period under a manager who I liked and respected and who rated me. When the management changed suddenly my style was not required. I didn't become a poorer player overnight, it was just circumstances and that is very common in the game. There was also the deterioration of team spirit that seemed to be as important as anything else in the downfall of both teams. You often hear players and managers talking about great team spirit and its importance – they are not exaggerating. I discovered that having a closely bonded group was rarer than I had expected, and that it is very hard to build but incredibly easy to destroy.

There are so many different characters, personalities and relationships at a football club it should not be a surprise that it is hard to maintain the right outlook from everyone. After all, only eleven players can be on the field at one time and all the others are almost certain to be a bit put out. That is when management is important and in football there are fewer who are truly proficient in this area than you might think.*

I was going to work for John King now, who valued my abilities and seemed to share my feelings about the game to some degree. I had spent a couple of months there and the spirit was good, I just hoped Kingy would stick around for a while – I didn't need another managerial change!

The next time I met Howard Kendall it changed everything between us. Each pre-season Everton would play Tranmere Rovers at Prenton Park in a friendly. One of my first outings for the Rovers would be against my former club. There was a moment in the second half when I was running up the wing at full speed being jostled by, I think, Andy Hinchcliffe. He nudged me and sent me flying towards the away dugout at full speed. I couldn't slow down and all I could see directly in front of me was Howard

---

* These days there are no excuses for poor management skills; there are management courses, libraries full of books on the subject and plenty of online talks. Have a listen to the ideas of the New Zealand rugby team from their great days and you will not go far wrong. For greatness you must have good values and understand the dichotomy of demanding the very best from yourself but also having the humility to know that, however good you are, you are only part of a team.

sitting, unable to move. My only way to stop now was to put my boot with six large metal studs up towards his head level and crunch it with a bang into the back of the dugout, deciding at the last second to miss his face by inches. I could have just about taken his head off!

I got up, uninjured, looked at Howard's startled face behind me as I jogged off and said, 'Tempted!' He beamed a smile and then laughed.

I had to do the same and winked back.

Epilogue

I honestly felt I was in the best form of my career at that point, but here I was leaving a top club to drop down a level. I had hoped that Celtic might have renewed their interest just then. For once there were no obvious advances from Celtic Park when I was finally free to go there. It would have kept me at a top-level club, this time in Scotland instead. Maybe I should have contacted them, because within a year they were back trying to sign me again! I couldn't feel down or get morose; I had a new club, which I knew I liked. I was still getting paid to play football, which I still loved doing and was acutely aware that it was still a massive privilege most people would love to have.

It also gave me a moment to reconsider what my priorities were. *Yes, I am married now and with a son to care for* (our beautiful daughter Lucy would soon join us), *but I can still do this job for the love of it, every training session, never mind game, can still be a joy. Undoubtedly there is a bit more pressure because of the family commitments but I can still hold on to that attitude for the time being. Others in desperate straits with no job or limited income don't have that luxury, so I must make sure I keep those thoughts at the forefront of my mind.*

One of the other reasons why I refused to be bitter about any negatives was that I felt far too many players around me spent too much time moaning about everything. That attitude always annoyed me. From not playing, or not being given a chance at a higher level, all the way to the quality of the hotels they were staying in or the food in the canteen. It was less of a problem at Tranmere, but I still found this whining unacceptable. I never wanted to be that person and hopefully never have been.

I had a mantra at the time: 'Being a footballer is what I do, not who I am.' It may sound trite, but it was important to me. If I could keep that thought in mind, then it wouldn't harm me psychologically to take a step down or even when I eventually stopped playing; it ensured a reasonable perspective. It had taken nine years, but I did grudgingly accept by then that this was my job and my career, for a while anyway. I would never allow it to define me to myself. It might define me to others but there is nothing I could do about that.

I had watched many other players struggle when their careers ended. Working with the PFA I knew how many ex-players failed to cope when, soon after their careers finished, the fame, adulation, money – and very often their partners – were suddenly no longer there.

I am happy I had that positive attitude because the second half of my career in the game after leaving Everton was if anything even more enjoyable than the first. It was certainly more interesting and the path was totally unpredictable, just the way I liked it. I thought less and less about finishing the degree as I was learning enough travelling through this life. I didn't get to graduate, but what I learned in my time as a student was more important than any piece of paper. The Caledonian University eventually gave me an honorary doctorate anyway, so I got the letters after my name in the end. Mum would have been proud.

People talk about their 'journey', how you have changed as a person and learned from your mistakes. Hopefully any cognisant human being does that throughout life anyway. Maturity, understanding and education by experience is the core of a worthwhile life, without forgetting to laugh at it whenever you can along the way.

I hope for something else on top of that. I hope that anyone who knew me as a youngster and who happened to meet me again all these years later would still recognise that same person. They would see someone who is not a slave to his ego, who still has the same care for his fellow men and women, especially those who have had less luck in life, and who retains an awareness that the world doesn't revolve around him. Huge wealth, love of power, constant search for material gain and cherishing empty fame are stupidly transient things and the world is getting more obsessed with them all the time. I have never thought that true happiness lies in chasing those external myths. It may be a long road, but it is important not to forget where you started the journey; it might not have been that bad a place.

I really didn't want to be a professional footballer, I just wanted to play football, so that is what I did. In the end I am blessed that I accidentally became a footballer and was able to do it for so long and enjoy the benefits of the profession, while dodging most of the pitfalls. I would love to explain to some of those in the game today that it is still possible even with all that money and attention, whatever some advisers may tell you. Check out the life that Juan Mata, of Chelsea, Manchester United and Spain, lives, for example. It can be done!

For some people it was considered the end of my real football career when I left Everton. But at Tranmere Rovers I played some of my best football and enjoyed it as much as anywhere, which was the crucial thing for me. I played more often for my country while at Prenton Park than I did at all my other clubs combined.

The football we played over the next five years was joyous and some of the games stick in my mind as clearly as any others in my career for the excitement, skill and quality. There were still big clubs and stadiums to visit in the second tier and we even had memorable wins against top Premier League clubs such as Aston Villa when we outplayed them at Prenton Park in the Cup. I didn't care if it was Bristol City not Manchester City; I was involved with a group who were in this together and had the right united spirit. The dressing room may have been full of laughter, but the commitment was there too.

Over the next few years little Tranmere Rovers had the most successful period in their history, getting to the cusp of the Premier League three times in a row. There were great people; I had sillier adventures; chairmanship of the PFA in England; a move back to Scotland; a spell as a player–chief executive in the top league up there – all to be followed by an entirely new career in the media and in journalism.

So being paid to travel to often exotic places to watch, talk about and write about football, is a joy. The characters I met on the way after leaving Everton were intriguing, maybe even more so than those I had come across before then. In the less rarefied atmosphere away from the elite level of the game it seemed more human and more real, and in many ways I preferred it. They were also a more eccentric and more diverse group of people than I had ever worked with before, so much so that at times I almost felt at home.

I didn't see that coming at all.

Chapter Titles Playlist

1. Do You Remember the First Time? Pulp
2. Kids MGMT
3. The Story of the Blues Wah!
4. Everything's Gone Green New Order
5. Don't Mess Up a Good Thing Fontella Bass and Bobby McClure
6. (I Don't Want to Go to) Chelsea Elvis Costello and the Attractions
7. Changes David Bowie
8. London Calling The Clash
9. A New Career in a New Town David Bowie
10. Eighties Fan Camera Obscura
11. Bigmouth Strikes Again The Smiths
12. This is the Day The The
13. Black Star David Bowie
14. All Together Now The Farm
15. Knives Out Radiohead
16. Back to Black Amy Winehouse
17. Fame David Bowie
18. Crash The Primitives
19. Kicker Conspiracy The Fall
20. New Dawn Fades Joy Division
21. Hit the North The Fall
22. Doubts Even Here New Order
23. Shine On You Crazy Diamond Pink Floyd
24. This Charming Man The Smiths
25. Here Comes the Summer The Undertones
26. I'll Be Honest The Spook School
27. Let's Stick Together Roxy Music
28. Leaving Blues Bombay Bicycle Club
29. With a Little Help from My Friends The Beatles
30. Take a Chance on Me Abba
31. Never Understand The Jesus and Mary Chain
32. Ferry 'Cross the Mersey Frankie Goes to Hollywood

Index

Aldridge, John 305–6, 308–9

Arran, Isle of 266–70

Arsenal Football Club 126, 162

Associates 179–80

Barnes, John 153, 243

Bates, Ken 74, 80, 82, 120, 122–4, 168, 173, 216, 218

BBC 97, 99, 100–1, 107, 240, 299

Beardsley, Peter 237, 298, 301–2

Boyle, John 271–3

Bradford City 159–60, 166

The Bridge News 98–9

Brown, Craig 55–8, 62–3, 69, 312, 320

Bulgaria 209–11

Bumstead, John 81, 106, 146, 163

Burrows, David 282

Butcher, Terry 51–2, 195

Cairney, Frank 40–4, 157

Campbell, Bobby 216, 218

Campbell, John 48, 271

Canoville, Paul 110–11, 129–33, 164

Cardiff City 115

Catholic Church 49–50

Celtic Boys Club 30–1, 32–3, 35–44, 49

Celtic Football Club 8–12, 22–3, 33, 35–6, 42, 69–70, 182, 227, 241, 272, 291–3, 332

A Certain Ratio 93, 108

Chadwick, Fiona 137, 138–9, 249–50

Charlton, Bobby 107

Chelsea Football Club 60, 65, 72–4, 80–92, 98–9, 101–7, 110–34, 147–8, 161–73, 181, 187–91, 194, 198–208, 211–19, 255–7

China 253–4

The Clash 149

Clyde Football Club 54–63, 65, 67–8, 82

Coates, Ralph 246

Cocteau Twins 92–3, 95, 151, 224, 258

Coe, Sebastian 57, 126–7

Connor, Frank 9–10

Cooper, Vince 275, 322

Cottee, Tony 225, 226, 231, 237, 246, 248, 297

Crystal Palace 110

Dalglish, Kenny 11, 33, 158, 192–3, 195, 197–8, 281–3

De Bruyne, Kevin 15, 302

Dixon, Kerry 80–1, 84, 105, 113, 120, 121, 126, 129–30, 135, 161, 164, 166, 178, 186–7, 204, 207, 257, 295

Dowson, Antony 137, 138

Droy, Micky 82, 122–4

Dundee United 33–5

The Durutti Column 93, 108, 258

Easterhouse 11–12, 19

Ebbrell, John 264, 295

Euro 92 Championship 304, 310, 316–20

Everton Football Club 161, 222–9, 231–9, 242–57, 273–92, 296–7, 300–3, 305, 309, 327–30

FA Cup 239, 241–2, 280

Factory Records 108

Fashanu, Justin 136

Ferguson, Alex 41, 158, 194–8

Ferguson, Craig 97

Ferguson, Duncan 311–15

FIFA World Youth Championships 72, 74–6

Finland 60–2

Galatasaray 273–5, 322–6

Gartcosh United 49, 50, 54–7

Gascoigne, Paul (Gazza) 152–3, 312

Germany 59, 318–19

Glasgow College of Technology 45, 47–8, 53, 59, 72, 84

Glasgow Rangers 49–50, 145, 166–8, 241, 292, 299–300

Guthrie, Robin 93, 258

Hansen, Alan 192, 195, 229–30

Harvey, Colin 222–3, 233, 237, 238, 249, 256, 273, 277–9, 292–3, 301, 324

Hazard, Micky 188

Heath, Adrian 288

Helm, Les 232–3

Helsinki 60–2

Heysel disaster 159, 239

Hill, Jimmy 107

Hillsborough disaster 239–42

Hinchcliffe, Andy 285, 297, 330

Hoey, Kate 181

Hollins, John 183, 185–8, 198, 211–14, 216, 279

Ingham, Mike 239–40

Inter Milan 181

Ipswich Town 51–3

Iraq 168–73

Ireland 208–9, 297

Istanbul 273–5, 322–6

Japan 251–2

Jardine, Sandy 68–9

Jasper, Dale 146–7, 163

The Jesus and Mary Chain 63, 92, 186

Jobson, Richard 94–5

John, Elton 140–1

Johnston, Maurice 25, 50, 298–302

Johnstone, Jimmy 28, 33, 154–5, 158

Jones, Joey 106–7

Jones, Keith 131, 167

Joy Division 70, 93, 108, 109, 175, 224

Keegan, Kevin 104, 105–6

Kendall, Howard 237, 279, 284–6, 291, 296–7, 300–3, 309, 328, 330–1

Keown, Martin 254–5, 273

King, Johnny 305, 307–8, 330

Le Saux, Graham 142–4

Lee, Colin 103, 129

Leighton, Jim 247–8

Lennon, John 99

Lineker, Gary 92, 166

Liverpool Football Club 280–3

Lumsden, Jimmy 9–10, 227

McAllister, Gary 313, 319–20

McAndrew, Tony 87–8, 201

McCall, Stuart 225, 237, 243–4, 284

McClair, Brian 76, 177–8, 182, 192–3, 248, 313, 314, 316, 317

McClean, Jim 34–5

McCoist, Ally 313

McDonald, Neil 225, 237, 286–7

McLaughlin, Joe 80–1, 129–30, 165, 201

McNaught, John 201–4

McNeill, Ian 73–4, 82, 125, 202

McStay, Paul 313, 314

Manchester City 107, 109, 160, 162, 190

Manchester United 161, 163, 250–1

Masterson, Danny 65, 68

Mauchlen, Ally 205–6

Melly, George 175–6, 178

Mexico 72, 74–6, 155–6

Millar, John 95–6, 142, 171–2, 217

Morrison, Jim 48, 67

Morrissey 258–65

Morrissey, John 308

Moyes, David 38, 39, 155, 227

National Front 112, 114–15

Neal, John 73, 82, 89, 90, 102, 104, 124–5, 127–8, 162, 166, 182–4, 204

Neil, Alex 29–30

Netherlands 317–18

Nevin, Annabel (Pat's wife) 67, 95, 121, 180–1, 223, 227, 229–30, 267, 281–2, 294–6

Nevin, Joe (Pat's brother) 21

Nevin, Kathleen (Pat's sister) 21–2

Nevin, Lucy (Pat's daughter) 332

Nevin, Mary (Pat's mother) 13, 18–20, 45, 325

Nevin, Mary (Pat's sister) 20–1

Nevin, Michael (Pat's brother) 21, 127, 252–3

Nevin, Patrick senior 11–17, 18–20, 22, 28, 39–40, 74, 104–5, 119–21, 125, 191, 209, 225

Nevin, Simon (Pat's son) 294–5, 322, 325

Nevin, Thomas (Pat's brother) 20, 26, 46

New Musical Express (*NME*) 63, 92, 93–4

Newcastle United 151–2

Niedzwiecki, Eddie 80, 163, 189, 208, 211

Paris Saint-Germain 215, 223

Partick Thistle 50–1

Pates, Colin 81, 102, 146, 163

Pearce, Stuart 154–5, 227–8

Peel, John 46, 72–3, 93, 97–102, 140–1, 175, 179, 210, 242

Poborský, Karel 248

Premier League 288–9, 307, 321–2, 334–5

The Proclaimers 94

Professional Footballers' Association (PFA) 114, 144, 288–91, 333, 335

Ratcliffe, Kevin 225, 237
Raymonde, Simon 95
Reilly, Vini 109, 258, 260, 262, 264
Rhodes 271–2
Rice, Brian 228
Robson, Bobby 51, 52–3
Robson, Bryan 163, 251
Roche, John 48, 66–7
Roxburgh, Andy 59–60, 157, 193, 199, 305, 309, 310–12, 315–17, 319–20

Saddam Hussein 169–73
St Andrews 127–8
St Jude's, Barlanak 25–6
Saville, Peter 108
Scotland 191–2, 195–8, 199, 208–9, 257, 304–5, 309, 310–20
Scotland Under-18s 59, 65
Scotland Under-20s 72, 74–6
Scotland Under-21s 155–8
Sharp, Graeme 225, 226, 246, 251

Sheedy, Kevin 225, 246, 247, 255, 256
Sheffield Wednesday 120, 164, 306
Shrewsbury Town 113
Silva, David 15, 302
Skinner, David 49, 51, 54
Smy, Suzanne 48
Snodin, Ian 225, 254
Souness, Graeme 195, 299
Southall, Neville 225, 245–7, 250, 253–4, 274–5, 276, 287
Spackman, Nigel 80–1, 106, 189
Spain 156–8
Speedie, David 120, 121, 129–30, 187–9, 191, 194, 197, 199–200, 207, 216
Stein, Jock 11, 12, 64–5, 156–9, 318
Steven, Trevor 205, 225, 236, 245–6
Still, Athole 215, 223, 224
Strachan, Gordon 195, 197, 311
Şükür, Hakan 324
Sunderland 165
Sweden 304, 309, 310, 319
Switzerland 296–7

Taylor, Gordon 114, 287, 288–90
Terry, John 107
Thomas, Mickey 106–7, 164–5
Thrills, Adrian 93–4, 147–8
Torbett, Jim 39
Tottenham Hotspurs 147–9, 162, 181
Tranmere Rovers 304–9, 321–2, 325–8, 330–1, 334–5

UEFA Cup 324–5
Umbro 315–16

Van Den Hauwe, Pat 204–5

Waddle, Chris 104, 153
Walley, Ernie 188–91, 200, 214–16
Warzycha, Robert 279–80, 298
Welsh, Peter 48, 222–3
West Ham 116, 135–6, 153, 283–5, 291, 320
Wharton, Kenny 151
Whelan, Ronnie 205
Whiteside, Norman 246, 250–3, 255, 259–60, 262, 264
Williams, Gwyn 85–6
Wilson, Ian 206
Wilson, Tony 27, 108–9

Acknowledgements

Many of the people who deserve acknowledgement are in this book already, but there are just as many who aren't mentioned by name. Certainly, most of the coaches and managers I had growing up in schools' football and in boys' clubs have my deepest gratitude for giving their time selflessly. Plenty of teammates, to whom I owed a great deal, again aren't mentioned, and some of those who are named probably deserve more fulsome and direct recognition. You each have my thanks here.

My teachers at school are shamefully missing in these pages even though quite a few were important positive influences on me. Dennis Lavery, Kathleen O'Rourke, John McLauchlan, Chris Nairn and Roddy Shaw are among those who might have the right to be angry with me for not getting a more complete name check, but you can't give me detention now, so you will just have to live with it!

I hope it is clear how appreciative I am for the efforts my managers Craig Brown, Andy Roxburgh, John Neal, Colin Harvey and John King made on my behalf. Each of them gave me huge support when others wouldn't have taken the time with such an odd outsider. They were also incredibly honest, honourable and good men to a fault, I have been fortunate to know each of them.

I must thank Vivienne Clore, who has been a friend for thirty-odd years, specifically for helping more than anyone else in getting this book published. Thanks for your wisdom, friendship, listening skills, advice, support and being the only person qualified to be my agent, even though it took me more than three decades to figure it out.

Jake Lingwood has been a brilliant aid in editing this book. His time, judgement and subtle influence have made this work far better than it would have been otherwise. I am not sure he added a single word, but his ideas on how I should go off and rewrite passages were invariably right. The entire team at Octopus helped superbly, even though we never met, mostly due to their work being done during the Covid-19 pandemic. To everyone from the designers to the marketing department, from the proofreaders to the legal team, thanks for the consummate professionalism.

A particular thanks to those working now at Chelsea FC who helped in the process of jogging my memory, sourcing pictures and providing information. I am indebted to Hugh Hastings, Paul Mason, Richard Godden, Steve Atkins, Neil Barnett and the peerless Thresa Conneely with her right-hand woman Caroline Mabey. Thresa, I am still not falling for the hard-faced act, the secret is out, we all know you are caring and lovely. I have known it since we first met at Chelsea in 1983 and nothing has changed my mind. You are the beating heart of the club.

Also, thanks to Paul at Scared to Dance for the DJ picture and the great nights with good friends down in Dalston. There are some friends who didn't make these pages, to them I honestly say your omission is not because I didn't care or have forgotten you. It is just that I couldn't fit your stories into the narrative or the space available.

To my family, who were the perfect influences as I grew up, my gratitude goes without saying. Well it has to, because we come from a generation of people who showed their feelings through their actions and not with gushing, overwrought sentimentality. A short, manly hug will have to suffice.

To every band I have loved, thank you for saving my life, my sanity, my heart and my soul on countless occasions. Artists never know just how much they help and how important they are to so many of us. When I need anything, I turn to your art and it has always been there to help me.

Thank you to my wife Annabel's entire extended family who have welcomed me into their lives. And of course to Annabel herself, who put up with me being stuck in front of a computer for weeks on end writing this, and still had the good grace to be supportive.